THE DNA OF RELATIONSHIPS FOR COUPLES

a book in

THE DNA OF RELATIONSHIPS CAMPAIGN

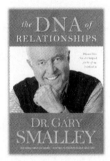

the DNA *of* RELATIONSHIPS *for* COUPLES

❀ ❀ ❀

Dr. Greg Smalley
Dr. Robert S. Paul

with

Donna K. Wallace

Tyndale House Publishers, Inc.
Carol Stream, Illinois

Visit Tyndale online at www.tyndale.com.

TYNDALE and Tyndale's quill logo are registered trademarks of Tyndale House Publishers, Inc.

The DNA of Relationships for Couples

Designed by Dean H. Renninger

Edited by Kathryn S. Olson

The author is represented by the literary agency of Alive Literary Agency, 7680 Goddard Street, Suite 200, Colorado Springs, CO 80920. www.aliveliterary.com

Scripture quotations marked NIV are taken from the Holy Bible, *New International Version,*® *NIV.*® Copyright ©1973, 1978, 1984 by Biblica, Inc.® Used by permission. All rights reserved worldwide.

Scripture quotations marked KJV are taken from the *Holy Bible*, King James.

For information about special discounts for bulk purchases, please contact Tyndale House Publishers at csresponse@tyndale.com, or call 1-800-323-9400.

Library of Congress Cataloging-in-Publication Data

Smalley, Greg.
   The DNA of relationships for couples / Greg Smalley & Robert S. Paul.
     p. cm.
   ISBN 978-0-8423-8322-6 (sc)
     1. Spouses—Religious life.   2. Marriage—Religious aspects—Christianity..   I. Paul, Roberts S.   II. Title.
   BV4596.M3S625 2006
   248.8'44—dc22   2005025596

Printed in the United States of America

24 23 22 21 20 19 18
12 11 10 9   8   7   6

Greg Smalley dedicates this book to his wife, Erin.
Thank you for the unconditional love you so
abundantly provide. I could not have written this book
without your sacrifice, encouragement, and support.
You are my last love and best friend. I love you.

Bob Paul dedicates this book to his wife, Jenni.
Thank you for all your years of patiently accompanying
me on this incredible journey. The extent to which you
have enriched my life can never be adequately expressed
in words. Because of you we will enjoy eternity together.

ACKNOWLEDGMENTS

THIS BOOK could not have been completed without the help of many friends and colleagues. Thanks to our families for all their support, encouragement, and patience: Erin, Taylor, Maddy, and Garrison Smalley, who give meaning and joy to Greg's life; and Jenni, Chris and Amara, Jessica and Chris Blackwell, Rebecca, and Nathan, who are God's gifts to Bob.

We need to give a special thanks to our collaborator, Donna K. Wallace, whose creativity and passion for this project were incredible. Donna, you breathed life into all the characters and their stories. Special gratitude goes to her family—James, Cierra, and Spencer—for sharing her with us for an intense twelve weeks. Cierra, we appreciate all your help with word crafting. It is truly an art.

Thank you, Gary Smalley, for your constant support and belief in what we are doing. You have created a wonderful legacy for us. You are truly a special friend and partner in this ministry.

Mark Pyatt, our behind-the-scenes partner: This ministry wouldn't be the same without you. You bring gifts to the table that none of the rest of us have. Thank you for your passion for marriage and your willingness to faithfully serve the Lord, this ministry, and the hundreds of couples we serve.

Many professional colleagues have left their unmistakable handprint on the development of the ideas presented in this book. Our current team includes Chris Arnzen, Tricia Cunningham, Dr. Shawn Stoever, Nathan Phillips, Jane Phillips, Dr. Robert K. Burbee, Dr. Brett Sparks, Cindy Irwin, Pat McLean, Tamara Hanna, and Gary Bruegman. Additionally, we have had the opportunity to work with a number of other incredibly bright, creative, and talented people over the years, including Dr. Scott Sticksell, Dr. Peter Larson, Dr. Kelly Vick-Morse, Sheryl Haile, Amy Smalley, and Dr. David Swift.

Thanks also to our faithful and devoted staff at the National Institute of Marriage: Sheila Brawley, Vicki Wrosch, Sara Newhard, and Shari Radford. Your daily investment makes our world go around.

We want to thank our incredible board of directors for their vision, support, and encouragement: Jack Herschend, Cary Summers, and Dr. Gary Oliver.

We would also like to thank some of our special friends at Chick-fil-A and WinShape Marriage—Bubba and Cindy Cathy, and Bob and Bev Maday—for their vision of great marriages and partnership.

We owe a lot to the many awesome people at Tyndale House. Special thanks to Jon Farrar and Mary Keeley for walking all the way with us from concept to completion. We were also fortunate to get to work with an amazing editor, Kathy Olson.

Thank you, Lee Hough, our agent at Alive Communications, for always watching our back.

AUTHORS' NOTE

The DNA of Relationships for Couples is based on the work and ministry of the National Institute of Marriage and therefore has many elements consistent with a four-day Couples Intensive seminar. However, characters are based on composites of personality types and are therefore fictitious. Any similarity to an individual case is purely coincidental. Any slights of people, places, or organizations are unintentional.

The purpose of this book is to educate. No individual should use the information in this book for self-diagnosis, treatment, or justification in accepting or declining professional advice and treatment.

The DNA of Relationships for Couples is set mostly in Branson, Missouri. Some of the landmarks, such as the Bradford House bed-and-breakfast, have been placed in their true settings but have been embellished for the purpose of readability. Other buildings, parks, and establishments are nothing more than figments of our imaginations. We hope those of you who visit will have fun distinguishing between the two.

"What? Marriage Should Be Thrilling?"

Greg's Story

"How am I doing as a wife?"

I wasn't sure how to answer that seemingly innocent question. But since Erin and I had been married only four months, I wondered how hard it could be.

"Fine," I said.

Have you ever said something that you wished you could immediately delete, like words on a computer screen? Erin's sudden lack of breathing made me wonder if "fine" wasn't really what she wanted to hear.

"*Fine?*" she echoed.

"What?" I asked. If I had been a batter in a baseball game, you would have just heard a gigantic *whoosh* sound as, for the second time in four seconds, I hit nothing but air.

"You think I'm just FINE!" Erin snapped again.

There it was again. The way she echoed my "fine" was somehow very different than I had intended it.

And then Erin asked me to do something that still gives me chills. "On a scale of one to ten, rate how I'm doing as a wife."

"Is ten the best?" My voice was shaky.

"You're stalling." *She's good,* I thought. Then I came to the sickening reality that I was actually going to have to answer her question.

"Well," I started, feeling like I was walking not just on eggshells but on the heads of chickens, "I would rate you as a . . ." And then it hit me. I had the answer! A confident smile pursed my lips as I said, "You're a 9.4."

I know what you're thinking: *Greg, you idiot, you blew it!* I know. But remember, you weren't there to wave your arms frantically and scream "No!" like the guy on the deck of an aircraft carrier waving off a fighter jet about to crash into the side of the ship.

You see, in my mind, God is a perfect ten, and since Erin isn't God and I thought she had a little room to improve, a 9.4 was pretty great.

I couldn't have been more wrong. It was as if I'd rated her .0000439.

"What am I doing wrong?" was her immediate (and let me emphasize the word *immediate*) response.

"What?"

Stee-rike three!

"Why don't you think I'm doing a good job?" Erin asked, obviously hurt.

"Honey," I begged, "a 9.4 is awesome. I meant that as a compliment."

"But I want to be perfect for you."

Erin and I lay in bed that night arguing about her score. We argued for a good forty-five minutes before we both rolled over and went to sleep unhappy.

My last thought before drifting off was, *And you wondered why I didn't rate you a 9.9.*

Erin and I hadn't done any premarital counseling or training; after all, we were "in love." Besides, I was the son of Gary Smalley, the famous marriage expert. We had a surefire ticket to a great marriage. I remember actually saying to Erin, "We aren't going to be like those *other* people who fight and argue all the time."

Sadly, I was very wrong. Erin and I had no idea what it took to develop a great relationship. It got so bad that three years into our marriage, I thought we were just one argument away from Erin's leaving me and going home to Phoenix. I didn't think she'd divorce me, but I was convinced that she didn't want to live with me anymore.

Eventually, Erin and I got some help. We learned ways to deal with our conflicts and experienced some improvement in our marriage. Sadly, though, our early brush with marital difficulties made us lower our expectations. We went from wedding-day hopes of marital bliss to mere relief at finding *some* happiness and experiencing *some* success. Being married was a lot more challenging than I had originally imagined, and I unconsciously learned to be content with having a "good" marriage. That is, until I began to work with Bob Paul.

Bob's Story

Like Greg, I came from a family of marriage experts and authors. I entered marriage with Jenni convinced that I knew the way to the Promised Land of marriage; all she had to do was follow me. As you might guess, we struggled miserably—for the first thirteen years of our marriage. During that time our four beautiful children came along, and we were blessed in many ways. But relationally things got worse and worse between my wife and me.

I have always loved Jenni and wanted to have a great marriage; still, no matter how many ways I attempted to fix our problems and point out to her what we needed to do differently, we got more hurt and disillusioned. Over time, the thought of having a "great marriage" increasingly became a question of whether or not we would even *have* a marriage. Our troubles progressed until the telling moment when Jenni made a statement that has forever symbolized for me the utter desperation of our marriage at that time. In a heated moment filled with hurt, anger, and disgust, she looked at me and declared, "The thought of ever making love to you again makes me feel like I'm going to vomit."

I had no idea what to do or where to turn. For years I was convinced that if Jenni would just do as I suggested, things would be great. Not now. I was no longer able to believe in myself. Proverbs 14:12 kept ringing in my ears: "There is a way that seems right to a man, but in the end it leads to death." I had tried my way for thirteen years, and now marital death was hovering frighteningly close. Fortunately for me, the complete hopelessness of the situation caused me to turn to God in a way I had never done before. I pleaded with God, "There must be something I need to learn through this pain and this mess of a marriage. I'm ready to learn whatever I need to in order to become a man you can be proud of. Teach me, Lord."

I spent the next two painful years on a path of incredible personal challenge and growth. Many times I became discouraged about whether my marriage and family would ever be restored, but I determined that either way, I was going to learn what it meant to love as God loves and to be a man after his own heart.

In my years as a marriage therapist since those days, I have had the opportunity to witness countless marriage miracles—transformations that defy the imagination. But my favorite one of all was the one that occurred in my own marriage. Two full years after my wife had closed herself off from me, Jenni was challenged by God to reopen her heart. Suddenly, without warning, she did . . . and I was ready! I had been given another chance where I believed there might never be one, and I was determined not to blow it.

Today, almost twelve years later, Jenni and I are thrilled— *thrilled*—with our marriage. It's not perfect, but I no longer expect perfection. We are imperfect people living in a crazy, mixed-up world.

So what's different? What caused our marriage to move from the brink of disaster to a relationship better than either of us had ever thought possible? Many of the answers are found in this book.

Like Greg, you may think your marriage is fine . . . or like me, you may believe your marriage is over. Either way, few of us truly believe that we can ever be "thrilled" with our marriage. But we can be. We know this is not a word you hear often—especially in tandem with marriage. But we want to show you how this can be your reality. Does it sound like a long shot? impossible? That's okay. Stay with us. We have yet to see a marriage fail when a husband and wife are dedicated to discovering all that God has intended for them.

Welcome to a New Experience!

We have walked this journey of hope with thousands of couples in a variety of ways—seminars, conferences, workshops, videos, and books—and we've had wonderful responses. But nothing else we have found comes close to our Couples Intensive program in helping couples understand God's hope for their marriage.

Consistently, people ask us for real-life stories to help them understand how to apply the principles we teach. We recognize the extraordinary power of watching relationship principles in action, so we've taken these requests seriously. We are excited to present this book, which is written to give you exactly that—an entirely new approach to self-discovery and application through story.

This book is unlike any other marriage book you will find. Rather than attempting to follow the steps of just another self-help book, you are about to enter into a fictionalized, true-to-life journey with us through one of our four-day Couples Intensive programs. Though it has the look and feel of a novel, you'll not find here a fantasy with neatly packaged, better-than-life romance. Instead, we invite you to step into our world, to engage with us in an unbelievably realistic journey based on authentic accounts of conflict, intrigue, and heartbreak—all the while receiving a guided tour through the awesome world of hope renewed and love redeemed.

How to Best Read and Enjoy This Book

You are about to be introduced to four couples who will arrive shortly for a four-day Couples Intensive in Branson, Missouri. They are normal people with normal problems, and all of them are struggling in their marital journeys. Their issues represent some of the most common types of problems we all encounter in relationships, the kinds of things most of us can relate to.

Imagine that we have asked you to fill our last guest reservation. One of the most powerful benefits of attending a Couples Intensive is discovering that marriage is challenging for everyone—and that the situations most of us encounter are startlingly similar. The details will vary, as will the severity, but the underlying challenges typically have more to do with our humanness and our attempts to conduct intimate relationships in a fallen world than they do with our specific differences. The four other couples in your group are a passionate, dynamic bunch who, like you, are looking for answers—who dare to imagine that their lives can be different. We invite you to enter into this intimate setting where you are privy to their Heart Talk involving their deepest concerns, hopes, and hurts . . . perhaps not so different from your own.

We realize that not everyone's marriage is in the same place as these seminar participants. You may not be on the brink of divorce or dealing with an affair, as Ryan and Becca are. You may not have a problem with unmet expectations like Rodney and Chelsea. You may not have a communication breakdown as Todd and Pam do, or a long-standing misunderstanding like Charles and Victoria. But you do need to learn to create a safe environment in your home so you, too, can express your heart to your family. We have found through our work with hundreds of couples that a relationship doesn't have to be in crisis to benefit from these powerful ideas and tools. Couples with *good* marriages discover ways to have *great* marriages.

We ask anyone who is considering attending one of our Couples Intensives to be open to God's working a miracle in their marriage. This is the one and only commitment we expect. We want to ask you, our reader, to make a similar commitment while you read this book. Refuse to be satisfied with mediocrity in your marriage or with having a "fine" marriage, as Greg was. Refuse to be satisfied with the status quo.

We realize that reaching the final destination—experiencing the ultimate marriage—requires two people committed to following the Lord's leading together, and you may not have a cooperative or interested spouse. The great news is that we've found a way for even one person to make a major difference by learning and using these principles.

Imagine

Do you sometimes feel as if you're living with a stranger? Has your passion ebbed like the tide? Perhaps you feel trapped in the same old arguments regarding finances or the kids. Life may seem to go on with its daily stresses, creating emotional distance between you and your lover. Possibly, boredom reigns in your bedroom.

You may feel alone.

Imagine if things could be different.

To engage in a story, one must imagine. And we invite you to do that. Place your preset expectations and judgments aside long enough to imagine your marriage being free of anxiety, void of misunderstandings, intimate, and filled with grace—as free-flowing as the movements of a beautiful ballet, or like a secret garden in springtime, fragrant and teeming with new hope and life.

Imagine what God hopes for you and your loved one.

Imagine if you were able to come to Branson, Missouri, in the early spring to spend four days with us as we coached you personally through the areas where you are stuck. . . . Imagine coming up the steps of a grand Victorian bed-and-breakfast tucked back off the main path, where you will be uninterrupted by daily chores, employers, children, or complications. Dare to imagine.

There are no guarantees of success, and we can never wrap up marriages with a neat bow. Each person will have to make a choice. What will it be? Come on in, kick off your shoes, and dialogue with us. These will be four days you'll never forget.

Rodney went to the kitchen window one more time. Stretching over the sink, he leaned closer and pulled back the curtain, as if he could will himself to see headlights bouncing toward him in the distance, indicating that Chelsea might be coming home. Everything was dark, save the little streetlamp at the end of the drive. She wasn't answering at the office or on her cell. Should he call the police? A mix of worry and rage—fear—crept into his throat. His wife might be in trouble.

He had played with the kids and fed them dinner, assuming she'd been held up at the office. Next he bathed the two toddlers, read books to them, and tucked them into bed. Still Chelsea was not home. He was getting nervous. The young dad watched several sitcoms and willed himself to wash the dishes—mainly so he could stay close to the window. Three more hours passed. Rodney didn't know what to do. It wasn't as if this was the first time his wife, a professional who refused to be controlled by anyone or anything, had arrived home long after she'd been expected. But not this late. She would be furious if he called the police.

Flopping onto the couch, Rodney paid little attention to the living room floor strewn with books and toys. Instead, images of his wife played out in his mind. Wondering, worrying, he fought with his suspicions. *She's been really loaded with work . . . she's been so annoyed with me . . . I know she goes out after work sometimes . . . pushing deadlines, that's all . . . there are all those attractive men in suits!* Hauling his large body off the couch, he went to look out the window one more time and then to check on the children.

Jack's cheek was mashed against his pillow, and his lips were pursed in an open-lipped pout. His chubby palm fell open, making him as vulnerable and innocent as any little human being could be. Hannah slept on her tummy in her crib with her knees bunched under her so that her padded bottom stuck up. Rodney leaned down to brush away her curls and kissed her temple.

Standing there watching his children sleep, Rodney felt even more desperate for Chelsea's return. At bedtime, little Jack had asked about his mommy and refused to be consoled until Rodney promised she'd give him a kiss as soon as she got home. These kids needed their mom. Where was she?

By the time Chelsea's SUV pulled up to the curb, the clock on the microwave read 2:13 a.m. Rodney's emotions had covered the gamut. With a mix of relief and anger, he knew this was it. He had to confront his wife about what was going on. He would meet her at the door and insist on an explanation. Her key was in the lock. He had waited up all these hours, and he fully meant to stand up and ask her, point-blank, what was going on.

The door opened quietly. Rodney panicked and remained paralyzed in his prone position. He heard his wife sidestep the cat and tiptoe quietly past the couch, where he was pretending to be asleep.

❀ ❀ ❀

"This is Julie. How may I help you?"

Rodney froze. Calling the Marriage Institute had seemed like a good idea, but now he wasn't sure what to say. "Um . . . ," he stammered, "a . . . a friend gave me your number a-a-and said I should call." He took a deep breath. "I don't know what to do. Several days ago, my wife moved out with the kids and said she is leaving me." The house was now barren. No laughter, no children squealing, no cartoons. He could hear his voice trembling, but he went on anyway. "I love my wife and kids, and I don't want to lose them. Can you help us?"

"I hope so," Julie said. "But first, tell me about what's going on in your marriage so I can help you decide if our programs are what you need and, if so, which one is right for you."

Rodney wiped his eyes on his sleeve. "My wife says I don't take any initiative in our relationship. It's not that I don't love her, because I do . . . with all my heart." He fought back tears. "I think it may be too late. I'm just not sure what to do."

"Are there other specific complaints or issues between the two of you?"

"Well . . . sort of . . ." Rodney explained that he didn't make enough money and that his wife claimed she wanted to be at home with their kids, but instead she wasn't coming home until late at night. Her resentment toward him continued to grow, no matter what he did. She hated the fact that he was still working at the Boys & Girls Clubs of America and pressed hard for him to go through management training or more schooling. "But I like my job. The work is steady, I have flexible hours, and I'm good with the kids. . . . I'm sorry for rambling."

"Not at all," Julie said. Her voice was pleasant, and she seemed patient. Rodney started to relax a little. "It's helpful to understand a little bit about what is happening in your relationship. It sounds like both of you are unhappy and feeling misunderstood. I can't help but wonder if maybe you haven't even gotten to the root of the problem."

That was exactly how he felt, but the idea of getting to the root of the problem was unsettling. Terrifying, actually. What *would* be discovered at the root of their troubled marriage?

Julie explained that the counselors she worked with, Dr. Greg Smalley and Dr. Bob Paul, were marriage specialists who helped people get to the root of these kinds of issues every day. They made sure both spouses felt safe before diving too deeply into their issues. She then described the Intensive programs available and encouraged Rodney to go to their Web site for more details.

A TALK WITH THE DOCTORS

Don't Go It Alone

We'd like to step aside just briefly from Rodney and Chelsea's story and talk with you, the reader, for a moment. Throughout this book, as you get to know our fictional couples and eavesdrop on their counseling sessions, we'll interrupt from time to time with words of encouragement, challenge, or clarification. These little "author asides" will be called "A Talk with the Doctors" and will be set apart in sections such as this one.

The first thing we want to share with you is that people were never meant to figure out how to create great relationships without help and support from others. Whether your relationship is good and you want it to be great, your relationship has occasional disappointments or challenges you don't know how to handle, or your relationship is a mess, don't go it alone. Reach out to others when you're grappling with relationship issues. There are many different ways to reach out to others. You can talk to a trusted friend or pastor, meet privately with someone in your Bible study or accountability group, visit a professional counselor, or attend a Couples Intensive like the one described in this book. It's often difficult for people to take the first step, just as it was difficult for Rodney to make that phone call. But your marriage is worth it—and so are you!

Maybe you're reading this book not because you have marriage challenges yourself but because someone you care about is struggling. If this is the case, we commend you for your compassion. We are confident that what you'll learn in these pages will better equip you to be that listening ear, should your friend choose to turn to you for help.

Whatever your personal situation might be, we invite you once again to come along with us as the fifth couple for this week's Couples Intensive in Branson. It is our hope and prayer that as you listen in on these fictional couples' lives, you will learn something about your own marriage relationship, and maybe even something new and exciting about yourself.

"An Intensive sounds like exactly what we need," Rodney told Julie, still nervous about the idea of discovering the root of their problem. "But I'm not sure Chelsea will even consider coming. Would you be willing to talk with her?"

Julie explained that just as medical doctors can't manipulate their patients to come in for checkups, their practice, for ethical reasons, wouldn't allow the staff to pursue clients either. They would simply have to wait until Chelsea was ready to contact them. "I'll be happy to discuss her questions, concerns, or hesitancy if and when she's ready. Does that make sense?"

"Rodney . . . ?"

As if his thoughts had conjured her up, Rodney suddenly heard Chelsea's voice. She had come in the back door, and he hadn't noticed.

"I just stopped by to pick up some extra clothes for the kids. I won't be long. Sorry to interrupt you."

"No, Chelsea . . . no problem. Um, I . . . was just talking with someone who might be able to help us. They . . . she wants to talk to you." He held out the phone, hoping against hope that she would take it. Looking a little skeptical, she did. Rodney slunk out to the porch and sat on the front steps to wait.

❂ ❂ ❂

"Hello? This is Chelsea."

Chelsea listened while Julie explained who she was and why Rodney had called. Impatient, the young mother worked around the kitchen while giving the woman on the phone a chance to describe a four-day Couples Intensive program and inquire as to whether this was something the couple would be interested in.

"You know . . . ," Chelsea started hesitantly, while reaching into the cupboard for the sippy cups, "to be honest, I don't know if I even want this marriage to work. I've tried hard for too long; I'm tired of hoping my husband will change. I don't know that I'm willing to put forth the effort to make it work."

Julie asked Chelsea if she was afraid to give her marriage another chance.

"Yes. I am disappointed with my marriage, and I just don't want to try anymore." She slumped down on an old stool in the kitchen. With a foot up on a high rung, she leaned her head against the wall. The cupboard doors needed to be scrubbed, food and crumbs had gathered under the table, and muddy scuff prints marked up the door. "More than anything, I just want to be happy, I want my children to be happy, and . . . I can't see how we can ever be all that with Rod in the picture."

Julie acknowledged that each individual has to sort through this kind of stuff on their own and that it was not her place to tell Chelsea what she needed to do, or not do, with her life or marriage. "That is strictly between you and God. And we're confident that you and he can sort it out." Julie went on to clarify how the goal of the counseling center was to come alongside couples in a way that would be useful to each person. "In fact, we really have only one question that we ask couples in order to determine whether or not we can work with them."

"Only one question?" With the phone wedged between her shoulder and her ear, Chelsea grabbed the broom and started sweeping up the mess on the floor.

"In order for us to feel confident that you are ready to enter our program, you need to answer yes to only one question: If God were to work a miracle in your marriage—even if the miracle is similar in magnitude to the parting of the Red Sea—would you be willing to receive that miracle? In other words, if God were to part the sea before you, would you be willing to walk through?"

Julie paused and then continued, "It's not necessary to believe the miracle *could* happen, or even to hope for it. The only question is, Would you accept it if it arrived? If your answer is yes, we are anxious to come alongside you both to see what happens. If the answer is no, we would encourage you to save your money and time."

There was a long pause. Chelsea glanced over at Rodney, who stood leaning against the door frame, looking a little anxious.

"Mhmm," was all she could summon. "I don't know what to think of all that. I guess if God wants to do a miracle, I'd be willing to receive it."

✦ ✦ ✦

Becca Stuart wasn't sure how she and her husband had arrived in one piece. They had originally planned to travel separately, but she soon thought better of it and decided it would be a good idea to spend a few hours together en route so they could get their stories straight. She and her husband, Ryan, had been separated for one month, and any kind of communication was impossible because of innumerable interruptions—and it proved no better while traveling across the nation.

"Right there on the sign, Ryan. We need Highway 65—you'd

better turn around here." No sooner had they found the right highway to Branson than Ryan's cell phone rang.

"That better not be the hospital," Becca said. The young physician and his wife had not been out of the Springfield rental car lot longer than five minutes before the hospital was calling *again.* "Can't they leave you alone?"

Ryan ignored his wife and continued the call. "Yeah, Monty. Tell me what her symptoms are again. I couldn't hear you." He shot Becca a dirty look.

Becca could hear Monty's voice through the phone's earpiece as he described the patient's symptoms: headache, nausea, stomach tenderness, bleeding, swelling, high blood pressure, and protein in the urine. She knew the symptoms for HELLP syndrome were serious. This situation called for immediate response from an ob-gyn. Becca could see her husband's frustration and knew he felt guilty for leaving the hospital when he was needed. Frowning, he replied, "I agree with your diagnosis, Monty. You'd better—"

"Ryan, you promised!" Becca was not happy. "Get off the phone." Though it was serious, she had no doubt Dr. Monty Burleson could handle this situation on his own.

Ryan shook his head in disgust and gave his wife a look that had become all too familiar—the look that said, "Stop nagging and leave me alone."

"You committed to this Couples Intensive, and now you're telling me you can't let the other doctors make the decisions for a few days?" She felt a familiar wave of desperation. "I can't believe I actually hoped this might work." On impulse, she yanked the phone cord out of the dashboard, where the phone had been recharging after a busy day of use.

They had been traveling all day, with several layovers between Southern California and Springfield, Missouri. Getting their two little girls settled with Ryan's parents before leaving for several days had been exhausting for Becca, and frankly she didn't care who was on the other end of that line. She had waited for Ryan's attention long enough. She needed him all to herself, just this once. This decision, as well as this trip, was long overdue—in fact, it may have been too late.

Ryan hardly broke stride in his conversation. Unfortunately for Becca, the phone had enough battery power for him to continue his conversation.

"Monty, I'm sorry about the interruption. Hold on one sec, please." He covered the phone and grabbed Becca's wrist. She knew by his expression that her behavior baffled him. "Stop being so dramatic, Becca. This will only take a minute. A woman's baby and her life are at stake." He pushed her hand back onto her lap, glanced at her, and rubbed his forehead. "It's not always just about you, you know." Ryan picked up where he had left off in the phone conversation.

In a fit of rage, Becca swung her body away from Ryan, stared out the passenger window, and began to read aloud the large billboard ads that littered the highway as they drove south.

"Silver Dollar City . . . ," Becca announced with sarcasm. "Maybe we should go there instead of to the Couples Intensive, since our lives seem to revolve around money." Leaning toward the phone, she shouted, "Hey, Monty, did you know there was a *famed* Highway 76? Cool . . . look . . . Andy Williams sings at the Moon River Theater. Ryan, wouldn't your parents just love it?"

Ryan was livid. He held the phone away from his face with his thumb over the speaker and whispered fiercely, "Are you finished yet?"

She wasn't. With every ounce of her energy, she would make it known to Ryan and anyone else within earshot how miserable he had made her life, and she didn't feel the least bit guilty for making his life a little uncomfortable in return. "Yakov Smirnoff has a show. Remember him from TV? Oh, my goodness," she mocked in a high nasal tone, "Shoji Tabuchi is in Branson too!"

"Monty," Ryan almost yelled into the phone, "I'll call you back in a few minutes. . . . Thanks." He gripped the steering wheel as if he needed to hold on to it to keep from hitting her. "Becca, what *is* your problem?"

"Oh . . . look who finally cares."

"Look, Becca, you know I have patients I've been seeing for close to nine months. I've told you—I don't know how many times—that I feel sick about leaving just when they are about to deliver. I can't just ignore the hospital." He glanced at her. "How would you have liked it if Dr. Jacobson had left town right before we gave birth to Michaela or Sydney?"

"Don't give me that. I'm not worried about Dr. Jacobson's marriage. I'm worried about ours. I can't imagine him working night and day, and—and then going straight to the gym or sailing or . . . or to the nearest break room for a little tryst."

Silence.

"Actually, your 'hero,' Dr. Jacobson, is divorced."

"Well, I'm not surprised." The delicate reality of their own wrecked marriage once again appeared insurmountable. "And that's exactly where we're headed."

"Whatever," Ryan muttered as he turned his attention to the radio dial.

"Wow, honey, you lasted a whole minute in the conversation this time before shutting down. I think that's a personal best for you." Becca knew she was pushing her husband over the line, but she didn't care.

"I never should have agreed to come to this marriage counseling," he said. "Are they going to help you accept the reality that you're married to a doctor? This argument is always the same. You want all the goods, Becca, but you don't want any of the inconveniences. . . ." He swore. "I'm so sick of this conversation. It's like we're caught in an endless cycle. There's a price we have to pay to have the things we want. Why do you think I work so much?"

"Because you're a pushover."

"Oh, that's mature."

Becca turned back to read road signs. A long silence ensued before Ryan spoke again.

"The real question is, will you ever trust me again?"

She had no response for that.

"You keep making the issue about my job, but I think your unwillingness to let up on some of your petty demands is causing huge problems."

"Have you completely lost your mind? The 'huge' problem in our marriage, Ryan, is the fact that you can't seem to keep your pants up. I'm not the one who keeps saying, 'I don't know what I want. . . . I've tried to stop seeing her. . . . She's the one who calls me. . . . I'm so confused.' Give me a break. And how about honoring God by honoring your commitment to our marriage—how about we start there?"

"Okay, that's enough. I'm done," Ryan countered. "I mean it, Becca. This is never going to work. We might as well go home."

Just then his cell phone rang again.

"Hey, Dr. Waterman," Ryan answered. "No, you're not interrupting anything important."

✦ ✦ ✦

Todd and Pam Davis were the third couple to arrive for the Couples Intensive. Pam was elated at the sight of their final destination. The Bradford House, a Victorian-style bed-and-breakfast built with elegant turn-of-the-century charm and furnished in characteristic 1920s style, was tucked off of Blue Meadows Road. Surrounded by giant trees, flowering bushes, and lovely spring flowers, its broad wraparound porch and double-door entry were unpretentious. When Todd pulled into the drive canopied by oaks and maples, it seemed to Pam as though they were out in the country, even though the inn was close to all that Branson had to offer. Quietly statuesque, the estate looked to her like a piece of paradise.

Her husband scowled.

The Bradford House, though expansive, was cozy and invit-ing, perhaps even romantic for those whose marriages weren't on the brink of disaster. What a contrast it was to their simple parson-age in Phoenix. *It all looks a bit fancy, but wonderful for hurting cou-ples,* thought Pam. Its shaded velvety lawn was framed with flower beds of tulips, daffodils, hyacinths, peonies, roses, and irises with large, plump blossoms ready to explode.

Pam knew Todd wasn't impressed. Such frivolity seemed wasteful to Pastor Todd Davis. The inn looked excessive, and he was a practical man. With her arms wrapped tightly around her thick waist, Pam hoped she could hold back the rising waves of nausea. "Todd, I feel sick. I better wait here in the car for a moment." Feeling ill had more to do with the person at the wheel of the rental car than the winding roads that dipped and climbed like a roller coaster. Pam had been trying to hide her excitement. These four days were for her benefit, but they came at an excruci-atingly high cost. Todd would expect her to show improvement equal to the sacrifice he'd made. She hated feeling indebted.

Her husband was still in a huff about the money he'd paid to register for their four-day getaway. This arrangement was not his choice. And though he never said it directly, his sharp tone clearly communicated that he hardly found her worth the amount he was paying to fix her up.

If I were a vehicle, he'd have traded me in a long time ago.

She watched as her husband slammed the car door and practi-cally lunged toward the welcoming entrance of their beautiful accommodations. He had made known his belief that this was a waste of good time and God's money. The sooner they got this first part over with, the better.

Wanting to hope, Pam felt fear clawing at the back of her throat. She cracked the passenger window of the rental car for a bit of fresh air. Maybe her blood sugar was low; she did a quick blood-level check. It looked fine. Her anxiety had to do with much more than the physical symptoms of her diabetes. Her mind and heart were in trauma. How could she receive help without being exposed when Todd was with her the entire time? What if the therapists only gave enough information to enable her husband to reload his guns to use against her once they arrived back home?

It wasn't long before Robert and Cristy, the Bradford House host couple, appeared on the front porch with Todd. Eager to personally greet each guest, they were friendly and helped with luggage while escorting Todd and Pam inside. Pam could hardly pay attention to the dialogue, however. Once inside, her fears were stowed away at the sight of the Victorian decor. These four days would be a treat for her regardless of what happened in counseling. How she wanted to explore! The inn had a delicious apple-cinnamon aroma, which made her want to find the kitchen. Her eyes followed the winding staircase, circling up past the arched entrance to the great room. For now, she obediently followed Rob and Cristy toward a massive mahogany desk. Pam would take a tour later.

Keeping the conversation light, Rob asked how the new guests had met. Without a thought, Todd answered with offhanded sarcasm, "I was witnessing outside a strip club." He laughed at his own joke and insinuated further that he'd been waiting for his wife's shift to end.

Pam was mortified, but Todd was oblivious to the awkward pause that followed.

With raised eyebrows, their hosts tried to cover her husband's ill attempt at humor by busily providing room keys and details about their stay.

❀ ❀ ❀

Pam was hurt by Todd's inappropriate response to Rob's question, but she didn't want to start a fuss as soon as they walked in the door of their room. Instead, she asked, "What do you think Cristy meant?"

"I don't know what you're talking about."

She was referring to what Cristy had said while they finished the check-in process. Cristy had mentioned that they should be sure to read what had been written on the inside of their closet. *And why did Cristy look directly at me and say that it would give me hope? If she only knew how far I am from hope!*

Todd left the room without saying when he'd be back. Pam sat still, with her eyes squeezed shut, making bargains with God. How was she going to survive this man?

Alone at last, Pam opened her eyes to admire their room in peace. She marveled at its lovely Old English furnishings. She lived a simple life, but she loved beautiful things. Feeling like a queen, she set about arranging her belongings and settling in. Cristy's words played over and over in Pam's mind. What did her host mean?

The room was furnished with a stately armoire that matched the cherrywood of the king-size bed, but she was drawn to the closet off to the side. In fact, her heart skipped a beat. Cristy had said that reading what was written inside her closet would bring her hope. *I could use a little hope.*

She opened the closet and adjusted her eyes to its dark interior. It seemed fairly ordinary—cool, cramped, a bit musty. At first glance, it didn't look like anything special. As beautiful as the rest of the historical bed-and-breakfast was, the closet had seemingly missed the last couple of face-lifts given to the rest of the inn. In fact, upon closer scrutiny, the inside of the closet looked shabby and scarred from hard use. Little attention had been paid to its upkeep. Not much hope there. Maybe she had missed a detail in what Cristy had said.

Poetically, Pam realized how closely this old closet resembled her life. A pastor's wife, now forty-five, with two teenagers and an eleven-year-old; she felt hidden, in a bit of disrepair, and empty—especially empty. Over the years her life had been filled with children, evangelistic outreaches, and church activities. She had been satisfied. Never could she have anticipated how painful and confusing raising teenagers would be . . . and the devastating loss when things turned bad.

Darkness threatened to sweep over her. No! She would fight it today. Battling against her thoughts, she busied herself with tasks around the room.

The big Jacuzzi tub looked awfully inviting, but Pam figured she should settle in first. Todd liked everything to be in order, and she wanted everything to go perfectly during these next four days. She was worth the investment, wasn't she?

First, she laid out Todd's study materials and Bible on the antique desk. Next, she carefully arranged their toiletries on the marble-topped vanity, just the way he wanted them at home. For a moment she leaned her elbows against the cool stone and looked deep into the blue starbursts of light in her eyes, allowing herself to imagine being here with a lover. A man who had gone to fetch her flowers, or . . . It wasn't like she had anyone other than Todd in mind; just the thought of such a man was dreamy.

Out of the battered suitcase she lifted the neat stack of clothes for the dresser and unzipped the vinyl hanging bag of clothes she had carefully ironed at home. She loved the smell of clean, freshly starched laundry. After noting which ones would need to be touched up again, she turned the closet light on and started to hang Todd's pressed pants and crisp dress shirts. That's when it caught her eye.

There on the back corner wall, the closet was covered with graffiti. It looked like the pages of an old yearbook, complete with dates, names of couples, and short messages.

Pushing aside their clothing, she moved to the back corner of the closet. Sure enough, several people had written special messages on the wall. When Pam read the first one, she was stunned.

"Given a chance for new life."
DAVE & NICOLE, APRIL 2006

She read the next one.

> *"God does touch the deepest part of your heart.*
> *Our miracle happened, yours can too!"*
> JAMIE & DEBBIE, DECEMBER 2005

Personal messages left for her from people in previous Couples Intensives. They must have stayed in this same room. Pam's heart began to beat faster as she read on.

> *"Emotionally, spiritually, mentally, physically . . .*
> *you can know the fullness of each other's heart."*
> JOAN AND RANDY, AUGUST, 2005

What appeared at first to be defacement of public property was instead warm oil soothing a deep crevice of pain. Pam's vision blurred with tears as she read each message. She had no idea who these couples were, but she glimpsed a tangible connection—a lifeline—in her crushing loneliness. She had been given literal love letters scribbled in a closet. She read how God had restored hope and healing in these marriages. "A chance for new life." That's what she needed most. *They couldn't possibly have been in the same poor shape we're in,* she thought. *Could they?*

❂ ❂ ❂

Victoria Templeton felt as if she had been sucking her breath through a tiny straw when at last she and her husband, Charles, drove through the gate to the historic bed-and-breakfast. Their travel had gone smoothly but had been marked by long periods of silence. Victoria was certain that they truly loved each other, but they no longer knew how to communicate it. Like the mono-grammed towels left hanging in the master bathroom of their sprawling home in Dallas, each nursed "his" and "her" own private pain. Without some kind of intervention, they would be driven further apart. Victoria didn't know how much further they could go before there would be no return.

Both husband and wife had agreed to come, but locked now in her own private thoughts, Victoria speculated about how well Charles would handle being confined over a four-day period with three other unhappy couples. The quiet bed-and-breakfast atmosphere, not to mention four days of intensive therapy, could prove daunting!

Once she could breathe again, Victoria felt at ease in the fashionable surroundings. While climbing the grand, winding staircase, she paused on the balcony and gazed through dramatic twenty-five-foot windows on all sides, which displayed a gorgeous view of the Ozark Mountains, lazy and blue in the late afternoon light. It was glorious. She would come back later for a better look at the view beyond the windows and the grand fireplace stretching from floor to ceiling. In spite of the pain in her heart, Victoria would enjoy the lovely change of scenery.

Husband and wife each went to their own rooms, reserved separately. Though it felt rather awkward, it was better this way. She knew her issues would get stirred during these next several days, and she wanted to ensure that she had her own space to work through them. She could think and pray more clearly when she was alone. Of course, Charles strongly disagreed.

It felt good to stretch after traveling for several hours. She stood in front of the lace-framed window to do some Pilates. Just then she saw an eagle soar over the trees against the backdrop of the picturesque hillside. She was sure that's what she saw. She craned her neck, hoping for another glimpse. How she would have loved to share this moment with her husband or even tell him about it later, but she knew her enthusiasm would be snuffed out when he tried to debate whether or not the area had such a bird.

She breathed deeply now, bending, stretching, twisting, angled in positions that brought her body relaxation and strength. This was her life: *solo, forte, moderato.*

Victoria had started reading the book *The DNA of Relationships* several weeks earlier and was captured by the simple yet profound metaphor of the Fear Dance. It so perfectly described her troubled relationship with Charles: how, against the backdrop of life's melody, they had fallen out of sync and little by little allowed themselves to push the other away. Being a dancer by nature, she longed to be free to dip and twirl, to move to her God-given rhythm—and she did, when she was alone. But when she invited her husband to join her, rather than together becoming a beautiful reflection of God's love in motion, they were a distorted image, crippled and twisted with pain and rejection.

She and Charles had come to the Couples Intensive with the hope that they could not only learn what was crippling their relationship, but also with the anticipation that they could learn new steps to freedom. She pulled out her book again.

❁ ❁ ❁

Victoria woke up cold and aching. The oversize pillow-top mattress of her bed seemed excessive for a woman all alone. Once she had located her glasses and perched them on her nose, the ominous glow on the clock focused to 11:38 p.m. She was hungry from missing dinner, but she had some dried fruit and nuts to snack on. Had Charles worried? Victoria sniffed. She was capable of allowing herself a good cry, but she fought it now. She had cried herself to sleep, and her bracelet had left a perfect imprint on her cheek.

The disturbing nightmare of crippled dancers that had plagued her brief rest continued to haunt her even now that she was awake. Her anxiety was aroused not only in anticipation of starting a four-day therapy session but also because she felt safe inside the walls of protection she'd built and she didn't want them to be torn down. She had learned to dance well by herself. *Lord Jesus, I need your peace.*

Finding her shower cap, Victoria took a long, hot bath in her Jacuzzi tub. After a few minutes in the warm bubbles and some time to pray, she began to feel sane again. She wasn't ready to ward off more nightmares, however. Wrapped in her wine-colored velvet bathrobe, Victoria decided to journal a bit until she felt relaxed and ready to sleep.

She pondered how humanity's original DNA had been woven together by the hand of God, the Master Creator, that we might dance in intimacy and freedom with him and the ones we love. She pulled out her journal and wrote thoughtfully:

> The DNA of relationships = our CODE for living = we are made for intimacy with self, God, and others.
>
> Our DNA determines the fabric of our being and the ways we are created to relate. Our DNA defines our movements through life, our life dance. In spite of the disappointments and pain we now experience as a result of being born into a broken world, we are undeniably woven together to live intimately in our Father's image.
>
> When we lose sight of our DNA of relationships, we can no longer recognize the beautiful image of God reflected in us, and we become crippled in our dance. We are designed to know and experience his perfect love in our relationships with ourselves, with others, and with him. But because of sin, we've learned to survive by acting out of distrust and fear, causing our dance to become a pained limp.

MONDAY, 8:00 A.M.

Clutching her folder, Victoria made her way down the broad, circular stairs of the bed-and-breakfast, along the hallway, and to the door marked "Private: Counseling in Session." The other couples gathered quietly with obvious apprehension, each finding a place to sit on couches and overstuffed armchairs in the small counseling room. The room felt tight.

Victoria, claustrophobic since childhood, had learned to plan escape routes, whether she was in a room, in a vehicle, or pulling a blouse over her head. Her eyes scanned the perimeter of the counseling room. With relief, she spotted two doors to the outside as well as to the stairway up to the main floor. Nonchalantly, she walked over and opened one of the doors just to be sure it wasn't locked or stuck. Silly, she knew, but now she could breathe more easily.

Each individual was welcomed personally by Dr. Greg Smalley and Dr. Bob Paul, both therapists dressed casually in jeans and seemingly as comfortable with the location and each other as they would be in their own living rooms. What a nice change from her staunch therapist back home. Though she was curious about

21

the others in the room, Victoria's attention stayed on the two men who would lead her through the next few days. She wanted to have a good feel for their style before it was time to reveal anything too personal.

"It's nice to meet you, Charles," said Bob. Victoria's husband had arrived, and Bob shook his hand firmly, placing his other hand on Charles's shoulder. Victoria watched the two men talk for a moment. Charles was handsome and stood tall and proud. He was slightly bent from life's lack of kindness, but he was well dressed and distinguished even in his retirement. Those enormous shining eyes—how could they not give away secrets?

Her husband was guarded but sensitive. Victoria felt a pang of jealousy at his instant male connection with Bob: making easy eye contact, showing little inhibition. How long had it been since she could hold her husband's gaze or be touched by him? With each passing day, the barrier had grown, leaving their marriage silent and cold.

Victoria chose a seat next to an awkward couple in their early forties with name tags indicating that their names were Todd and Pam. The husband, Todd, was as stiff as a cardboard figure. Next to him sat a plump lady with a dimpled smile that seemed tacked into place like artwork on a school bulletin board. Victoria nodded to them without feeling the necessity to make small talk.

"Chelsea, Rodney, so glad you made it in," said Greg to a young couple who was just arriving. They entered the room at the same time, which was the only indication they belonged together. "Here are your name tags. You can sit anywhere you find most comfortable. But whatever you do, don't sit on Bob's lap; he's real sensitive about that!" Greg gave them a big, warm smile. "I'm so glad you guys are here. We'll get started shortly."

A disjointed trickle of pleasantries followed, mixed with pauses and a lot of staring, while they waited a few minutes for the last couple to arrive. Bob and Greg's lighthearted approach brought remarkable ease to the tension in the room. They both definitely loved to laugh.

Victoria busied her mind with memorizing the words on a couple of posters hanging on the wall. One read, "Life is relationships; the rest is just details."

The other was titled *DNA of Relationships*:

1. We are made for relationship.
2. We have the capacity to choose.
3. We are responsible for Self.

The words rang familiar from the book she had completed just prior to coming. Upon discovering her own capacity to choose, she had called and enrolled. She needed some help on implementing the rest.

Fashionably late, the California couple, Ryan and Becca Stuart, came thundering down the stairs in a whirlwind of Ralph Lauren's Romance perfume and the Marc Jacobs spring collection in chartreuse; Tommy Hilfiger for him, a breast enhancement for her; both tan and model perfect.

Victoria had heard one of the other couples mention that Dr. Stuart and his wife's late arrival was due to difficult travel arrangements. She welcomed the diversion of the "supermodel" couple. Perhaps with their entrance, she would attract less attention. She had learned to accept the many situations in which age and color set her apart from the rest, and she was more than happy to stay out of the spotlight. Even with their late arrival, they must have been one of the first couples up that morning, judging by the way they were so meticulously manicured, blow-dried, pressed, and curled. *Does that girl actually plan to keep her makeup from smearing? This is therapy!* Victoria smiled.

After taking special care to see that everyone was settled and as comfortable as could be anticipated, Bob settled into his chair and stretched out his lanky six-foot, four-inch frame. *He could play some decent basketball,* thought Victoria. Bob kicked off his shoes and crossed his feet at the ankles, resting them on an ottoman. Victoria found his bearded face friendly and his dark eyes expressive and trustworthy. Bob's was a face that would be memorized by the end of the four days; it somehow ensured a sense of safety.

"We're glad you all made it," he said. "We imagine that if you're like most people, you're probably wondering what in the world you got yourself into! As a matter of fact, I can promise that if you found yourself dreading coming here, you're not alone. Most people do, but believe it or not, by the end of Thursday they actually dread leaving. You may find that hard to imagine at this point, but it's common enough that we don't mind saying it up front."

Both therapists introduced themselves and talked a little about their history together and their mission.

Victoria noted that Bob's partner and the founder of the Marriage Institute, Dr. Greg Smalley, was short in comparison to his lanky counterpart. He had a boyish face with distinct features etched in a light complexion and hair the color of wet sand. Leaning forward with his elbows propped on the arms of his chair, his voice was soothing and steady. He gave no indication of needing to put on airs to establish himself as a "specialist." Victoria was drawn in by how Bob seemed to openly admire his partner, who, like an expedition guide, looked ready to take on the twists and turns of the marriage journey, pointing out landmarks and pitfalls that would otherwise go unnoticed.

"What I love about these Couples Intensives," said Greg, "is that we will talk about things that revolutionized our marriages and our love for our wives. Bob and I both are filled with confidence and hope for your journey through pain because we remember our own. I feel honored to be invited into that place with you."

Dr. Smalley transitioned into the next segment of the morning with an opening prayer. Nothing fancy. He simply asked God for guidance and protection, then paused and asked each person to focus inward and take a moment to pray silently for their loved ones.

Tears were already beginning to flow, and Victoria was relieved to find a tissue box within reach. She took extras to hold in her lap and tried to focus on praying for her Charles. All she could silently utter was, *God help us.* Tears dripped down onto her handful of tissues. Yet in the midst of a sea of doubt and confusion, she felt at peace.

"Amen."

Ready or not, they were about to begin.

Bob began. "Few of you may realize yet the history that will be made in this room. It is your sanctuary away from the throes and battles of life. This little room has been the location where miracles the size of the parting of the Red Sea have taken place."

Victoria wondered what this meant for Rodney. He had nudged Chelsea. When his wife turned toward him, he searched her face, but it held no expression.

The two counselors were kind. With their thorough approach to allaying as many fears as they could right up front, Victoria began to breathe a little more easily.

Bob took care in explaining the details of their approach. "We want you to know that we don't follow a formula here. Instead, we work diligently to follow the leading of the Holy Spirit. Our intent is to help you find your way to what you want, as opposed to us telling you what we think you should want and how your marriage should be. We do not fully know yet what is needed for you in particular. That being said, our days together will not only be a relational process but a spiritual one as well. Without knowing the details of your faith or worship preference, I want you to know that Greg and I have been praying for you and we know our place—needing to be guided by the Holy Spirit."

Greg nodded in agreement and said, "Let's dig in." He then

asked each couple to introduce themselves. "Tell us what brings you here and what you hope to accomplish during the Intensive. Both your point of view and your tears are welcome. Please tell us your concerns, as you see them. It's okay if your perception is radically different from your spouse's; that's fairly normal.

"As a matter of fact," Greg went on, "Bob and I hardly ever agree on anything. Of course, we're not married . . . !" Greg kept a solemn expression while spouting off dry humor before betraying himself with a broad smile. Victoria felt Charles stiffen next to her. Though others in the room laughed, she knew her husband would not be easily amused until their issues were resolved.

Bob chuckled and got down to business. "Who would like to go first?"

A TALK WITH THE DOCTORS

Asking for Help

It's always hard, in any situation, to admit that we need help. Just as the participants in a Couples Intensive are often reluctant to speak up, you will likely feel that way in your situation. Sharing your struggles and heartaches with another person is messy and painful. We always say, "This isn't the fun part!" But we can't stress enough the importance of opening up to someone you can trust—a close friend, a pastor, someone in your small group, or a professional counselor. It's so necessary, so important, if you're going to start the healing process.

And if you're not personally experiencing struggles in your marriage, it's almost guaranteed that you know or care about someone who is. If you are entrusted with someone else's pain as he or she seeks answers, remember how hard it was for that person to ask for help, and offer all the support and encouragement you can!

✵ ✵ ✵

Looking around the room, Pam marveled at how incompatible the group of couples appeared to be. With ages spanning several decades, some were handsome, some wealthy, and others not so much—that would be her: plain and not so wealthy. The striking contrasts made her feel especially self-conscious. Surely Bob and Greg couldn't have coordinated such a collection of people on purpose! Under any other circumstance, the four couples occupying this small space may never have considered sharing four minutes together, let alone four intimate days of revealing their most private agonies. Pam's hands grew damp. One thing was obvious: They all had shattered dreams. Tight and distant, their tension filled the room.

Pam sat quietly, hoping someone would volunteer soon. Even after twenty years as a pastor's wife, she never could get comfortable with these stretches of waiting for someone to speak up. She knew her husband would break the silence, and she didn't feel at all ready to talk about herself yet.

"I guess we can go first. Is that all right with you, Chels?"

Rodney couldn't possibly know what a relief it was to Pam, an anonymous woman sitting across the room, that he was finally the first to speak up. Slouched in the corner of the couch, he had been nervously twisting the hoop earring in his left earlobe. Pam smiled at his oversize T-shirt with a worn picture of Elmo and a caption that said, "Tickle Me," which covered his inner tube–shaped tummy and low-riding gym shorts. He looked to her like a big, gentle pet. His wife, on the other hand, sat erect with perfect posture in a chair next to him, with noticeable distance between them.

Pam wasn't so sure about the young man's wife. They looked as mismatched as a Saint Bernard and a Chihuahua. Rodney's trim, athletic wife weighed no more than one hundred pounds and had hair the color of a new penny. She was well kept and looked to be in perfect physical shape. Though dressed casually in jeans and a hooded sweater, it was with purpose. She looked anxious to start. "Sure, I'm ready to start," she said.

Looking around the room, she made eye contact with each person. "I'm Chelsea Conner, and this is my husband, Rodney. We live in Springfield, Missouri—just about an hour from here. We've been married seven years, have two kids, and are now separated."

Her knee bounced in quick time.

"Our story is that we married way too young, and now that I know what I want in life, I realize we are totally wrong for each other."

Pam nodded in spite of herself.

"Rod is a good guy, but he refuses to grow up. I need a husband who will lead our family and bring in a decent salary. But all Rodney wants to do is hang out with his friends and play ball, music, and video games. We've been to a couple of counselors . . . and he makes pathetic, halfhearted attempts to change for a while, but then we're right back to where we started. I want to be home with our kids, but I have to work because Rodney doesn't make any money and he won't look for another job. He won't even try."

Fury flashed in her green eyes. From where she was sitting, Pam could see the look of disapproval Chelsea was giving her husband. In fact, the interaction was so intense that Pam glanced down at her hands folded on her lap.

"It's not working. The truth is, I can do better on my own— it's one less mouth to feed."

Based on the size of Rodney, that was no small matter. Chelsea's sharp words were obviously familiar, judging by the grieved look on her husband's face. It didn't take much imagination for Pam to see Rodney's tendency toward apathy and unresponsiveness, but he seemed earnest in his love for Chelsea.

"What was the next thing?" Chelsea asked. "Oh, yes. What are my expectations and intentions?" She shifted and folded one leg under the other, softening a bit from her initial self-righteous attack. She glanced at her husband.

Fear flashed across Rodney's face, and he looked away, as if he couldn't bear the words that would come next.

"I love Rod . . . he's my friend. After all, he *is* the father of my children, and we've had some good times. But I need someone to help me make decisions, someone to dream with and build a future with. I'm not his mother." Quietly but firmly she stated, "I want a divorce."

"What do you hope will happen over these next four days?" asked Greg.

"I conceded to coming because it hurts me to see the pain this is causing Rod and the kids. They love being together, and having our home torn apart is terrible for them. I want healthy closure, but now that I'm here . . ." Her voice trailed off.

"Go ahead," Greg encouraged. "I'd like to know what you're thinking."

"When I spoke with the lady over the phone, I said I was open to a miracle. But, honestly . . . ? I was hoping that the miracle would be for Rodney to see why we can't make this work. Now that we're all jammed together here in this room, I feel like I'm going to be pressured into making our marriage work regardless of what I truly want. I want to leave."

Greg appeared unfazed by the young woman's directness. "First of all, Chelsea, how you feel makes total sense to me. I'd want to leave too if I felt I was being pressured into making a marriage work. We want you to know that we're here for you, not the other way around. You are actually free to leave at any time."

Chelsea focused in tightly on the therapist, as if no one else were in the room. "I'm not sure we married for the right reasons, and I can't imagine how problems that haven't changed in seven years can change enough in four days to make a difference."

Greg nodded. "Sounds like you do need a miracle. Frankly, I don't know how that will happen either. All I know is that we see those kinds of miracles taking place here every week. The question you have to ask yourself is, are you willing to walk this out with us over the next four days to see if one occurs? I wish we could offer you a guarantee. At this point all we really have to offer is a lot of faith. I appreciate your honesty."

He paused for a moment to allow closure. Chelsea's leg was still bouncing, and it looked to Pam as if she was ready to bolt.

Next Greg turned to Rodney, nodded, and encouraged him to begin his side of the story.

Rodney shuffled out of his slouched position and started doodling circles on his folder. Getting choked up, he simply said, "I don't know what to do. I'm losing my wife." He looked as if he couldn't catch his breath.

His head was shaved, and his high forehead bunched up before he smoothed over it with a wide hand. "I don't measure up. I'm not the highbrow 'suit' she wants. She's already decided what she's gonna do." He leaned forward and shrugged one shoulder, holding it up near his ear. "So, I figure you can work your magic on me, but my marriage will still be over. She's already started the paperwork." He took a quick glance over at his wife, who sat with her lips pressed tightly together, memorizing the pattern on her Reeboks. "I'm willing to do whatever it takes to save my family," he said, rolling his lower lip and biting on it so that the small tuft of hair under his bottom lip stuck straight out.

Greg seemed to recognize the feeling of hopelessness in Rodney's voice. "Thanks, Rodney." He paused and then asked, "Okay, who's next?"

❂ ❂ ❂

Rodney wanted to cry, but he wasn't about to let his guard down this early in the show. He took a deep breath, willing himself to numb out. His first notion was to reach out for his wife's hand, but he knew that would be about as detrimental as sobbing at this point. He hardly noticed that Greg had asked for the next couple to start.

"We're Todd and Pam from Phoenix, Arizona." Todd's voice filled the small room, making Rodney snap to attention. Hard lines of consternation had formed deep crevices on the man's face even though he looked to be only in his midforties. Rodney didn't figure tenderness was a central theme in this guy's repertoire. As Todd began to talk, he seemed to hold every defining aspect of life under tight control, except his unruly bone-colored hair, which insisted on coming loose in the back, regardless of the strength of his hair gel.

Before continuing, Todd leaned back with a stern expression. His face was severe, with narrow-set eyes and deep pockmarks at his temples. His eyes blinked rapidly while he placed his palms flat together in a meditative position, his thumbs resting under his chin with the edges of his forefingers rubbing the tip of his large nose. "I'm the senior pastor of a small Bible-believing church." He shifted positions and picked an invisible piece of lint from his pants. His worn Dockers were pressed with permanent lines in the legs, and his green, collared shirt was starched stiff.

"We've been married and in the ministry for twenty-one years now, and never did I anticipate being in a therapy session such as this. In fact, I've always taught against it." He sighed loudly and sat up straighter. "I only agreed to come for my wife. Pam needs me to be here. She's been having a lot of personal trouble lately, and it is beginning to take a serious toll on our family." He spoke in a sermonish drawl, with accents placed carefully for emphasis. Such as saying *a* with a long sound, as in, "Pam has been having *ay* lot of trouble . . ."

With a quick scan around the room, Rodney could see that there was a good possibility that different personalities would put a rub on each other before the four days were up. He saw the Asian-looking guy whose name tag read "Ryan" frown and press his lips together in a straight line with obvious disdain at the minister's words. And the blonde with him, who looked like a model, had a momentary look of surprise before her face contorted into an unmistakable frown.

Todd plowed on. "Our daughter who is fifteen is doing fine. In fact, she's an honor student and a wonderful musician. . . ." He took the liberty to tell how his "pride and joy" played the piano in competitions and at church. "And our younger girl is a good kid too, but she's struggled with some things." Here his face darkened. "There's added pressure on pastors' families. We are prepared to deal with that . . . but I guess we're here looking for some practical answers." As an afterthought, the pastor looked at Chelsea and added, "Unlike other couples in this room, the word *divorce* is not in our vocabulary."

Now it was Rodney's turn to be infuriated. This creep had no idea what he was talking about! Immediately, he was drawn to the plight of the minister's wife, Pam. She looked sweet but frightened. He felt sorry for her and wondered what Dr. Smalley and Dr. Paul could possibly do to make her husband less obnoxious. She sat respectfully angled toward Todd, with her feet crossed at the ankles and her hands folded in the lap of her plain dress. When signaled to begin, she wrung her hands. Her short hair was pinned back with barrettes, which quivered slightly, disclosing her fear.

Staring straight ahead, Pam inhaled a shaky, little breath before beginning. "Like Todd said, we're looking for some helpful, practical answers. I do believe God gave us everything we need in the Bible, but we need to know how we can apply his truth to our daily lives. We're not like other couples in that we don't fight." Her eyes were empty and very sad. She explained that both she and Todd agreed their primary concern was for their kids. "But we're hoping this Couples Intensive will put both of us on the same page, so to speak, so we can return home with a united front."

"And what do you see as the issues, Pam?" Bob asked gently.

Her whole body shivered as if she were out in the cold. Rodney handed her a throw, which she draped across her lap. She nodded, and drawing in another breath, glanced at her husband before looking at the floor. She nodded and in a half whisper said, "I—I've been depressed. . . . You see, we have another child the preacher didn't mention."

There was an awkward pause while Pam hung her head in shame.

"Our oldest son has chosen a life of debauchery and sin," stated Todd flatly. "When he refused to be repentant, I had no choice other than to ban him from our family and the church. My wife refuses to forgive me for this, but I'm accountable to God and the church. And Zachary's behavior has upset the girls terribly."

After Todd finished speaking, the group sat stunned.

Greg suggested they take a short break. The couples shuffled and stretched, and several refilled coffee cups or got water bottles from the refrigerator in the small adjoining kitchenette.

Rodney lumbered outside as quickly as his large body would move. Any overt show of conflict was hard on him.

Bob took advantage of the brief stretch break to make a quick phone call on his cell. No sooner had he stepped outside and walked a few paces when in the background, the clicking of stiletto heels sounded on the asphalt. Rodney watched as Bob half turned toward the flash of pink—the doctor's wife was running toward him with her hands flailing in the air. Bob motioned that he was on the phone, but she didn't seem the least bit deterred. With her frantic gestures, she appeared to have every intention of interrupting his call. Rodney turned away, intending not to overhear their confidential dialogue, but their voices carried.

Bob asked his caller to please hold.

"Bob." Breathless from her fast pursuit, his guest persisted. "We do *not* belong in a group setting. Our issues are too complicated and—and humiliating." She continued, "My husband is having an affair, for goodness' sake! It's too private, and we need serious help."

Rodney swallowed hard and turned back toward the two.

Bob managed to sign off the call and assured the flamboyant

woman that he certainly understood she didn't want to talk about their private business in the group. With genuine compassion, he explained that they dealt with issues of infidelity as much as any other single issue.

She looked shocked. "Really?"

"Unfortunately, yes. I can imagine how painful your situation might be. But what we talk about will be completely up to you. However, I have a hunch you might be hoping we can provide you with some help. It will be your call, but I'm game if you are."

The woman—Rodney recalled that her name was Becca—halted all motion, as if she wasn't sure what to do with that response. Rodney watched with fascination. Would she leave? One could anticipate being nudged or pushed to stay, but Bob had just assured her that there would be no pressure. The stunning woman of five feet ten still appeared uncomfortable with the situation yet at the same time seemed relieved by Bob's relaxed confidence. Rodney guessed a woman that beautiful must have grown accustomed to being on the defensive with men trying to manipulate her. But Bob had just given her full control of the situation. She merely looked at him and nodded before making her way back to the counseling room.

❂ ❂ ❂

Before Becca had gone to find Bob, her husband had bolted upstairs. He had nowhere in particular to go, but Becca was certain Ryan needed a serious time-out. He was so miserable about being here, she couldn't imagine that he'd be willing to share his counseling time with the couple who had just introduced themselves. What had Todd said about his son? A life of debauchery? *Just wait till the Reverend gets a load of us!* Ryan's true colors were sure to flare to the surface before long. She just hoped they wouldn't ignite into something ugly. Ryan had promised he wouldn't use profanity in the counseling room, but she wasn't so sure he'd be able to keep his controlled image intact. He had endured years of militaristic demands from his father while he was growing up, and he wasn't willing to put up with any heavy-handed or legalistic demands now.

While taking his seat, Ryan bent down to move his folder, and Becca looked into a face stormy with frustration. Refusing to make eye contact, he looked as if he wanted to hit something or, preferably, someone. Beads of sweat formed along his thick, black hairline. She knew just how to let off some of that steam.

"We'll go next. I'm Becca Stuart from Newport Beach, California, and this is my husband, Ryan." With a smirk, she slipped her feet out of her four-inch heels.

Ryan's jaw clenched as he lowered his head.

"While we were driving into the parking lot, my heart was racing. I literally felt sick to my stomach." Becca popped her gum. " 'Why am I here?' I asked. Well, I'll tell you why I'm here. . . ." She punctuated her answer with a dramatic pause, while tucking a strand of hair behind her ear with an index finger and then pointing it directly at the accused. "My husband has ruined my life!"

❂ ❂ ❂

Rodney watched as Becca reached for the Kleenex box and ripped out a tissue with an exaggerated flick of her wrist. Her diamond-studded bracelet flashed as she wrapped the tissue around a long, nicely manicured finger and dabbed daintily at the corners of her eyes.

Rodney's doodling had come to a halt when she started talking. He was paying close attention now. From across the room, he didn't think Becca looked as if her life was ruined. In fact, she may have been about the prettiest woman he'd ever seen. Her tan skin was caramel satin in contrast to her platinum-streaked hair. It hurt him to see her so upset. To make matters worse, her husband was all but ignoring her. Rodney could guess who was the jerk in this relationship.

Becca's face twisted in anguish. "I get so furious when I think about all the things I've had to put up with—feeling worthless, undesirable . . . alone." She continued crying and twisting her tissue. With a helpless gesture, she threw it to the floor and whipped another from the box.

"But nothing has hurt as bad as Ryan's *ongoing* affair. It makes me want to *puke* to even think about it." If she'd had any reservations about making their story known just moments earlier, she showed no signs of it now. She pressed her knuckles against quivering lips.

Rodney could feel the sweat trickling down his sides. With the blatant and painful reality of Becca's situation being laid out before him, he could no longer deny the same possibility in his own life. Though he didn't know for certain, he, too, feared that his spouse had had an affair before their separation.

"There, now it's out. My husband has been cheating on me, okay?" Becca cried quietly and then balled her hand into a fist. "I feel so stupid! I have a right to divorce him, but God hates divorce, and I want to honor him. I've tried to be sane, but honestly . . . ? I'm a total wreck."

She sniffed loudly. "Anyway, that's why we're here." She looked at Bob for the first time since she'd started speaking. "You know, I think we'll stay, Bob. We need a miracle too, and we need it now!"

"Thanks, Becca." Bob gave her an affirming look before signaling for her husband to begin.

Ryan seemed unusually indifferent toward his wife. Rodney wondered if some of Becca's exaggerated behavior was to get her husband's attention. He evidently did not want to be at the Intensive. His jaw was rigid, and he sat flexing his fingers. Everything about his body language communicated that he was a private person—that he could think of nothing worse than being in this group. Pointing to his name tag, he wasted few words.

"I'm Ryan. And I guess I've caused a lot of pain for my wife."

I guess you probably have, thought Rodney.

Ryan paused. "But as you can see," he took a deep breath, obviously put out, "Becca tends to be sensational and . . . really quite paranoid. With just a few details, she can let her mind run wild with suspicions and crazy ideas." With his fingers locked behind his head, his biceps bulged. Rodney tried not to show that he noticed, but it didn't matter. Ryan seemed unaware of his own appearance. "My wife can be very demanding. I've certainly tried to make things right."

At this, Becca threw her head back on the couch cushion and rolled her eyes up to the ceiling.

Rodney looked from one to the other. Ignoring the woman next to him, Ryan went on to describe how he'd tried to make things right but nothing was sufficient. He claimed that after their two daughters had been born, everything changed and their marriage started to die. With all their fighting, they had pretty much killed whatever was left. "As for the affair? That's not the *cause* of our marriage failing; it's merely a by-product."

At this Becca sprung to the edge of the couch. "Am I supposed to just sit back and listen to all this because it's his perception? Whatever happened to reality?"

Bob stepped in. "Becca, I know you are hurting, and your feelings matter greatly here. . . . We are committed to doing everything in our power to help you achieve what you're here for. However, we also need to hear from Ryan. His feelings and perceptions matter too."

She rolled her eyes again and turned her body away from Ryan, but she forced herself to be quiet and let Ryan speak. Rodney began to think maybe there were two sides to the story.

"And what are your expectations for these next four days, Ryan?"

Leaning forward with his elbows on his knees, Ryan poked at the carpet with the tip of his shoe. With his head hanging low, he murmured, "I don't know. I'm at the end. I guess I want to hear your diagnosis so I know how to proceed."

Bob seemed genuinely willing to honor Ryan's request. "We'll be interested in learning more about what you want and how you hope things will turn out."

❂ ❂ ❂

"Charles, Victoria, thank you for your patience in waiting to go last."

Bowing her head, Victoria listened for the whisper of the spring breeze through the trees, the sound of her heart beating in her chest, the hum of the refrigerator in the accompanying kitchen lounge. In time she focused on the print in the furniture. Upon closer scrutiny, the pattern, which was subtle from a distance, was a detailed scene of an old country estate. A young boy was golfing in a mix of pale blues and browns. *This fabric pattern is Charles,* she thought. Indeed, Charles was not an outwardly demonstrative man, but at a closer look, he was complicated, like an intricate country scene.

Even now his expression was as somber as the dark jacket he wore. In stark contrast, Victoria wore deep, vibrant hues of fuchsias, violet, and sunflower yellow. Designed to laugh, dance, and love freely, Victoria knew her rhythm, and though she knew how to dance solo in the privacy of her mind, one of her most haunting pains was the unshakable reality that she couldn't get in step with her husband.

Sitting at his left side, Victoria raised her eyes to Charles's face in search of comfort, but she found none. Instead she saw the cruel reminder of his recent inner agony: a heavy, two-inch scar gouged into the flesh of his cheek. Victoria wanted to slide closer and take Charles's hand, but she didn't dare. She wouldn't allow herself to trespass across the invisible barrier of his grief. Though he shared the love seat with her, he seemed forever distanced; they might as well have been on two different continents. Actually, they had been recently, and it had been far less lonely for Victoria.

She was beginning to feel whole within herself, yet a cold, empty void remained when it came to Charles's portion of her heart. She couldn't risk his rejection. Neither was she ready for what he would need from her when he was ready to welcome her again. The ongoing conflict within her was too much to bear.

Charles sat silent. When it came time for him to speak, he formed his sentences with great care, as if he feared being held to account for every word's pronunciation. But Victoria let the words pass her by. They were a grim reminder of what was all too raw: a house and a life made up of rooms, cruelly echoing their empti-ness—the daily reminder that she and Charles were alone.

When it came time for her talk, she fretted about how she could describe the harsh reality that she was never so alone as when she was with her husband. Surely, those sitting in this room were much too young to understand. She didn't know how to begin to articulate her thoughts . . . how her husband was like a giant vac-uum that could suck all the joy from her life.

No, she had never been able to say it right. Oh, to have the audacity of that young doctor's wife, showing every ounce of her fury as she threw her head back, making wild gestures with her slender, jeweled hands and pulling herself up to a perched posi-tion, with her feet squarely in the middle of the couch. Well, per-haps that was going a bit far.

Panic set in, and Charles's wife of thirty-two years felt faint. The room seemed to be closing in, and Victoria kept her eye on the door. *Maybe this group therapy wasn't such a good idea!* The other couples' stories were unearthing her own buried pain. Although it had been six years since they'd lost Isaac, it still felt like yesterday.

Her mind raced through disjointed thoughts. Memories of ice-cream cones, laughter, wrapping her little grandson in his flannel quilt after his bath, rocking him in the night. . . . Her Isaac was gone—and with him, the soul of dear Charles.

But life continued—at least hers had. In the midst of the lingering pain, their other grandchildren now filled their lives. If only Charles would open up enough to embrace them.

Charles was saying something about how his wife was cool and distant. Unresponsive. Victoria conceded to this and nodded slightly. Over the years, she had been as available as she knew how to be. Now she wished she hadn't, because it only fostered his resentment. This was her pain too. . . .

She heard Greg asking what her expectations were for the week.

With deep sadness, she answered softly, "I hope we can find answers, Dr. Smalley. Our lives have been forever changed. I died too that day. But I want to live again."

"Our prayer will be that we can help you find the answers you're looking for, and that you'll experience the Lord touching your broken heart." Greg paused. "Thank you for being here, Victoria. I'm concerned that you may not feel safe yet and therefore aren't able to fully engage with what's happening. Safety is a huge priority with us," Greg went on, looking around the room. "We want to do everything we can to make this feel like the safest place you've ever been. Sounds like a tall order, doesn't it? We are asking you to join us in making this room feel safe."

Bob instructed how one of the best ways to make things feel safer is to try to keep judgment out of the process. "People feel wary of truly opening up when they are afraid of being judged. So check your judgment at the door on your way in. If you're really attached to it, you can pick it up on the way out, but while you're in here we want you to feel safe.

"Now, before we take a short break," Bob went on, "I want to thank all of you for your honesty. I know how hard this first day can be. In fact, I often say, 'If every day was Monday, I'd get a new job!' But because I know Wednesday and Thursday are coming—

when we're going to see what miracles God has in store for this group—I know it's worth hanging in there. And I want you to know that too. The first day is tough and messy. This isn't the fun part! But it's really a necessary part.

"We hold fast to the promise God made in Isaiah 61:4: 'They will rebuild the ancient ruins and restore the places long devastated; they will renew the ruined cities that have been devastated for generations.'"

Victoria found herself smiling as Bob quoted one of her favorite Scripture passages. She believed that promise—oh, how she believed it. She prayed that its truth would shine upon her dear Charles, too, before the week was over.

"One more thing." Greg was soft spoken, but he continued to hold everyone's attention. "Honor is a legacy given to us by my father, Dr. Gary Smalley. And no matter what, we will practice and uphold honor and respect in this room. We will also keep confidentiality after we leave. Again, we want this to be the safest place you have ever been. We are bound by our professional code to keep everything that goes on here confidential. While you are not bound in the same way, we do ask that you make a commitment to never mention anyone here by name once you leave this place."

3

Chelsea wanted to run and hide. She had just endured hearing three other couples describe troubles every bit as bad as her own. No way did she have the energy to respond to anyone else in the room! How could Bob and Greg possibly cover all they needed to in four days? She was going to have an anxiety attack right on the spot.

When Greg had said, "We want this to be the safest place you have ever been," Chelsea almost ran out screaming at the top of her lungs. Of course, she would never do such a thing. She was pinned by the forces that be. She'd never considered herself a fatalist before, but she'd never been this stuck either. Not only was she frantic about not having enough time to work through their issues, she was sick with the realization that she had taken off precious vacation time and allowed her mother to use her hard-earned savings for the Intensive session and travel. For what? For these two guys to convince her to stay in a marriage she didn't want?

And Greg wanted her to feel safe? Right!

Nothing was safe. The tape in her head of Mother scolding her and demanding that she do the right thing was stuck on "continuous play," she didn't know how she would make ends meet, and she was afraid of her recent sin being exposed—everything inside was revolting. She simply could not face the thought of remaining married. As if imprisoned by a steel trapdoor, she was desperate to get out.

Here she sat immobilized when she should have been jumping into action: demanding to get her money back—something! Beyond all the commotion going on in her head, she heard Bob's voice saying her name.

"Chelsea? You look like you're having a hard time. Is there anything I can do to help?"

She hadn't noticed that the others had stepped out of the counseling room for a break and only she and Bob remained.

Chelsea studied the floor while he sat down across from her. "I'm feeling forced in a direction I don't want to go—where I . . . I can't go. I literally do not have the strength." She picked at her lip. "The irony is I think I am a much stronger person now than I was prior to my decision to leave Rodney. I can't figure it out." She felt pulled in every direction—and worse, as if she was failing at everything. "I cannot hold it together. I think I'm seriously losing it." She glanced quickly at Bob without meeting his eyes. "I am finally at a point where I can move beyond my parents' demands and disappointments with my choices . . . but I can't see a way out that will make God happy. I feel so condemned. I've tried to do things right, but what happens when it doesn't work out and you're totally stuck?"

"I think maybe you're putting the cart before the horse," Bob said. "Even though we call this a *marriage* Intensive, there is no way at this moment I would recommend starting this week by trying to decide whether or not you and Rodney should stay together. With all the conflict you have going on inside, if that decision is on the table this first day, you are sunk. There's no way that feels safe."

She remained guarded as he leaned forward and waited for her to get past her skepticism and look at him. She wanted to, if only she could quit resisting.

"I'd be willing to talk through some of this stuff with you if you're interested, but go ahead and cut yourself a little slack. You don't need to make a decision about it right now. I'm not saying put it off indefinitely, just not today. Free yourself of that weight. We ought to focus on you and your needs for a while. What do you think?"

It sounded good. Chelsea raised her eyes with a despairing look. "I'm not a quitter. I just don't have the energy to fight this thing out. My children are more than I know how to care for right now."

"Yes, I hear loud and clear that you are exhausted, and I'd love to see if we could help you sort this out . . . without the *fight*. We're here to help you find some answers you can not only live with but be excited about, okay? Let's put your staying-married-versus-separating thing aside for the moment, okay?

"Our goal is for both Rodney *and* you to walk away from this experience feeling good about yourselves as individuals—a more complete expression of the man and woman God created you to be. The only way for you to experience healing is to open yourself up to God's guidance and concern for you as an individual. This has to be first and foremost. And if in the process you and Rodney figure out that there is a way you can do this relationship together, then you may want to do so."

When the other guests returned about ten minutes later, Bob was lying on the floor with his feet propped on the couch, chatting easily with Chelsea. She could almost forget that he was a therapist; his demeanor was so relaxed. He had a way of dealing with the difficult stuff and then moving right on to talking about his kids or music or dogs.

Before starting again, Bob explained that Chelsea was feeling stuck and wasn't sure she wanted to stay. She could see that others had fears too. Bob put them all at rest by assuring them that they

never had to cover up their emotions, that it was much more bene-
ficial to explore them together. "If it's okay with you, let's explore
this a bit further, Chelsea."

She was ready.

"I realize this may sound different from other teaching you
may have heard, but we are confident that it is biblically sound.
And as with anything you hear from us, if what we say doesn't
match up with Scripture and is not confirmed in your spirit by the
Holy Spirit, then for goodness' sake, throw it out."

With a shrug of her shoulders, she agreed.

"I'm not sure why marriage and freedom are exclusive from
one another for you right now, but temporarily putting your relationship with Rodney aside, I think the more pressing issue for
you, Chelsea, has to do with your personal needs. It seems like you
are seeing this—even your being here—as a choice between you
and the marriage."

"At this point, it is."

"Why?"

Chelsea felt utterly powerless to make her life turn out right.
Anything she opted for was going to be terrible. Whether she
turned tail and returned home to all the messes or left for good—
being the one who walked out—she knew the kids would suffer.
Either way, her mother and God would be displeased. "I've been
put in a place where I have to choose, and I can't. It's like I have
only one option: Be married and *get* happy. That's what God
wants." Feeling overwhelmed, she started to cry.

"I do believe God wants the best for you. Unless I'm mistaken,
you are his child and he loves you."

She knew that. Just like her mom loved her . . . and made very
clear that she would control what Chelsea did at every turn in her
life.

"You still have choices," Bob said. "You may not like them,
but they're there."

"Right. Like what?"

"If you actually had to choose between you and the marriage, and that was the only option, I'd tell you to choose *you*."

"What?" Chelsea's head snapped in his direction, and she met his gaze with disbelief.

"Well, you do feel as if you have to choose between you and the marriage now, right?"

"Uh-huh."

"And what *are* you choosing?"

"I have chosen me, even though it's wrong." Her mind flashed over her most recent choices while she traced the pattern in the couch with her pointer finger.

"Wait. Even though you want to judge yourself, I'm not willing to join you in that judgment. For now I want you to know that without question, I'm encouraging you to choose *you*. Do you know why?"

"No."

The room was suddenly so quiet Chelsea could hear the others breathing. He was encouraging her to choose *herself*?

"Before I say more, let me preface my answer. Chelsea, do you have a clear sense of what my life's work and ministry are all about?"

"Saving marriages?"

"Yes, saving marriages is my passion. With this in mind, listen carefully. I have come to the absolute conclusion that the well-being of an individual is always more important than the well-being of a marriage."

Rodney's pen stopped midstroke. He raised one eyebrow in a questioning slant. With a quick look, Chelsea could see that her husband didn't like where this was going. It even made her feel a bit unnerved. They had paid this guy good money to save their marriage, not to encourage her to go out and discover herself.

Chelsea demanded to know the answer to the question every other person was wondering. "How can you say that?"

"Because Jesus came to save people, not marriages."

Rodney looked bewildered. Todd, the minister, was turning crimson.

She had no more time to worry about what Rodney or the others thought. Chelsea needed to figure this out for herself. "How can you break it down like that? I've entered a sacred covenant under oath to God. If I had the freedom to make that choice, I would always choose me. That's not gonna work!" She folded her arms. "For me to choose *me* means not having Rodney in my life at all."

Rodney shrugged his shoulders up to his ears and examined his pen.

"I think you are turning this whole deal into a choice you don't have to force. I am saying we start with taking care of Chelsea."

"But how can four days do that?" Her glimmer of hope was quickly fading.

Bob explained that he understood Chelsea's time concern and conceded that it was certainly easier for him to feel more relaxed about the process. "After all, what have I got to lose if it doesn't work out? But I figure you're here because you hope we just might have something you haven't heard or tried. I imagine you've already tried everything you could think of."

Greg spoke up. "Wouldn't you be just a little disappointed if we merely said more of the same things you've already heard?"

"I suppose so," she said, still a bit unsure. She wanted to trust these guys, and she knew they were godly men, but she wasn't sure about the direction they were taking her. Most of all, she didn't want to be played. After visiting with Bob, she was fairly confident that he'd shoot straight.

Bob went on. "We're suggesting you consider some of what has helped other people whose marriages were in pretty rough shape. And beyond that, it has made a huge difference for Greg and me personally. One of our biggest commitments is to teach only what we can make work in our own lives. It's got to be more than a good theory. We know it works because we live it. So here is what I would like to suggest . . ." He was pretty much no-nonsense and clearly stated that either the Intensive was going to work or it wasn't. "In order to walk this out, you don't need to have the kind of faith that I have. As a matter of fact, as far as I am concerned, you can piggyback on my faith if you need to, just long enough to check it out. That's the biggest risk you have to take right now. I'm hoping you find a place in this moment where you can relax and not worry at all about how or when we are going to arrive at a solution, or even how God is going to work. All you have to do is be willing to put one foot in front of the other."

Chelsea remained pensive.

"Do you remember our measure of what makes a marriage a success?"

"Both people walk away thrilled?"

"Yes."

"Bob, I've never even used the word *thrilled* before, let alone used it in the same sentence as *my marriage*."

Most of the people in the room could relate, and they laughed with Chelsea at her candidness.

Bob chuckled too. "Well, this is my favorite place to use it—in the context of marriage! We are not at all interested in helping people endure misery or mediocrity for the rest of their lives. Period. Either couples are thrilled or we haven't succeeded. And to have a successful marriage, you must have the opportunity to be fully true to yourself, to be able to express yourself to the fullest."

Greg spoke up then. "Chelsea, I'm concerned that you may have marriage and freedom defined so narrowly that there really is no way to have both—you are in a position where you have to choose between the two. And the easiest way right now seems to be leaving the marriage. Can you see the dichotomy you've created? We want to encourage you to open up your definition of freedom a little bit so that you have the possibility of having both."

"Let me ask you this," Bob interjected. "What do you believe would enable you to finally have freedom?"

That was an easy one. "Not being married."

"I don't buy that."

What? "Then what is it?"

"I'm not sure yet. But we can try and figure it out. I just know the answer isn't 'not being married.' I know plenty of people who are not married and aren't free. It has to be something else."

Chelsea could feel her face grow hot. What did Bob know about her life? He obviously didn't know what it was like to wake up after a few crummy hours of sleep, rush through a morning routine after dragging two sleeping children out of their warm beds, pack lunches and extra clothes, and shove food into them while sitting in traffic. Not to mention having to look just right, stay in shape, and push hard all day trying to convince the firm of her ambition.

If that wasn't enough, then she had to remind Rod to pick up the dry cleaning or the kids, or she found herself nagging, calling, looking for him, or apologizing for him when he didn't show up places . . . all before collapsing into bed to the sound of his laughter as he hung out with his friends. Rod looked all sweet and mild sitting over there now, but she seethed at the thought of how many times she'd had to drag herself out of bed to tell the guys to keep the noise down so the kids could sleep—so *she* could sleep, for goodness' sake! What did Bob know about living with a man who took zero responsibility for bringing the kids up in the faith?

Any kind of break would be freedom. Being able to sit on this couch for ten minutes without having to wipe a nose or make a decision was freedom! Divorce would mean one big chunk of stress would be out of her life and *he'd* have to take his turn with the kids—another chunk of stress relieved.

Chelsea was beginning to shut down; all she wanted to do was run hard and fast away from here—away from life. But Bob was right with her. "Chelsea, how are you feeling toward me right now?"

Totally caught off guard by the question, she glanced around the room and said tentatively, "Actually, I'm getting pretty annoyed with you." Feeling bolder, she straightened. "How would you know what I'm feeling or what I really want?"

"I don't," Bob shot back, without missing a beat. "But from what I hear you saying, you don't want freedom from responsibility; you just don't want to do it alone. You want a partner who will work *with you*, but Rodney seems like just another big burden to carry. It sounds like you're incredibly disappointed—maybe even heartbroken—that the man you hoped would stay on the adventure with you staked his tent early in the journey and said, 'That's as far as I'm going. I like it here. You can go on if you want. By the way, you paid the mortgage, right?'"

Okay, so Bob did know. She was still annoyed. "I do feel that way, and I'm not taking this anymore. I hate who I'm becoming, and I want to get out before it is too late! We're sitting here trying to make ourselves clear, but the fact remains, when this week is over, it's over, and so is our marriage."

❈ ❈ ❈

Rodney, who just wanted everybody to love one another and be okay, was embarrassed and hurt by his wife's defensive argument. Her words cut deep into his heart. They had argued and said mean things in private, but hearing her say these things to another person, with so much passion, sapped the life out of his soul. He was beginning to think maybe this Intensive was all a mistake. Was he going to have to sit here through four days of humiliation and hurt just to kiss his marriage good-bye? He sat holding the pieces of his pen that he had unknowingly disassembled.

Bob's tone of voice went unchanged as he forged ahead. Rodney kind of hated him right then. "I just want you to know we are committed to you and your ultimate well-being," Bob said. "You alone will have to determine what that ends up looking like. In the end it'll be between you and God, and whatever you two work out will be fine with me. I just see you in conflict over the whole deal."

Greg spoke up again. "You said you'd be open to a miracle. Can you trust God in this? What do you need in order to feel comfortable about moving forward?"

Chelsea sighed deeply. "I want to honor God. And even though Rod infuriates me, I do love him. I want to keep him in my life—especially for the kids—but I think we will be happier apart. I know couples who are. I don't want him to be hurt, but I want him to grow up. That won't happen when he's with me. I don't see why God can't be okay with that."

"I can see that you are done living in turmoil, but you do not sound resolved at all," came Bob's interesting reply. Rodney covered his mouth with his hand and tried to figure out what on earth this therapist was trying to do. Bob had more curveballs than any pitcher Rodney had ever played against.

"What do you mean?"

"You are resolved about not wanting turmoil anymore, but I can hear loud and clear that you are not resolved about your feelings for Rodney."

"Why?"

"Because I hear you saying you genuinely love him. I have a hunch that it might even be useful to take the time to sort out how you actually feel about him."

Rodney's shoulders relaxed a bit—perhaps a bit prematurely.

"Bob, I've already *done* all that! I do love him, but I really resent him, and I don't respect him." She turned her body at a sharp angle away from her husband. "Bob, my whole marriage—my future—was built on a warm, fuzzy childhood romance. I was with Rodney at age seventeen. We were two romantic nomads dreaming about how the world was fueled by love, sex, and weed. I had two little children before I realized I could really use a paycheck. I was just young and stupid, and I didn't want to end up where my parents were. But guess what? Here I am. I was totally checked out when I met Rod. I didn't even know what my choices were then. I didn't know what I wanted."

"I get that you were idealistic and wanted to live without any regrets. You wanted to believe that life was fueled by love, that there had to be something better than what your parents had settled for." He smiled a knowing smile. "I was part of a whole generation that felt the same way.

"Now you must feel like the brunt of some huge cosmic joke. Yet there is still a little flame flickering in your heart that says there's still got to be a way to be free. I realize that there's conflict there now. Part of you wants more: more status, more security, more growth, etc. And in some ways that feels like growing up. But I sense that you haven't fully given up on some of the things that you valued back then. I wonder how different you really are, deep down, from that love child. I think I can relate more than you know. I was a radical, long-haired, rock drummer who gave serious thought to moving to a commune. A lot of those dreams of peace and love and strong community still exist in my heart. Sometimes I can't reconcile some of the ways my life has taken me away from those values.

"Whatever we do, I don't want you to feel as though we are forcing your hand, as if we are maneuvering this thing and mushing it around until you no longer have a choice. What you decide about whether you stay or leave is between you and God. No matter what we explore and no matter what we discover.

"Whenever you do feel pressured, let us know and we'll stop immediately, okay? I'm guessing you tend toward being very responsible. So when you start feeling those old emotions of, 'I'm here, I've got to do this, even if I won't be able to live with myself,' all of a sudden you hear the gun cock by your ear. If you feel a gun pointing to your head, let us know. I don't want to be party to that. How does that sound?"

Chelsea looked relieved, and Bob continued, "I am confident that I could take one of my children and force them to go anywhere I want them to—even if they didn't want to—if I held a gun to their head and demanded they do as I say. It would be terribly abusive though."

From across the room, Todd grunted and folded his arms so his fingertips were sandwiched under his armpits. "I can't keep listening to this garbage! The Bible is crystal clear about divorce. I don't know how you can call yourselves Christian counselors and sit here telling this woman that all that matters is whether she is okay. Why aren't you showing her what the Lord has directed through his Word? All your psychobabble does is support her selfish desire to do what she wants and have her conscience relieved."

Everybody in the room was instantly on edge, unsure of what was about to happen next. Rodney did all he could to remain quiet. This guy's demeaning approach had to go.

Bob turned to address the minister. "Todd, how do you feel about swimming?"

"Swimming?" The whole group was jolted. "I like it well enough." Todd blinked in a series of longs and shorts, as if he were sending Morse code.

"Are you a good swimmer?"

"Yes."

"Can you imagine yourself standing on the edge of a pool but not knowing how to swim?"

"Sure." His arms remained tightly crossed.

"How would you feel if you were forced to jump into the deep end?"

He shrugged. "That happened to me. My swimming instructor pushed me off, and I discovered I could make it just fine."

"Was it traumatic?"

"I was terrified, yes."

"Okay. What if your instructor didn't push you but instead swore to you that it would be fine?"

His eyes narrowed with suspicion. "I still would have been frightened."

"What if I were the instructor and held a gun to your head and through gritted teeth promised that you would be fine? Now, jump!" Bob made a make-believe gun with his thumb and forefinger and pointed it at Todd's head.

A flicker of understanding crossed Todd's expression, but he squeezed his lips tight and refused to respond.

"We are talking about some stuff here that is really frightening," Bob said. "And for some, it may turn out that you already have all the skill needed to jump in. For others, this may not be true. We need to be sensitive to those who are terrified of jumping—even if everyone else is running down the board and high diving.

"And Chelsea, it would be just fine with us—in fact, preferable—if we just eased you into the water. You may need to just stick your toe in and test it or hang out on the steps a little bit, wade around in the shallow end with floaties. Hey, I am totally good with that. I would rather you do that, and when you feel safe enough to go swimming in the deep end, then we'll go. I want this to be that kind of experience for you."

Rodney liked how animated Bob became while interacting with his clients. He caught yet another glimmer of hope. He was beginning to see what Chelsea was up against and how sensitive the counselor was being to his wife. Chelsea's response was remarkable. Instead of shutting down and leaving, she was actually staying engaged with Bob. Maybe this was a good thing after all.

"Like Todd, you might find out you would do fine if you were pushed in, but it is a traumatic way to learn how to swim. And it's not necessary. It's also a rough way to do life. If I were you, I would want assurance that it is never acceptable for me to go forward in a relationship at the expense of my safety." Bob explained how he would like to find a better way, a safer way, to move forward and address their precarious issues together. Rodney noticed how Bob gently continued to talk until he saw the tension leave Chelsea's shoulders. Only then did he turn again to the minister.

"Todd, my experience is that God is a gentleman. He gives us the freedom to make choices. And he also says we will be accountable for those choices. I'm aware that it is not my place to judge Chelsea, nor am I convinced that I am wise enough to ultimately know what is best for her, or for any of you. But I am completely confident that every one of us here in this room is fully capable of sorting this stuff out with the Lord directly.

"That said, I will do everything in my power to assist you here in sorting things out with God. But I will leave the final decision to each of you. Todd, you don't have to listen to a thing we say, and certainly you don't have to believe it. But I wonder if, since you are here and we both know Jesus as our Lord and Savior, if you might be willing to simply see where this goes and hold off on making a final decision about me, my work, and my theology. I appreciate your concern and your commitment to truth. My hope would be that, as we work together, your concerns about us and what we do here will be eased. What do you say?"

Todd didn't look at all convinced to Rodney. His rigid body language communicated his serious concern about what he was hearing. Would Bob's lack of defensiveness, combined with his willingness to talk directly about the Lord, make it possible for Todd to consider Bob's request before writing him off as a humanistic heretic? Rodney wasn't sure.

A TALK WITH THE DOCTORS

A Safe Environment

We've been doing Couples Intensives for more than seven years. And we know that after hearing guidelines for change, people by nature tend to resist. We've come to anticipate the most frequent objections and have learned to walk people through the swampy places where they most often get stuck.

Much of Chelsea's resistance in this story is based in fear, and the only way to ease that fear is to honor her resistance. By showing that he is okay with it, Bob establishes a sense of safety so she can drop her guard long enough to stay and find help. In order to find healing, Chelsea needs to experience a certain level of trust. We often need to have the option of saying no before we feel safe enough to say yes.

If you are like us, you long for relationships in which you feel completely safe. You want to feel free to open up and reveal who you really are and know that the other person will still love, accept, and value you—no matter what.

Yet many of us struggle with various aspects of intimacy because it requires openness, and openness makes us instantly vulnerable. We're not quite sure what others will say or do, or how they'll use what they learn about us. This is why a lack of desire to connect—or an avoidance of intimacy in general—usually has to do with attempting to avoid pain, humiliation, embarrassment, or just plain discomfort.

As a way to lower the risk, people come up with many strategies to try to connect without getting hurt. We put up walls and try to project an image we think people want. Like Chelsea, we may keep parts of ourselves closed and protected. We may ignore or deny how we actually feel. We may get angry or demanding as a way of distracting ourselves, or our spouse, from our own vulnerability. There are a whole host of options we may use to attempt to avoid relational risks.

Unfortunately, these strategies limit the intimacy of our relationships. The foundational component of a deeply intimate relationship is a truly safe environment—one that is safe physically, intellectually, spiritually, and emotionally. And so we do everything we can to create safety when we are together for our Couples Intensives. We know that people are, by nature, inclined to want to be open and connect. Openness is the default setting for human beings. No state of being takes less energy to maintain than openness, which involves being yourself and just relaxing. Maintaining defenses, walls, and fortresses takes tremendous energy, as you will see in the next several chapters as our guests try to work through their issues.

Our approach is to create a safe environment for intimacy, and it is astonishingly effective. When two people feel safe, they will be naturally inclined to relax and open up. Then intimacy will simply happen.

Warm, midmorning sunlight filtered through the blinds. Victoria loved how the dust particles danced in a sunbeam, but there was little time to think about those things now. The second session was about to begin. Shoes were being kicked off, and Greg removed his light sport jacket and draped it over the back of his chair. He perched on the edge of his chair and squirted water from a water bottle into the back of his mouth before leaning forward to address the group.

"The first day is usually messy, and couples aren't quite sure what they've signed up for. The group often feels real awkward. You've had to sit back and listen to couples you've never even met talk about their deepest pain and suffering without knowing what to do to fix them, and things just don't feel too pleasant right about now. But it's okay. We've heard everyone's introductions, and now we have a pretty good idea of who you are and where we're starting. Now we want to begin with some work."

At this, Victoria felt her heart speed up. She wasn't alone; everyone in the room looked restless and miserable. Several of the men—especially Charles—looked as if they didn't want to hear any more lurid relational details. It was a bit like being in a stranger's bedroom overhearing a couple's most intimate dispute. The benefits of the group dynamic remained a mystery.

Bob took over. "We will work with one couple at a time, and in this first round most people give us a little bit of history. We will do that until we feel a sense that we've reached a good place for a pause, and then we'll let things settle a bit. This is when we take a few minutes to check in with everybody. You are each other's assistants. During the process, chime in as you feel led. Sometimes Greg and I will be facilitating or directing the process, and sometimes we will work it out as we go. It is kind of organic and free flowing. We will be your guides, but we are really relying on all of you to be engaged with us."

Victoria was intrigued.

"So, who is willing to go first?" asked Bob.

Becca's legs were crossed, and her foot started swinging a mile a minute. The lovely Californian appeared to be especially anxious to begin, and the words practically flew out of her mouth: "We'll go first." She flipped her hair over her shoulder as if she were born ready for confrontation. Just watching her was enough to wear Victoria out; no wonder she was so thin.

Bob nodded and looked over at Ryan. "Are you up for it, Ryan?"

Victoria's son was the same age as the young physician, and though Ryan's attitude needed a serious adjustment, she wanted to see him get help as much as she hoped for Becca's wounds to be healed. As a mother, she understood a young man's desire for freedom and knew what a fatal flaw that could be when combined with an entitlement philosophy that says, "I deserve this."

An excellent communicator, Ryan explained how serving in the role of a physician meant he continually carried the burden of responsibility for many lives. He described how brutal his residency had been and that he was finally in a place where he could live for himself a little. He even admitted to hoping for easy answers because he didn't have the "relational stamina" to do anything that took much effort. In fact, he hoped the counseling sessions would make a divorce seem like the best choice. Pointing to the little redhead, Chelsea, he boldly stated that he just wanted out, like she did.

"After Becca had the kids, her whole personality changed," he said. "She was sick and tired during the pregnancies, which was hard but manageable. She's always struggled with her self-image, and that whole thing just got out of control, like her eating disorder, which came back too. Yet the biggest deal was her extreme shift when she took on this 'mother image.'" He said it with marked disdain.

To Victoria, Ryan's story sounded a bit stretched. Perhaps it was the collision of images that was throwing her off. After all, the woman sitting in front of her looked more like a runway model than a mother. Beauty for Becca obviously took no effort. She hardly looked like she'd been bogged down in mothering. She didn't appear to have ever carried a child, inside or out. Sitting perfectly groomed and manicured in her size-two designer fashions, her role as a mother was hard for Victoria to imagine.

❂ ❂ ❂

As anxious as she'd been to begin, Becca hadn't anticipated Ryan doing all the talking. She wanted to yell, "Stop! We've changed our minds. Someone else can have our turn." She felt exposed and too closely analyzed with everyone looking at her. She grabbed a pillow and hugged it tight to her middle, feeling as nauseous as if she were stepping off the spinning teacups at the carnival. *I didn't think he'd say so much! Can't someone shut him up?*

"Becca's sense of adventure is gone. She doesn't want to be playful anymore," continued Ryan. "She's more into the kids and her friends than being with me. It's like she *thinks* she wants to be with me, but when it comes right down to it, she can't get out of 'mother mode.' The kids are the only thing we have in common anymore. I work long hours every day, and when I come home there are emergencies, crying kids, and situations that need my immediate attention. Then she accuses me of not spending time with our girls. When she tells me about something cute they did during the day, she starts out happy then ends in an accusing tone, like, '. . . and *you missed it.*' But she sure appreciates the paycheck!"

Becca's mask started to crumple.

"And okay, since she was the first to bring it up, making love has become a major ordeal. I'm tired of trying to figure her out. I know I've blown it, but I'm over it. I've been jumping through hoops and performing for a person who can never be satisfied with what I have to offer. There's no way to please her."

"Let me get this straight," Bob said. "Were you jumping through hoops before the affair, or just after?"

"No, I've always jumped through hoops to please my wife. But now the stakes are even higher. It's ridiculous."

Bob reiterated that it sounded as if Ryan and Becca had in fact had this system in place for a while and that when Becca discovered the affair, Ryan used the same system at higher volts to try to please her in order to reestablish trust. "But it doesn't seem to be getting you anywhere. It seems like no matter how many things you do to try to convince your wife of your loyalty, she is still going to be suspicious."

"Right. And quite frankly, it's this kind of stuff that makes me want to take off and do something really crazy. I just keep jumping and jumping until I can't take it anymore. Then I get resentful, and when she's pushed me too far, I say all sorts of mean things. I take off in the car, and it starts all over again."

Shifting his weight, Ryan tugged at his snug pant leg and nervously glanced around the room as if he'd momentarily forgotten anyone else was there. But he still had more to say. "We do great when it's just us, but when we mix with others or when I'm away from her, it's horrible. She freaks. I don't know what to do; my job demands that I be away from her."

"And you feel there's no way for you to actually succeed and pull this off? Perhaps you're thinking that no matter how hard you try, she will never be truly satisfied," Bob said.

"Yeah, I hate to admit it, but I am starting to seriously doubt it."

"So, what do you want?"

"I think I want what she wants, but I don't know how I can fix it or what I can do to satisfy her needs. This is what I've been dealing with during the last few months. She freaks out and I feel guilty, so I ask her what it is that she needs. Then she gets nasty and makes a bunch of accusations like I should automatically know what she's thinking or feeling. I just start doing stuff for her, and it appeases her for a while. But I never get to think about what it is that *I* need. I mean—even with this Intensive—we're here because *she* wants us to be here."

"Ryan, I asked *what do you want*, and you first told me what it is she wants. And I then I think I heard you imply, 'This isn't working for me.'"

Ryan wet the tip of his ring finger and rubbed it across his bottom lip. "That's exactly right." He tried to explain how guys just want to deal with stuff immediately—how they want to make amends and then have it be done. "I mean, I was willing to say this affair happened and will never happen again. I was ready to move on. But she won't let me. It makes me so crazy I end up screwing around again. Bob, I don't think we can fix this thing." He threw up his hands in surrender. His easy demeanor quickly turned to rage, and despite his earlier resolve, profanity flew. "Our marriage is not only broken, it's smashed to bits! I'm not sure why we're even here."

"Let me ask you this," Greg interjected. "How well do the two of you understand what is really happening? In terms of not just *what* has happened with your affair, but *why* it happens and *why* it won't happen again."

"Why? She pushes me into it." He nodded. "Yes, for the most part I feel like I understand exactly why things happen," Ryan said.

"I don't!" Becca was trying so hard to stay quiet and let Ryan talk—he needed to if this was going to work—but . . .

"Wow. I'd say that is pretty important," Greg said in a disarming and remarkably even tone. "If I were in Becca's shoes, there would be no way I would feel safe if I didn't know why the affair happened in the first place, because I would have no way of knowing whether or not it was likely to happen again."

Glaring at her husband, Becca couldn't stay quiet. "It's not that I don't feel safe. I feel like an idiot. An absolute idiot!" Hot tears streamed down her face.

"Why is that?" Bob asked.

"Now that I am in this situation, I regret everything," Becca said, doubling over. "I have always said that if my husband ever cheated on me, I would be out the door. Now here I am in this position—begging him to stay with me. I'm so angry! I trusted him!" She pounded her fist into the pillow. "And now I want him back? It doesn't make any sense. That makes me think I am an idiot.

"I don't get any support from him or any understanding. Bob, he's not even sorry. Look at that face—no remorse! He's just bummed that he got caught. He had such a good thing going. . . . 'Oops, I got caught'—that's all the more sorry he is. And as for the hoops? I am not expecting him to do what I want, but I am expecting more than what I am getting. Is that too much to ask?" She sniffed. "I am filled with so much hate right now, I can hardly stand myself."

"So what is it that you need or want?"

"For one thing, I *need* him to go to a doctor. I need to make sure that nothing is going on. He's been with some low-life tramp who sleeps with married men. That's my opinion, and I'm sorry if

I've offended anyone." She looked squarely at Todd, the pastor. "I want to make sure that he doesn't have anything. He says he wore a condom, but he's lied so many times, I don't know if he did or didn't or whatever. I don't care. He needs to go to the doctor. I had to. Do you know how humiliating that was? You'd think that he'd want to make sure his family is safe. But no, he's too proud!"

Becca insisted in no uncertain terms that she did not want him kissing their daughters or being anywhere near her until she knew he was clean. She had no way of knowing where his mouth had been. "I want him to go to a doctor. I am trying to protect him, which I totally shouldn't be. But you know what? His pride is more important than his family. He's a doctor. He knows the health risks. And yet he doesn't want to be embarrassed among his peers."

The others in the room sat in disbelief. Becca could see that their scenario was a bit more raw than they had probably anticipated. Charles was visibly uncomfortable, and Victoria eyed the door several times. At least one other set of eyes narrowed with disgust.

"He says that I am punishing him by withholding sex and making up a bunch of hoops he has to jump through? Let me tell you something. I went out of my way to have somebody find a doctor *far away*. That doesn't sound like a hoop to me. I think he shouldn't even question this. Has he even considered that he's being so self-centered that he's robbing *me* of sexual pleasure? I am a highly sexual person, so his need for anything more than I can provide is absurd! I don't get it. Isn't this the kind of weird thing that happens to people who've been married forever and sleep in separate beds? Punishment? This is not punishment. I want him checked."

"Why?" asked Bob, without skipping a beat.

"Why what?" She reeled with astonishment.

"Why do you want him checked?"

"What if he has something that shows up later, like AIDS? I'm concerned about him." She was unnerved that Bob would even have to ask. "And I don't want to get a disease!"

"You're afraid that not only do you have to experience the pain of the affair and betrayal but in addition you could end up contracting a venereal disease? That would just be over the top, especially if it was something preventable."

Becca tucked her hair behind her ear and nodded, relieved that he actually did understand her.

"I am hearing you say," Bob continued, "that this is really scary for you, and you need to know the truth. You need to feel safe. And when he won't cooperate, it's terrifying."

"Yes, it freaks me out. I'm afraid all the time. Bob, I have these scenarios that run through my head . . ." Becca swallowed and shuddered. As warm as it was in the room, she wrapped her arms around her middle as if she were sitting in a freezer.

Bob turned his head. "Ryan, I think I'm hearing genuine fear. What do you think?"

With a tilt of his head, Ryan gave a nod.

"How does that make you feel?"

"Terrible." Shifting again, he rubbed his palms up and down his thighs.

Bob leaned in. "Okay, but do you feel manipulated by your wife's emotions right now, like she's trying to get what she wants or punish you in some way?"

"No." His tone was flat. "She's really frightened. I can't stand seeing her hurting like this." Then all of a sudden, with a shocking show of emotion, he blurted out, "I can't handle it, okay?" He stood up and faced the window.

"How long has all this been going on?" Greg asked.

Becca was the first to respond. "Since June of last year, as far as I know. I don't know for sure how long it's been going on."

"Do you feel as if you know the extent to which things went on?"

She had no idea. He'd been working with the other woman

for over two years and had several other conquests along the way. As far as she knew, she was the only one who had ever questioned or confronted him. "I asked him. I looked in his eyes and knew." Tears pooled in her eyes before spilling down her cheeks. "He was shocked, but I knew something was going on. So I looked into his eyes and told him, 'I know something is going on, just tell me.' Can you believe he looked at me point-blank and lied? Not once, not twice. What, Ryan, fifty, a hundred times? Then he would make fun of me, verbally abuse me, and say that it must be all in my head, that something was wrong with me."

❋ ❋ ❋

Tears were running from Becca's big blue eyes down her tanned face. Rodney reached over and tucked a fresh tissue into her hand and gave it a pat.

"I knew stuff was going on." Becca wept softly. "But I couldn't check his schedule—it's never a straight nine to five, so he can lie whenever he wants. How could I confirm the truth? Nobody in the hospital would ever reveal him."

Rodney felt as if he had rocks in his chest. He ached for this hurting woman who sat traumatized beside him, yet all the while his own fears and suspicions were building. He had been so trusting of Chelsea. Maybe he'd been played for the fool. *For how long?* Becca paused, looking exhausted, and pressed her fingertips to her lips. She straightened and pushed on with determination.

"He says I mean the world to him, but . . ." All of a sudden the fire left, and Becca's whole posture crumbled. "How could I mean the world to a man who wanted me to believe I was crazy, just— just so he could do this?"

Bob gave her a moment and then gently said, "It sounds, Becca, like you can hardly tell what is real anymore, and that is extremely disorienting. How do you know when it is real and when it is not?"

"I don't. Basically I was ashamed to ask anybody for help. It was so embarrassing, I had to figure it all out on my own. One day I finally went to his office, walked right in, and said that I couldn't be married any longer to a cheater—that there are too many other guys out there who would love me the way I need to be loved. I said I was leaving him, but I wouldn't go until he told me the truth. I couldn't just break up our—" her voice caught on a sob— "family on a wild hunch, just because he made me feel crazy."

Rodney wiped the beads of sweat from his head.

"Why are you still with him?"

"I threatened to leave him, divorce him, whatever. But he promised me we would be fine. We would go away on vacation, the affair was over . . . he loved me . . . he wouldn't be with her or anyone else ever again. I believed him. You know how hard it was to believe him again? He said we were going to work this out. But—" teetering on the edge, she laughed an insane laugh— "come to find out, he was still cheating on me."

Rodney felt paralyzed. Somehow he had led himself to believe that Chels just needed space, that after a little freedom and time everything would be fine. He couldn't imagine living life without his woman.

"I begged him to tell me the truth. I said we couldn't ever be friends again but we would go through this and be fine. I told him, 'I can be okay with someone telling me the truth, no matter how horrible it is. If you need to mess around, fine—just don't do it to me. Care about me at least enough to let me leave with some dignity. But tell me the truth. I can't live with a liar.'"

"What do you think the issue is here?" asked Bob.

Becca seemed stumped. "With me?"

"No, with him."

With a look of astonishment, she exclaimed, "He's a liar, Bob!"

Shredding a tissue into a pile on the floor, Becca described how her husband went to great lengths to get everybody to like him. She explained that she didn't know how far he would go to protect his self-image. And how frightening it was not to know what else he was hiding. "He could be a sex addict, for all I know." She went on to describe in detail several other questionable events. "He even failed a polygraph and still won't admit it." She waved her hand toward the tissue box that was out of reach. "I never wanted to say these things publicly. We're Christians, for crying out loud!"

The pain in her eyes was so intense, Rodney had to look away.

"I'm not making up stories. I am certainly not imagining these things. Believe me, I have questioned whether or not I am going crazy, but I'm not. I'm not crazy at all. He blatantly flirts, gives sexual innuendos, and charms the ladies to boost his self-esteem."

Turning from the window, Ryan took an open seat nearby and pushed his hand through his thick hair. His voice was wooden and distant. "Becca's radar is so tuned to the slightest thing that everything comes up coded as cheating. I told her the affair was over. I happen to be her worst demon, and *that*, Bob, is our biggest problem. We can't get past it. Everything will be looking great for a week or a month and then the tiniest thing comes along and *bam!* It's a total setback. I'll get a call on my cell phone and she questions why I need to answer it. A friend will ask me to go sailing and she wants to know which women we're taking. She's angry if anyone at all breaks into our life. I mean, if somebody does happen to call, it's a fifty-fifty shot that it will be a woman, right?"

"So what do *you* want at this point?" Bob questioned.

"I want her to realize I'm not doing anything."

"You want her to trust you?"

"Absolutely."

"And she doesn't."

"Right. It is ridiculous to the point where it is now having a negative impact on my practice." He described how he'd worked his whole life to get to his position. "But I can't even accept an emergency call without her being rude and interrupting. It's gotten so bad she even wants me to fire my female assistants."

"Why would you say that she should trust you at this point?"

"She just has to, that's all."

"Are you trustworthy?"

"Yes."

Rodney saw Becca roll her eyes as if to say, *And you're gonna believe that?* Rodney's reaction exactly. Even Bob looked a bit stunned.

"One hundred percent?" Bob asked.

"Absolutely. I know I've blown it in the past when I told her she needed to trust me, and I feel horrible about that." Ryan leaned back with his hands behind his head.

"So, why do you think she is having a hard time trusting you now?" asked Bob.

"For all the smoke screens I blew. I think that's where the problem is. But how am I supposed to get from there to here—to the point of wanting to start over? Maybe I can't explain things right, maybe I can't talk to her enough. I don't say the right things, and if she hears a buzzword, it brings her right back to that terrible time."

"Let me get this straight. You are saying that there is no possible chance that this could ever happen again, under any circumstances, for the rest of your life?"

Throwing his hands out from behind his head, Ryan seemed baffled. "How can I say for sure that it couldn't happen?" Exasperated, he leaned forward again on his forearms. "I mean, I feel bad. It hurts me to see her so upset and to see how this has consumed her whole life. But—"

"Given the circumstances," Greg cut in, "and kinda where things are at now, you feel like you are 100 percent trustworthy, but on the other hand, you can't guarantee it won't happen again. Here's the problem: Even though you can't guarantee that there is no possibility that it could never happen again, you want your wife to trust you. How or why should she trust you when she can't be sure that it will never happen again?"

"This is different."

Charles made his feelings known by getting up and leaving through the side door, as if to say, "This mess is hopeless." Rodney could relate.

Undeterred, Greg continued, "I want to address the issue of trust for a moment. Before we can ever have a healthy, thriving marriage, there must be trust. When there is no trust, there is no relationship. Does that make sense?" There were nods around the room.

"The real question, then, is this: Is it possible to ever rebuild the kind of trust that is necessary for you to feel safe in your marriage? What would you two say you ideally want for yourselves and for your marriage?"

Becca looked far across an imaginary horizon. Her teary eyes scanned back and forth as her thoughts formed. "I want a faithful husband who is honest. I want what we had. Maybe I was living in a fantasy world, and maybe I didn't see all the times he was going up to the office, sneaking around, but I want to be back where I thought we had a great life—I want to be happy."

"As in happily-ever-after happy?" asked Greg.

"No, not marital bliss; I just want him to be my best friend again. We were so close."

"So you want a deep connection."

Rodney found himself blinking back tears as he watched Becca's anger recede. In its place a stunning, childlike beauty came over her face, and she looked at Greg in utter vulnerability. "To be honest, I want something beyond that."

"Like a soul-type connection, heart-to-heart, that kind of stuff?"

"Yes. Isn't that what most people want?"

Greg looked full of sympathy for this broken woman. He nodded slowly. "And how about you, Ryan?"

Ryan shifted and showed a slight hesitation as if he was afraid of getting cornered by all the "creative" dialogue. Though Rodney could see that Greg was intentional in what he was asking, there was nothing threatening in his tone.

"I think that's what I want," Ryan mumbled.

"Did you know that when you peel away all the other stuff, we are all wired to want exactly that?" Greg asked, looking around at the group. "God put a deep longing in our souls to crave intimacy. And on some level we know that in order to have it, our hearts must be open, because true intimacy is when people share the deeper parts of who they are with each other. That kind of sharing is a heart-to-heart experience. That can happen only when people feel safe enough together to be willing to open up."

After a natural pause, Bob picked up where Greg had left off. "Intimacy can be shared only between two open hearts. But here's the rub: If you open up your heart, you are totally set up. The moment you open your heart to another person, you are vulnerable; you are set up to be hurt, set up to be disappointed. That's why caring in and of itself is risky business. The deeper you care, the greater the risk.

"We long for that intimacy, and we know it takes openness. But I see some people attempting to get there by using one of two approaches, both of which are the hard way. The first approach is to read about and study intimacy, hoping to create intimacy by becoming an intimacy expert. The second approach is to focus on getting your heart open. Some people simply throw open their hearts and rush headlong into a situation, hoping and praying they don't get crushed. This option feels careless to me, but a lot of people do it.

"Others use what I like to call the 'crowbar approach,' because it is very much like trying to pry open a manhole cover while standing on it. Part of you very much wants to be intimate and open, and a part of you is saying, 'no stinking way, this is too dangerous!' I absolutely see both of you trying this approach to intimacy. It's just a hard way to go.

"Yes, Becca. There is a part of you that desperately wants to be open to Ryan and trust him, and there is another part of you that is saying there is just no way, it is too risky. There's a battle raging inside. It's a war you've never had to fight before, and it's killing you because it doesn't appear there is any way out of it. I mean, how can you ever really trust him?

"Ryan, you, too, are waging a brutal war inside. You want to be trustworthy, but the stakes are high. You have to somehow prove to your wife that you are capable of doing something you've failed at numerous times. You're not sure you are strong enough, and furthermore, you're not sure you want to be enslaved to such demands. I can't say that I blame you. It's a losing battle. I don't think you can win.

"I want to suggest another alternative. Thankfully, it's a far easier approach. I always prefer to look for the easiest way to do things; life is hard enough as it is. This approach is simply to devote yourselves to creating a safe place for each other. When two people truly feel safe together, their hearts will naturally open. And when two open hearts are in close proximity to each other, intimacy happens without force, without effort, without energy. People always prefer to be open when they feel safe, because it just takes so much less energy to live that way.

"Becca, Ryan, are you tired enough yet to be interested in finding a way to be together that isn't so exhausting?"

They both nodded their heads slowly.

"Then you might want to consider focusing all your time and attention on making your marriage a sincerely safe place." Bob went on, "Ryan, I'm still not sure where you are with all this, but I want to suggest a couple of things that each of you can do to actually create this space." He looked around the room. "This is for all of us, because most of us don't realize how easily damaged or destroyed the emotional security in a marriage is.

"Your marriage is definitely damaged, but it is not destroyed. It's up to you to decide what you'll do with it from here. Now, I want to talk about trust, because it is the key element here. And believe it or not, this issue right here—trust—is why I have hope for your marriage to survive!"

Rodney couldn't believe what he was hearing. He watched as several other sets of eyes in the room widened. The issue of trust was the reason Bob had hope in Ryan and Becca's marriage lasting? Maybe he'd misheard. Rodney had never heard of a situation in which trust had been more trashed than this number Ryan had worked on Becca! The last thing he would have expected was for anyone to still have hope for the Stuarts' marriage. It really seemed as if it was way beyond any hope at all.

"There is a myth we have about trust, and it's getting the best of you right now," Bob continued. "The myth says, *Trust can be earned once and for all in a marriage.* The hope is that if you are trustworthy long enough, trust is fully established and complete from then on. But that's just a myth. The truth is that *in human relationships, trust is never earned once and for all.* It must be continually established and maintained."

Bob remained quiet for a moment. Rodney figured their counselor was giving them all time to absorb the impact of what he'd just said. Charles slipped back in quietly and remained standing.

A TALK WITH THE DOCTORS

Building Trust

Issues of trust touch all relationships in one way or another. We may have difficulty trusting others, or we may be frustrated that others don't trust us. Whether dealing with a jealous spouse or facing a teenager who wants the keys to the car, you must deal with trust issues. In marriage we often view trust in overly narrow terms: Can I trust you to remain sexually faithful? However, the issue of trust is a much broader, further-reaching concept than that. And it powerfully affects our relationships.

We were all created with a longing to be intimately connected to others. This connection works best when we feel completely safe. We are then able to relax, let down our guard, and just be ourselves without having to worry about being hurt, judged, ridiculed, or rejected. It is in this open, honest, and exposed state that deep intimacy truly flourishes. Much like being with someone in a beautiful garden where the weather is ideal, there is no hint of danger and you feel completely safe. The experience is totally peaceful both inside and out. You are able to achieve this state as a result of trusting your surroundings and the honorable intentions and commitment of the person you are with.

Even though the prospect of creating a relational Eden is a bit idealistic, this is the environment in which we were created to exist, and it is something we can consciously strive toward (even if we know we won't be able to pull it off perfectly). If we commit ourselves to creating an umbrella of safety over our marriage, we will have a shelter under which we can relax and openly and intimately enjoy our life together. Our relationship becomes a sanctuary, a safe harbor, a place we long to come home to.

Before we go any further, we want to offer a definition of the term *trustworthy*. You are trustworthy when you fully grasp how valuable and vulnerable another person is, *and* you treat that person accordingly. To the extent that you treat the person as precious and irreplaceable, you are trustworthy. And to the extent that you don't, you're not.

Bob tells a story to illustrate this important point. When he was eighteen years old, he had an opportunity to work as a handyman for a rich, eccentric psychiatrist. This guy was a classic psychiatrist. He came from Vienna, had a German accent, and was one of the most unusual characters you would ever meet.

He was a wine connoisseur and an art collector, and his house was different from any place Bob had ever been. One hot summer afternoon, he asked if Bob would give him a hand. He had carpet cleaners coming in to work on the living room carpet, and he needed Bob to help remove some items. The first thing Bob grabbed was a little antique clay figurine. It was about the size of a football, and it had arms and legs sticking out like a child reaching for his mother. As Bob walked out of the living room, he must have swayed a little bit at the doorway. He just barely bumped the toe of the clay figurine on the doorjamb . . . and the leg fell off. It landed on the floor with a thud.

Bob was just a kid, and he had no idea what to do. So Bob called the guy over, and when he took one look at the clay figurine with the hole in it in Bob's hand and then spotted the leg lying on the floor, he totally lost it. He started screaming at the top of his lungs, waving his hands, and jumping up and down—totally out of control.

Bob was afraid for his life at that point. The man finally looked him in the eye and shouted, "Do you have any idea how much that thing is worth?" He grabbed it out of Bob's hand, saying that the weird-looking thing was worth thousands of dollars and that it was thousands of years old. Then he reached down, grabbed the busted leg, and exclaimed that one of the things that had made it so incredibly valuable was that it was in perfect, flawless condition.

Bob was stunned. The man then wanted to talk about what Bob was going to do to pay for the damage, and all Bob knew was that he needed to get out of there fast. He was so upset he didn't know what to think. So he went home as quickly as possible. To this day, Bob is thankful that when he told his parents the story, they had enough presence of mind to call an attorney friend. He assured them that as this man's employee, Bob had no financial responsibility for the damage, and that if the crazy psychiatrist hadn't bothered to have the figurine insured, that was his problem, not Bob's.

Every one of us has a part of us just like that clay figurine: of infinite worth and value like a priceless work of art, yet easily damaged and easily devalued.

We are trustworthy to the extent that when we have access to that precious part of another human being, we "get it"; we understand and we treat them accordingly. To the extent that we do, we are trustworthy. To the extent that we don't, we are not.

"Ryan, if you think of trustworthiness as never, *even for a moment*, forgetting how valuable and vulnerable Becca is and always treating her like that, can you say you are 100 percent trustworthy right now?" Bob asked.

"I guess not," Ryan said, as the impact of the realization began to sink in.

Bob turned toward Becca. "How about you, Becca? Are you 100 percent trustworthy toward Ryan—always remembering how valuable and vulnerable he is, always treating him like that?"

The sudden shift of focus surprised Rodney. He had been so caught up in thinking about how wrongly Becca had been treated and how justified she was in her anger and hurt that he hadn't even considered her behavior . . . or his own, for that matter.

Everybody in the group appeared struck with the importance of what had just occurred. Rodney was especially anxious to see where Bob and Greg were going next. On the one hand, there was the new realization that his own relationship was not completely safe. Yet he wondered if Ryan was getting off the hook too easily.

"Hi, Mommy. Are you far away?"

"Not too far away. I'm coming home on the day you have dance class."

"Is that tomorrow?"

"Not quite." *When do children begin to grasp the concept of time?* Becca wondered.

"Is Daddy there too?"

"Yes, darling."

"I want Daddy to come home too."

"Yes. We're working on that."

"I miss you, Mommy. I miss Daddy, too. Grammy doesn't read my books right."

Becca smiled. "I love you and I'll see you soon, okay? Give your sister lovin's. Promise?"

"Okay."

"Michaela?"

"What, Mommy?"

"Do you feel cozy and safe?"

"Uh-huh. I have Suzy Bunny in my backpack."

"Wonderful. Let me talk to Grammy now."

"Bye, Mommy."

Becca wiped her eyes. Her precious girls. Through all the turmoil, they still felt safe. *Thank you, God.*

Her Michaela was such a bright child, with the vocabulary and inquisitive mind of a college student. Becca had been missing her girls, and now she ached to hold them tight. At the break she had dashed out of the counseling room to call her mother-in-law. She knew Eho wouldn't ask many personal questions—not of her, anyway.

For the sake of the girls, Ryan had moved out . . . one week prior to Sydney's first birthday. She was thankful they were young enough not to know the pain and deceit. For now. How long did she have to figure this out? Michaela asked a slew of impossible questions. Her heart broke all over again—this time for her innocent little girls. They needed their daddy every bit as much as she needed her husband.

Ryan had been good about coming home to tuck Michaela and Syddie in at night. His work had been demanding and he'd been away so much, they really didn't notice any difference after he moved out—*that's telling, isn't it?* It didn't take a math genius to figure out that he'd been running around on her at the time they conceived Sydney. Some mothers might resent a child in such a situation, but Becca didn't. She had always wanted sisters, and she received this second baby girl as a gift especially for her.

Sometimes she imagined having herself as her mommy, and it made her feel better. She imagined getting a phone call like the one she'd just made from her mother. Maybe her mama had wanted to say those things too, if her mind hadn't been so trashed on booze. Becca was having a hard time wrapping her mind around this whole idea of being valuable and trustworthy. It would take a while for the truth to penetrate the hard shell of protection that had formed around her heart. Right now Bob's words were still bouncing off her heart like little pellets instead of the high-powered bullet she needed.

❂ ❂ ❂

"How many of you feel as if you are completely emotionally safe in your marriage?" Bob asked as the group reconvened after their late-morning break. "In other words, you feel as if you can tell your spouse anything—including your deepest hurts, fears, and concerns—and completely trust that the information will be handled sensitively and carefully, and that you will never regret having told him."

Pam ducked her head. She couldn't imagine feeling completely safe with Todd. She thought about how relieved she was whenever her husband wasn't around to be critical of her every move and decision. Even in his silence she felt his dissatisfaction.

Each person made it clear that they did not feel completely safe in their marriages.

"So this is clearly a big issue for most of us," the counselor said. "How many of you would love to find the keys to creating a truly safe marriage—one that would enable each of you to say that being in the presence of your spouse feels like the safest place in the whole world?"

Pam smiled weakly. For her to feel safe with Todd, he would first have to *be* safe. How could that ever happen, when obviously he didn't think any of this even applied to him? She looked over at her husband, whose expression remained unchanged.

"As I said before," Bob continued, "there are two commitments that we each can make that together create an emotionally safe place. The first commitment is to devote yourself to being trustworthy. In other words, when you have access to any of the deeper parts of your spouse's heart, body, mind, or spirit, to remember that they are priceless and easily damaged, just like that antique figurine I broke. Commit to handling them as a priceless treasure, with great care."

To illustrate his point, Bob picked up a little white teddy bear. He explained that it represented the part of a person that is of infinite worth and value, like the soul—the part of a person that lives in the "holy of holies" of his or her temple. He pointed out that people are trustworthy only when they can hold that part of another person in their hands, fully understanding what an honor, privilege, and responsibility it is. Their behavior toward the other person must reflect that. To the extent that this is a person's attitude and behavior, that person is trustworthy. When someone forgets or even momentarily loses sight of this, he or she is not.

"Trustworthiness is an easy thing for us humans to lose. Let me give a silly example to show you why. Let's say my wife, Jenni, and I are walking out of the house, and by some strange happenstance, the door slams and catches both of our fingers in the door at the same time. I guarantee you that in that moment I would be far more focused on my finger than I am on hers. I might know she is hurting, but I am feeling my own pain. In that moment I would be thinking more about myself than I am about her. And anytime I am not fully aware of how valuable she is and do not treat her accordingly, I am not trustworthy. Because I am distracted by my own pain, in that moment I am not fully trustworthy.

"Now let's say in another circumstance we are both upset. I can guarantee that I will be far more focused on my own upset feelings than I am on hers, and though I know she is upset—I can see, I can hear that she is upset—I am engrossed in feeling my own 'upset' because it's in my body. In that moment, I am thinking more about myself than about her. In that moment, I am not trustworthy to her.

"So I want to ask again, Ryan: Are you 100 percent trustworthy? Meaning that in every moment of every day, when Becca gives you access to that precious part of her, you never for a single moment lose sight of how valuable and vulnerable she is and you always treat her with the utmost care and respect?"

"No."

Pam could see that Ryan was starting to get it.

"How do you really feel about Becca, and what do you want for her in life?"

"I want nothing but the best for her," he answered without emotion.

"Well, if you want nothing but the best for her and you are not 100 percent trustworthy, why would you ever ask her to trust you?"

A dramatic pause followed.

"This is one of the things that most dramatically changed my marriage. From the day I first asked myself this question, to this day, I have never once asked my wife to trust me again, ever. Instead, I have devoted myself to the best of my human ability to being trustworthy—to showing her as best as I possibly can, when I have access to that part of her, that I understand how valuable and how vulnerable she is. Knowing I am capable of failing over and over again and of hurting her, but doing everything in my power to avoid it.

"I have to decide to let her determine the extent to which she feels safe opening up to me. All I can do is devote myself to the task of being a trustworthy husband to her.

"I say this because I'm hearing you, Ryan, asking your wife to trust you, and I don't think you've got what it takes to pull it off. Not because you are not a good guy but because you are a human being. This is not a male-versus-female issue, and I'm certainly not giving you license to fool around. What I am saying is that this is a human being issue. My wife is not capable of pulling it off with me either. She is a human being, wired to focus on herself. So this is commitment number one: Devote yourself to being trustworthy to the best of your ability."

To Pam, Ryan looked deep in thought, while still holding some reservation. How she wished her son, Zach, could hear Bob's teaching about becoming trustworthy. She knew that like Ryan, her son didn't find infinite value and worth in women, his girl-friend, or anyone, for that matter. Instead, he had, in essence, been told that he was not worthy of ever being trusted again. Her heart broke all over again.

Bob was still speaking. "Commitment number two is actually harder for most people. When I extend this vulnerable part of me to another person—" Bob held out the little stuffed bear—"sometimes he or she will kind of look at it and say, 'Ah, isn't he cute?' and all of a sudden, oops!—" he let the bear fall to the floor—"'I've been dropped.' It's brutal, and it has happened to all of us. What can we do to protect this invaluable part of ourselves that God so loved that he sent his Son to die for? We find the answer in commitment number two.

"Commitment number two is this: Anytime I extend this valuable part of myself, my 'holy of holies,' to another person and they grab hold and start doing one of these numbers—" Bob started flipping the bear recklessly up in the air—"I immediately pull the bear back in and say, 'Excuse me. Apparently you have lost sight of how valuable I am, but I haven't, and I can't let that happen.' Sounds a little dorky at this point, but you'll get the hang of it.

"Now, you have a couple of good options when this happens: One, you can hold your heart close and build a thick barrier around it for protection, no longer allowing any access. This is a pretty good option, but you should know that while barricades certainly keep the threat out, they don't allow for anything to pass between the two warring factions.

"The next option might be to erect a wall with peepholes, where you can peek out and pass provisions through—basic necessities only. It's really a safe alternative, but it can get lonely inside that wall all by yourself.

"All of us have known people who haven't got a clue about handling others with care and aren't likely to get a clue anytime soon. With people like this, the peephole allows me to say, 'Hey, how are you doing? Nice to see you. How's the weather on your side of the wall?' and that kind of thing. But do they have access to the part of me that really matters? No stinking way, never! If this part of me is so valuable and they are not safe, this is absolutely an appropriate option.

"But I must warn you: This peephole kind of living means death to a marriage. Have you ever tried to hug a person when they are on the other side of a wall? It's not a warm and cozy experience.

"The other alternative is more like building a friendly little fence or drawing a line in the sand. When I extend this part of me, holding the bear out over the fence to my wife, Jenni, and she gets a little careless, I say, 'Excuse me, honey, I'm taking this back.'"

A TALK WITH THE DOCTORS

Trusting

We want to emphasize again that trust is not something that can be earned once and for all. Trust is warranted by consistent honor and care toward another. Trust can be betrayed in an instant. Becoming caught up in your own feelings and forgetting—even momentarily—about the ultimate well-being of the other person is all it takes to become untrustworthy. Thus, focusing on being trustworthy toward other people is far more useful than focusing on getting them to trust you. When you additionally make respect and honor of you a prerequisite to allowing someone access to your own vulnerable places, you begin to trust yourself. You feel deeply cared for and self-confident. Then even if another person forgets to care about you, even for a moment, at least you know that you won't forget!

This commitment requires that you recognize and respect your own incredible worth. See yourself as God sees you: valuable and precious. Require anyone you allow access into your inner sanctuary to proceed with honor and care. Whenever you let someone have access to the most sensitive part of you and they start getting careless, you must take back that part of yourself. Essentially, you are saying, "Excuse me. Apparently you've lost track of how valuable and how vulnerable I am. But I haven't, and I can't let that happen."

All relationships involve choice. When people treat you badly, you can choose to be trustworthy to yourself in a couple of ways. You may need to build a wall and shut the person out, at least for a time. That can be very appropriate. Some people have no clue and are not likely to get a clue anytime soon. You can treat them cordially, but you don't need to give them access to the most vulnerable part of you. They can shout over the wall, but that's it. The problem with this tactic, of course, is that it hinders a deep relationship. It makes connection impossible. You can't hug someone standing on the other side of a wall.

Another alternative is more like drawing a line in the sand. You say, "Hey, I'm safeguarding this part of me because I can't trust you with it right now. But I do want to have a relationship with you. Therefore, I will give you repeated opportunities to try again. But I need you to know that the next time I let you in, and every single time thereafter, I'll be requiring the same thing: that you show me, through words and actions, that you understand how valuable and vulnerable I am and that you act accordingly. To the degree that you do this, let's be friends. But when you forget, I need you to know that I won't forget."

Your ability to feel safe in a relationship depends more on the second part of trustworthiness than on the first. When we remain trustworthy to ourselves, we can afford to give others a lot of freedom in relationships. We know that others are going to forget, that they *are* going to have moments when they stop being trustworthy. We can live with that, however, because there's always someone taking responsibility—*we* are. When other people act in unsafe ways, when they get caught up in themselves, we take the most vulnerable part of ourselves back and protect it. And when they regain their trustworthiness, we can say, "Let's try this again."

We've been given great wisdom in Proverbs 4:23: "Above all else, guard your heart, for it is the wellspring of life."

The concept of guarding her heart and being able to choose how she would respond to Todd was entirely new to Pam. She had never really considered his role in her unhappiness. She'd always believed her husband was the authority—that he was right and it was she who needed to change. But Bob was describing an entirely different way of looking at their relationship. She would have to take some time to ponder all this.

"I would also say something to this effect," Bob said. "'I want you to know, Jenni, that I love you and I want to have a close relationship with you. However, I need you to know that it is not okay to treat me carelessly. I am going to give you some chances—repeated chances, most likely—but I want you to know, the next time I let you hold my heart—'"

Bob interrupted himself. "Keep in mind, I'm never going to give my heart away. I may share it, but in essence, my hand never leaves my heart."

Then, resuming his imaginary conversation with Jenni, he went on, "'. . . And every single time thereafter, I'll be requiring exactly the same thing of you—that you show me through your words and actions that you get how valuable and how vulnerable I am. And to the extent that you do, that's great; let's relate. But when you forget, that's okay, because I won't forget, and I am taking this part of me back. I am responsible for it.'" Bob pulled the bear back securely to his chest.

"So let's review." He wrote on the whiteboard:

Commitment #1: Commit yourself to being trustworthy.
Commitment #2: Require others to be trustworthy
     toward you.

"These two commitments are what being trustworthy is all about. And when you get two people who are doing both of those things, each person devoted to being trustworthy to the best of their ability—and both of you committed to being trustworthy to yourself, watching out for your 'holy of holies'—you will find a hedge of safety, a hedge of protection, that surrounds your relationship. The best part is this: You will discover that without a fight, you are open and ready for intimacy. Isn't that a marvelous plan?"

Pam thought that it most certainly was. If only it would work . . .

"Why does it work?" Bob went on, as if reading her thoughts. "Because we human beings prefer to be open and intimate, given the option. Openness is our default setting. Openness takes less energy to maintain than any other state of being. What really takes a lot of energy is maintaining walls, fortresses, and force fields. Or projecting images of who you want people to see. This is why the one thing most people have in common when they arrive here is that they are absolutely exhausted. All this protection takes work. When you have an option that allows you to feel safe, I guarantee you will always find a desire to be real, open, and relaxed without having to put on any pretenses—a desire to just be free."

"Does this make sense?" Greg asked, looking at Becca.

"Complete sense," Becca responded. "I've been giving my 'bear' to Ryan and praying that he will take good care of it. I've definitely taken my hand off of the bear. But I thought that is what we are supposed to do in a marriage—give ourselves to each other. Right?"

"You are exactly right," Greg answered. "This is what we are taught. This is what we see reinforced throughout our culture—hand yourself over to others and pray they handle you with honor and care. But this is a total setup for pain and misery."

"As a matter of fact," Bob jumped back in, "of these two commitments, do you have any sense which one is more important?"

"Well, after hearing your descriptions of both," Becca said, "I'd say that it has to be commitment number two—being trustworthy to yourself. Am I right?"

"Not even close." Bob laughed playfully. "Just kidding. You're *exactly right*. Without question, it is number two: Require the other person to treat you with honor and respect. And I'll tell you why. If I don't trust myself to take care of me, and if my well-being is dependent on how well Jenni takes care of me, what will happen when she gets caught up in herself? Who is watching out for Bob? Nobody.

"However, if I am devoted to understanding how valuable and vulnerable this part of me is—" he held up the bear again—"when I begin to grasp the profound implication that this is the part of me that Jesus died for, I learn to protect it and take great care of it.

"When I extend this part of me to Jenni during a time when she is not fully focused on my well-being—which as a human being she is going to do—or if it goes the other way around, our hearts are never left unattended. There is never a time that this part of me is not being cared for. And I pray that she is consistently watching over *her* heart, because there will be days when I'm forgetful and distracted. I hate to admit it, but there are going to be days when I get careless with this treasure—her heart—that is so priceless it should never be put in harm's way. I pray that when those days come, she is caring for herself, because I never want her to be damaged by my hand. I don't want her heart to be damaged by anybody, but I can't bear the thought that I hurt her there— and I have—deeply. I pray that it won't happen anymore."

Ryan's expression remained hard. His brow furrowed, and he stepped out immediately after Bob was done speaking.

Pam thought Becca looked exhausted but relaxed. She was grateful for the young woman's boldness. Interestingly, when Becca was not in the spotlight, her actions were as hushed as if she had stepped backstage.

Never before had Pam heard anything like what Bob and Greg

were describing. While she could see the beauty and value in others, she'd never acknowledged such a thing in herself. Come to think of it, she had always focused on caring for others—but never for herself. She felt as if a window shade had been inched up ever so slightly and the light that had always been there, blocked by the shade, was now spreading across the length of her heart in a bright beam. For the first time, Pam realized that whenever she felt ragged and worn out, the last thought to come to mind was whether or not she herself was trustworthy with her own well-being. Instead, she'd either push harder or slip into depression, admitting defeat.

A TALK WITH THE DOCTORS

Safety

When two people mutually commit themselves to being trustworthy toward each other and require that they be treated with honor and respect, the relationship begins to feel safe. Both will tend to relax and open up, creating greater opportunities for deep and satisfying intimacy. If you consistently act in a trustworthy manner, others will be far more likely to choose to trust you. After all, don't most of us want to live in a state where we are safe enough to relax, open up, and just be ourselves? And isn't the ideal relationship one where entering into the other's presence feels like coming home, entering the safety of a garden?

In every interaction between you and your spouse, you have a choice between two paths. You can move toward creating and maintaining a safe environment for your relationship, or you can fall into the steps of the Fear Dance—the trap of reacting to one another in ways that make the relational environment insecure and unsafe.

In our Couples Intensives, we take great care to create a safe place, where participants can be free and open, while at the same time learning to keep a secure hold on their hearts. Individuals first entrust the intimate details of their lives and relationships with us therapists because we are safe. Then they usually begin to share with others in the room and soon feel close and connected with each other, too.

We want to encourage you to make these same efforts to create safety in your own marriage. Optimally, your home will one day feel like the safest place on earth, where your heart can thrive and beat with life.

❂ ❂ ❂

Almost two hours had passed, and both the humidity and the temperature had risen, making the room slightly stuffy. Victoria hardly noticed; she had been so entranced by the exchanges taking place.

"Now, before we break for lunch," Bob said, "we have a short assignment for you." As Bob spoke, Greg began handing out photocopied packets to each person. "These are worksheets we want you to fill out before the next session. You are not going to hand these in to us or even show them to anyone else unless you want to, so don't stress out about your answers. Just fill out the information so you'll have it on hand in case we want to refer to it later."

Victoria glanced at the top sheet of the set of pages Greg had just handed her. "Identifying Your Fear Dance," the heading read. Sounded intriguing.

She stood as the others began filing out of the room. It felt wonderful to straighten after being tense and breathless over the past hour. She stretched and stepped out into the midday sunshine. The others were going to lunch, but she wanted a few minutes to process all she'd heard. Her mind reviewed piece by piece the dialogue and the new lessons they were learning about being trustworthy and safe. There was so much to consider.

While walking toward a bench under a fragrant dogwood,

with petals fluttering down around her, Victoria replayed the Stuarts' scenario in her mind. Her heart ached for them, and she paused to say a prayer for their specific needs. While praying, a Scripture verse came to mind: Psalm 4:8. "You alone, O LORD, make me dwell in safety." Oh, she did hope this for Ryan and Becca. They were both so wounded. *Oh, Lord, for all of us.*

Victoria had never considered her own home unsafe. But she recognized now the recurring sense of relief she felt whenever Charles left. Year after year, one stone had been laid upon another until they had just a little peephole in the barricade of protection between them—just as Bob had described. The ever-capable wife envisioned the thick, gray prison walls surrounding Alcatraz, isolated on an island unto itself, separated from the mainland of San Francisco, and often enveloped with the heavy fog that hung over the bay. What a chilling contrast this was to the Garden of Eden— God's perfect setting for his creation.

"Isn't the ideal relationship one where entering into the other's presence feels like coming home into the safety of the garden?" Greg had asked. Victoria shuddered to think how people allowed themselves to become imprisoned. Leaning back against the garden bench, she closed her eyes as warm tears trickled down her cheeks. She breathed in the sweet, pungent fragrance of the earth as it sprang to life. Bees buzzed around the tree blossoms, and tiny birds flitted and bustled about in the limbs.

For the past year, Victoria had been having a recurring dream in full, vivid color just as she was waking up. In her dream she was a little girl on a perfect summer day, barefoot and chasing monarch butterflies through a meadow filled with wild daisies, orange poppies, and tall purple lavender, while walking hand in hand with her dearest friend. Falling into the tall, soft grass, they tumbled and rolled and lay giggling. Breathless, they watched as clouds puffed overhead, lazy in the azure sky. . . . No hint of danger or fear or disappointment.

As her mind wandered, it was pure bliss—and so far from her

reality with Charles. Would she ever be able to feel safe and vulnerable with this man she had vowed to spend the rest of her life with? With her palms, she wiped the tears wetting her face. Deep down she knew she had been created with this longing that had haunted her for so many years. It was her birthright. This was what God had intended all along: She was fashioned to be intimately connected with others without inhibition. For so many years, she had pushed this knowledge aside in the name of duty.

Victoria didn't anticipate Charles could ever feel this way—he was wired so differently. She couldn't imagine her husband ever being by her side laughing without care or defense. It went against everything she knew about men. But Greg and Bob insisted that both men and women were created to know intimacy.

Suddenly, a new thought flashed across her mind: Perhaps Charles had never felt completely safe *with her*—never able to relax or let down his guard, to fully be himself without having to worry or feel self-conscious. *Why?* She had done her part in erecting those foot-thick prison walls. Though they had made love for many years before their recent cold spell, she had always operated under the premise of duty only—never feeling open and honest with her husband.

She remembered more of Greg's words: *"Even though the prospect of creating a relational Eden is a bit idealistic, this is the environment in which we were created to exist. . . . If we commit ourselves to creating an umbrella of safety over our marriage, we will have a shelter under which we can relax and openly and intimately enjoy our lives together. Our relationship becomes a sanctuary, a safe harbor, a place we long to come home to."*

How Victoria longed to come home to the garden.

✸ ✸ ✸

"Um, Bob, can I tell you something?" asked Greg with an elaborately casual expression after all the guests had left the room.

"Sure, what is it?"

"You took your hand off the bear." He did a volley spike with the little stuffed animal.

"Hey, gimme that!" Bob grabbed it off the floor, stuffed it into his shirt, and ran laughing up the stairs toward the dining room.

MONDAY, NOON

It was lunchtime, and the guests made their way up from the counseling room located on the lowest of the three levels at the Bradford House. The dining room of the inn had windows on all sides, which gave the feeling of eating outside against a backdrop of huge oaks, cedars, and beautiful dogwoods blooming with their pink and white flowers. Guests could opt to eat in the more private dining room, where marble-topped tables were intimately set for two, but most of the Couples Intensive guests congregated in the main dining area, where they shared one common table.

Something delicious was always being concocted in the large, sun-filled kitchen where the cooks hustled about making certain all the meal preparations were under way. Unlike some bed-and-breakfast kitchens, this one was open for guests to come right in to serve themselves at a smorgasbord layout at the large island in the center of the room. The twenty-four-hour coffee and snack bar was kept well stocked with pastries, finger snacks, tea, cocoa, coffee, water, and soda. Certain guests frequented this area more than others—namely, Rodney. He had crossed paths with the sweet lady named

Pam a time or two while en route. He could appreciate a woman with a taste for good pastries and a cup of tea.

Rodney's wife, Chelsea, was never tempted by food, and the tantalizing lunch display held no power over her. At the break she grabbed some fruit and crackers and split for the balcony outside. She wasn't one for much conversation, and Rodney was certain his wife, who could run a marathon, would have little energy to make others more comfortable with small talk.

Chelsea's presence wasn't missed by anyone other than Rodney. All the other guests seemed to be absorbed in their own modes of survival. Rodney wanted nothing more than to have Chelsea by his side, but he had learned to let his strong, independent wife go. When she needed space, he knew the worst thing he could do was try to hang on. Though he had conceded to it, he didn't like it.

He had just turned toward the dining room after piling his plate high when Pam came briefly to the kitchen to put together a plate of sandwiches and fruit to take to her room. Her husband, "Preacher," as she called him, was developing a migraine. After her brief explanation, she said little while bustling about her task. Rodney gave her an extra-warm smile. Just fifteen years his senior, she looked like she'd endured lasting disappointment.

Rodney watched as Becca and Ryan each grabbed a nutrition bar and used the lunch break as a good excuse to get away. Ryan looked miserable as he followed his wife toward the front door. Becca had announced to everyone within earshot that she needed nail polish remover, and it seemed that accompanying her was sufficient enough of a mission for Ryan. They could be heard spatting as they exited the main entry of the bed-and-breakfast.

Rodney, on the other hand, found the dining room comforting. He missed the noise and activity of the kids back home. In fact, he was ready to go out and shoot some hoops or toss the football around. But the food was delicious, so he piled it high and joined the few who were willing to brave the community dining experience.

At the far end of the table laden with long-stem crystal and folded linens sat the striking African-American couple. Victoria was dressed in expensive textures and colors. Not too flashy, her outfit was arresting in contrast with the others' casual jeans and tennis shoes (with the exception of Becca's outfits, of course).

Small talk came easily for Rodney, and soon they were having a nice conversation, though Charles mainly nodded and remained quiet. The older gentleman was neatly put together. Everything he did was proper but utterly genuine. The way he held his silverware, the placement of the napkin in his lap. Somewhat stoic, he seemed to wear a "do not disturb" sign on his face. He obviously didn't feel the need to go out of his way to keep the conversation light.

"How's your lunch?" Rodney asked. He jiggled the ice in the bottom of his glass after draining his serving of sweet tea in a couple of long gulps.

"Fine, thank you. The salad is delicious," said Victoria.

Sunlight shone on Victoria's shiny, close-cropped hair. Rodney missed his mom. It was nice being in Victoria's presence. "So how is the weather in Dallas this time of year?" he asked around a mouthful of food.

Greg and Bob eventually joined them too. They were usually easy to find if they were together. With their steady stream of laughter and heckling, they were like two off-duty comedians. They casually chatted with the guests and kept the atmosphere light while eating their salads topped with tomatoes, eggs, avocados, and grilled chicken.

Greg told about how his son, Garrison, had humiliated him the day before. Greg was buying a gift certificate for his wife, Erin, and the woman helping him was, well, rather large. She was making small talk with them when she asked Garrison, "Are you having fun with Daddy?"

"Yes, and Daddy said I could ride the helicopter!" Garrison explained, referring to the small kiddie ride out front.

"I love to ride that," said the lady, trying to keep Garrison engaged in a conversation.

Garrison took one look at her and said, "You wouldn't fit—you're too big!"

Greg laughed and said he almost died. "Garrison, that's not a nice thing to say!" he'd said.

Without skipping a beat, Garrison returned his judgmental eye toward the woman. Pointing at her stomach, he asked, "Do you have a baby in there?"

When Greg asked if anyone else had come to lunch, Rodney said he had seen Pam in the kitchen earlier. *But I didn't see her cranky husband.* Rodney didn't finish speaking this thought out loud. As sweet as Pam appeared to be, he didn't care much for Todd. If there was anyone here that Rodney would have trouble liking, it would definitely be him. In fact, several times in the past, Rodney's intuition had proven correct, and he wondered if his uneasy feeling about Todd was accurate this time too. Something was definitely up with that guy.

Greg and Bob ate quickly and went to attend to some business with the bed-and-breakfast staff. A short while later, Charles politely excused himself, drawing himself up to his full height of six feet three. The presence of this middle-aged gentleman was nothing short of intimidating, though he did have a certain pleasantness about him too. Rodney had learned from their brief dialogue that Charles was a retired attorney. The younger man was grateful he'd never had to oppose Charles in a court of law.

Charles and Victoria had been polite with one another: helping to pull out chairs, removing a jacket, passing the salt and pepper, but they were definitely chilly. It took Rodney a while to realize the distinguishing trait: They never made eye contact with each other. He couldn't help but wonder why they were here and if they'd ever been in an all-out screaming-yelling-throwing battle as he and Chelsea had.

As soon as Charles departed, the climate warmed almost

immediately, and Victoria's shoulders seemed to relax a little. They were the only ones left at the large table, but Rodney wasn't in a hurry to leave Victoria's company. He was drawn to her smoky Southern voice and was curious about her story. She smelled fresh, like orange trees in spring. Still, he figured she would want to be alone, and the outdoors was calling his name. He wanted to explore a little bit before the afternoon session began. After thanking the wait staff for a delicious meal, he stepped out into the bright sunshine.

❀ ❀ ❀

Pam was eager to start when the group reassembled an hour later for the afternoon session. A French-looking butler named Galen, handsome in his full-length blue apron, brought down a platter of cookies, candies, and fresh coffee. Yum! Maybe she'd stash a couple of cookies for later. It still felt bizarre making small talk with people who had just shared their most intimate details earlier that day. Rodney found a spot on the floor and started sketching cartoon figures on the back of his notebook.

Looking as if her insides had been shaken too hard, Chelsea took her place again on the couch next to Pam. Chelsea's demeanor was less businesslike but a far cry from relaxed. Pam received an awkward smile from the woman sitting next to her, then offered Chelsea a box of tissues, knowing they might come to good use before the session was done. Chelsea's toe tapped out a rhythm that seemed to say, "We only have four days, let's get this thing rolling."

"Who'd like to go next?" asked Greg.

Chelsea and Rodney looked at each other. Together they quickly said, "We'll go."

They seemed surprised to hear each other's voice. Pam suspected it was the first time they'd agreed on anything in a long while. Chelsea drew herself up and wrapped her arms around her knees. This face-off between the "Chihuahua" and the "Saint Bernard" promised to be an interesting one.

"We, um, we're obviously trying to figure out about ourselves as individuals in addition to as a couple and as parents," Chelsea began. "We've been to counseling . . . and actually I've tried a lot harder at this than Rod, but that's no surprise. I think he just anticipated that I'd make everything work out and he was going to be cared for no matter what. So yes, it looks like I'm the one walking." Her eyes narrowed with disgust. "He's scared spitless because I've literally held his world together. He doesn't help with finances, the housekeeping. . . . He eats food straight out of the can without heating it. . . . He doesn't know the cost of our mortgage or how we even got it! He's basically the entertainment committee on a good day."

"How does that impact you, Chelsea?" asked Bob.

"I never thought about it, but at first I liked being in control. I've always been very responsible and focused, and when I met Rod, he made me laugh and helped me relax. He was artsy and offbeat, and I was young and stupid enough to think that love made the world go round. Well, then I got hungry and then I got pregnant, and then I wanted to accomplish something with my life . . . and guess who didn't want to grow with me.

"I want him to be my friend. I want him to be in our children's lives. I just don't want to be married to him anymore. I know that sounds totally juvenile. Right now, I don't think I even want any other relationship. . . ."

Pam wondered why Chelsea's face all of a sudden grew flushed.

"Bob and Greg, I know you have high hopes for all of us in here to stay married, and I want to feel safer with all this. But I need serious resolution. Marriage is taking the life out of me."

"You look worn out and exhausted," Greg noticed.

"That's exactly how I feel." Her shoulders sagged. "I've read *The DNA of Relationships* and found a lot of good stuff in there, but quite frankly, we're not looking at *communication* problems. Rod and I have MAJOR *personality* problems.

"And when I look at my parents . . . Well actually, I can't think of a single couple I know who is happily married. Not one. And the longer they stay together, the more zombied out they get. They sleep on opposite ends of the house, bicker all the time—it's pathetic!

"I'd rather live out loud and tell the truth. Like, 'Hey people, we're screwups, okay?' Not only that, I love being separated. I'm only twenty-four years old, and I have freedoms I've never had before. I know my kids are safe when they are with Rodney. Though he's like a big oaf, quite frankly he's good with them. I know this is not how a wife and mother should talk, but I never got to play. I started working at age fourteen, was an honor student, and except for the couple wild and free years I had after meeting Rodney—well, even then I took care of things—but other than that, I've never really let go of the reins."

She paused and fiddled with her hair tie. Addressing everyone in the room, she said, "I know you think I'm being horrible and selfish, but I'm tired of being cranky all the time."

"It seems like what is so painful," Greg said, "is having to be someone you're really not. You've had to become something different—something worse."

"That's exactly right. This is not who I am. I can be fun too, when I'm not solely responsible for holding everything together, nagging, and taking care of the family. The kids squeal and run to their dad when he gets around to dragging his sorry self home—I never know when it's going to be. And he doesn't see how sad they are when he doesn't show up! That's another thing about the separation—it has made Rod get serious and grow up a little. He can't just be the 'family fun factory' anymore. I'm not there to mother him and the kids 24-7. He's got to make some decisions. I think it's the best thing that's happened to us."

Pam was not surprised to hear Rodney crack his knuckles

loudly. His displeasure at what Chelsea had just said was obvious, but he didn't say anything in response to having just been blasted.

"What happens when you are together?" asked Greg. "Are there ways you are different when you are apart than when you are living together? Rodney, do you think you get complacent and take things for granted when you are together?"

"Yeah. But I wasn't always like that." Chewing on a straw, Rodney rubbed a flat spot on his kneecap. "I think I messed up by being too open—by telling her how I feel. I was too open."

"How do you mean?"

"I think Chelsea used to have a romantic view of who I was. I *am* romantic . . . and funny, laid back—I brought our relationship balance, like she said, but now she thinks I'm an idiot. I've always been pretty much antiestablishment. I've never really fit with mainstream society, and she thought that was cool until she got a job at that accounting firm. Then I wasn't good enough anymore."

He chomped incessantly on the straw, which gave Pam the shivers. He pulled it out from time to time to examine its destruction. "She fell in love with me—with who I really am—" *chomp, chomp*—"but now she's got this John Wayne image of what a *real* man is. I'm just not it. I cry, I'm soft, I love kids. . . . I'm not a 'suit.' This is who I've always been—a free spirit. I don't want to lock myself down to the world's definition of bigger, faster, and more, more, more." The large bohemian shrugged. "If that means I'm a loser, I guess I've failed her."

He kicked off his Birkenstock with a bit of vengeance. "I thought it was okay for me to be vulnerable, to share my insecurities and my pain. I like when she's strong and initiates—'female superior,' if you know what I mean. She liked it too, but then she started hating me for it. I guess I started grossing her out."

Bob stepped in to the dialogue. "I want to come back to this. It's really important. But first I want to address another issue. Could I make a suggestion? I'm hearing several things, but one thing is for sure: I'm hearing a lot of judgment from both of you. I think we'd best start there. Rodney, I was watching you while Chelsea was talking, and I noticed how you bristled at the judgment not so well hidden when she was talking."

"Was it that obvious?" Rodney said somewhat sarcastically.

"I imagine that when you both start feeling judged by the other, you almost always end up in a heated argument, which leaves you both feeling hurt, attacked, and alone."

They both nodded their heads in agreement.

"The ironic thing is that you care deeply for one another. If you didn't, Rodney, you wouldn't care what Chelsea said, and Chelsea, you wouldn't care how Rodney behaved. Right?"

"I guess so," Rodney reluctantly agreed.

"The question is this: How can you create a safe environment, where neither of you feels attacked and you both feel loved and cared for? Actually," Bob went on before either one could answer, "is that what you want—to feel safe, loved, and cared for?"

"Sure," Rodney said.

Chelsea agreed with marked hesitation. "That would be nice." Then the tiny Chihuahua made another lunge at the gentle beast sitting near her. "But Rodney will never—"

Bob cut her off. "It sounds like you were about to go to a judgment, Chelsea. So, before we go there again—because it doesn't sound like that is getting you where you want to go—perhaps trying something different might get you different results. What if you both suspend the judgment and instead adopt an attitude of curiosity—even fascination—about what makes the other tick?

"Judgment closes people up and shuts them down. When people feel judged—as Rodney does when his wife talks to him about his lack of relational assertiveness—they usually end up defending themselves and maybe even go on the attack. Right?"

"Yes!" Rodney said, with as much enthusiasm as Pam had seen yet.

"Much better things tend to happen when we suspend judgment—on both ourselves and others—and replace it with a genuine interest in the other person. People usually act and feel the way they do for good reasons. Perhaps Rodney really is passive within the marriage—but maybe he's that way because Chelsea believes he never will measure up or because he feels like a failure. Maybe he sees himself through a distorted lens. What if, deep down, he tells himself, *I will never measure up to be the kind of husband and father Chelsea wants me to be?*

"Imagine what might happen, Chelsea, if you expressed genuine interest in Rodney rather than judging him—if you assumed that he is passive for valid reasons. Notice, I'm not saying you have to agree with the reasons. It's not a matter of deciding whether those reasons are right or wrong. This will lead to more judgment. Either Rodney will defend himself or he will shut down. Either way, the marriage loses."

"You're right, Bob," Chelsea agreed. "That's exactly what happens."

"Chelsea, don't tell Bob he's right so fast. Make him work a little harder than that," Greg ribbed. "You'll give him a big head!"

Bob smiled and pressed on. "Curiosity actually creates safety. Remember, when we feel safe, our hearts open and intimacy happens naturally—it's nothing we have to create. Curiosity also helps us get to the real issue. Chelsea, you've made the issue Rodney's passivity. But that's not it at all. That's the surface issue. It's just the tip of the iceberg. The real question is what is underneath.

"Rodney, do you think you are just basically passive by nature? Does that capture your true underlying personality?"

"I don't really think so. I am laid back, but I think I've become more and more passive because I never feel like I'm good enough for Chelsea. I never really feel like I measure up to what she now wants me to be," Rodney responded without defensiveness.

"Do you see what happened here?" asked Greg. "When Bob suspended judgment and expressed a genuine interest in Rodney, he created an environment of safety."

"Rodney, did you feel safe when I was asking you questions?" asked Bob.

"Sure."

Bob looked at Chelsea. "When you hear Rodney's view of himself, you have an opportunity to understand his passivity. That discovery, hopefully, will lead you to feel compassion toward your husband, not judgment. And you know what tends to happen when people sense compassion, don't you? They usually open up."

Pam saw a man who had become passive as a result of constant criticism . . . and then he'd been judged for being passive. She wondered if her husband saw any of the parallels to their story that she did.

A TALK WITH THE DOCTORS

Suspending Judgment

Compassion and understanding create a tremendous amount of safety. When someone refuses to judge our motives and instead tries to understand why we did a foolish or hurtful thing, that person's compassion encourages us to open up—and our relationship grows. The wall starts to come down, and the conflict decreases.

Judgment tends to foster defensiveness and close down relationships, while curiosity inspires openness and safety, giving life to relationships. When we express our interest in someone, something energizing occurs. Have you ever met people who are awesome listeners? They seem fascinated with everything you say. They hang on every word. They ask good questions and clearly express an interest in getting to know you. You almost can't help but walk away from people like that thinking, *Wow, I really like that person! I felt so cared for. She seemed so interested in me.* You might not even remember the people's names, but you've already decided they are great. Why? Just because they seemed curious and interested in you.

Judgment writes people off, bangs the gavel, and sentences them to fifty years of hard labor. That kind of judgment shuts off discovery. It's as if they've already heard everything they need to hear in order to render their verdict: "That's it. You're finished."

Curiosity says something quite different. It says, "I don't know enough yet to render a verdict, so I'll forget about sentencing for a while. It's true that I don't like what has happened. But I still need to open the door to discovery." One lifetime is not long enough to really know the true beauty of another person. Besides, everyone makes major changes inside every year, so you'll never be able to really know everything about one person.

The process of discovery gives life to relationships. If you stay fascinated with your spouse, your friends, your children, your colleagues, your neighbors, you'll never find the end of your opportunity to learn—both about them and about yourself. When you choose to suspend judgment and foster a spirit of curiosity, you keep the relationship safe and alive. You encourage it to grow and deepen.

Greg stood and stretched. "Let's back up for just a moment. Let's talk about what is really going on between Rod and Chelsea. I hear a loud cracking and rumbling from underneath the surface. What we've seen is just a glimpse of a giant iceberg a couple of hundred feet below the surface. Do you know what this iceberg is? *Fear.*"

"Fear?" they both said in unison. Pam was just as surprised as they were. What could Greg be getting at?

"You heard me right. It's fear."

"Greg, did you happen to notice that I'm six three and weigh over 250 pounds?" Rodney asked. "This may be hard to believe, but I'm not exactly afraid of Chelsea."

Pam laughed along with the rest of the group as Rodney's wisecrack broke the tension.

"I'm not sure," joked Bob. "Chelsea is pretty feisty, Rodney. She might be able to take you!"

Greg continued, "Seriously, this is where most people get confused about fear. I'm not talking about fear in the sense of being afraid for your physical safety. That can be an issue, but here I'm talking about emotional fear. So don't get hung up on the word itself. Many people don't perceive themselves as afraid. They are more inclined to use words like *concerned, worried, anxious, stressed, annoyed,* or *uncomfortable.* When we talk about a fear, we are referring to the thoughts and feelings that trigger defensive or protective reactions in us. This fear may take many shapes: fear of failure, fear of abandonment, fear of rejection, fear of inadequacy, fear of you-name-it. Do you ever wonder why you do and say certain things that you wish you didn't—things that seem so out of character with who you'd like to be?"

Pam recalled that Chelsea had said this very thing.

A TALK WITH THE DOCTORS

Fear Buttons

If *fear* isn't a word you connect with, another way to look at this is to talk about *buttons.* We all have buttons that can get pushed, and we all have typical ways we react when our buttons get pushed. You know what I'm talking about: When someone pushes a button, either we want to go after that person or we want to retreat.

Think for a moment about a wild animal that gets cornered or surprised. What does it do in response? One common response is for it to get quite ferocious, baring its teeth and growling. Another common response is to freeze or run away. God's creatures were created with these abilities to quickly respond to emergency situations.

Scientists call this the fight-or-flight response. Humans are no different. In fact, the hormone adrenaline courses through our bodies in moments when we don't feel safe, helping us get ready to respond and protect ourselves. What you may not realize is that an emotional experience of feeling unsafe in your relationship can trigger powerful reactions as well. And while the fight-or-flight response is great for survival, it is lousy for promoting intimate connections!

Almost always, our fear buttons exist prior to marriage. We come into a marriage relationship with hurtful messages having been written on our hearts. Looking back to previous relationships, especially with our families and parents, we can often gain some awareness of what those messages are.

None of us like fear. But as an emotion, fear can be a useful source of information. By acknowledging and discussing fear, we can actually open the door to intimacy. On a personal level, the key is learning to recognize and understand the fear and what is going on for you emotionally. On a relational level, being willing to be vulnerable enough to share our fears with one another opens the door to experiencing compassion, understanding, and love—in other words, intimacy.

People like Chelsea aren't impressed by how many marriages stay intact, and quite frankly, I'm not either. Only about 12 percent of married couples claim to have ever found anything close to what they were looking for in a marriage. The rest remain stuck. Yes, it *is* pathetic, but not because they choose for it to be that way. I'd venture to say that with all the self-help books, teaching seminars, and counseling methods out there, people have tried desperately to get themselves free.

I contend that there's a particular reason *why* we get stuck. We get trapped by our own relationship dance and cannot break free from it. We have named this destructive pattern the Fear Dance. The Couples Intensives work, to a large degree, because we help couples identify and break the rhythm of their own dance.

The fear buttons or triggers are not the problem. The problem is how we choose to cope with them and the dance we get stuck in. Here's how the Fear Dance works: When someone pushes our fear buttons and then we respond with unhealthy reactions, a destructive dance has begun.

"Let me illustrate what we call the Fear Dance," Greg went on. "At conferences and speaking engagements, my audience will often request to hear a particular story of when Erin and I got into our dance, so I'll share it again with you." Greg gave a shy grin.

"My wife, Erin, is a nurse, and on occasion her nursing duties require her to work the evening shift. On one such night, I felt alone and bored—and when I get bored, I like to change things.

"I decided to rearrange the master bedroom. I moved the bed, repositioned the knickknacks and their shelves, relocated the dresser, and generally gave the room a new look. Then I went to bed and turned out the lights.

"Erin didn't want to wake me when she got home, so she kept the lights off. She tiptoed into the bedroom and immediately smashed her shin on a little table that, until a few hours before, hadn't been there. She tripped and crashed into a pair of antique skis, which in turn tumbled onto a shelf containing all her beloved Precious Moments figurines. The skis shattered most of her treasures, then continued to fall until they smacked into my head.

"The combination of breaking glass, falling objects, my wife screaming, and a blow to the skull made me think, *Robbery!* Now it was fight or flight—and in the dark, I had no desire to fight anyone. Instead I bolted from bed, forgot that I had moved everything, and ran straight into the wall, bloodying my nose.

"When the lights came on, Erin instantly criticized me for moving the furniture without first talking about it. Her angry words made me feel like a failure, so I started to defend myself. I minimized her concerns, rejected her opinions, and made the argument ten times worse." He paused and looked around the room. "Does any of this sound the least bit familiar?"

Pam noticed that many of the participants were nodding or at least looking quite alert.

Greg went on, "As Erin and I look back, we see a similar vicious cycle playing out in every major argument of our marriage. We recognized the pattern early on, but we didn't know how to break it. The real issue in our conflict wasn't my decorating decisions. The real issue was our core fears, as well as how we reacted when our fear buttons got pushed. My core fear, for instance, is the fear of failure.

"If I feel I'm failing—or even if I feel I'm at risk for failure—I cope with that feeling by turning to certain unhealthy strategies like defending myself, trying to fix the problem, rationalizing my behavior, or minimizing Erin's feelings—to name a few. These things usually push Erin's fear button. Her core fear is feeling invalidated. She wants me to value her feelings. But when I'm defending myself, I'm not valuing her. I'm focused on me, so she feels invalidated. She reacts by criticizing, escalating, blaming, or being sarcastic. In the end, usually one or both of us withdraw. While things eventually calm down, we always seem to return to the same frustrating spot.

"The very fact that couples engage in the Fear Dance shows us that both partners want something. I, for example, want to feel successful and avoid failure. Erin wants to feel valued for who she is, for her feelings, and for what she thinks. When we cue up the grating music and start our Fear Dance, we labor under the illusion that by coping in such unhealthy ways, we'll get what we really want. But it never works out that way.

"To try to move ahead, we learned some good communication skills and became adept at putting pieces back together, but still we could not get over the hump. We simply could not understand why our discussions so often ended in explosions. We seemed to act out the very same script, time after time.

"Our habits didn't change for the better until we finally

understood that we had become mired in a destructive relationship dance. We remained shackled until we recognized that certain identifiable fear buttons set us off and start us on yet another futile round of accusations, attacks, and rationalizations."

Greg then asked if Rodney and Chelsea were open to diagramming their Fear Dance with the group. They agreed.

"Rodney and Chelsea, here's how your dance plays out. First, you are both distracted by surface issues. Chelsea, you talk about being married way too young and how you realize you are totally wrong for each other. I believe this is nothing but a surface issue."

Pam saw Chelsea narrow her eyes.

RODNEY'S FEARS
Failure
Inadequacy
Not measuring up
Not being good enough

CHELSEA REACTS
Criticism
Judgment
Anger/escalation
Running/fleeing
Rebellion
Ambition
Pursuing status
Self-focus

RODNEY AND CHELSEA'S FEAR DANCE

RODNEY REACTS
Being defensive
Going into fix-it mode
Being passive-aggressive
Keeping the peace
Abdicating to Chelsea
Lack of ambition
Withdrawing/shutting down

CHELSEA'S FEARS
Being trapped/helpless
Being powerless/controlled
Being taken advantage of
Being judged

Greg continued, "Chelsea feels resentful toward Rodney because she wants to be home with the kids but has to work for financial reasons. She feels Rod isn't adequately providing for the family. Furthermore, she is frustrated by his lack of drive and ambition. She wants him to grow up and be the leader of the family—spiritually, emotionally, financially, etc.—and she feels angry at her husband.

"I heard Chelsea say, 'I need a husband who will lead our family and bring in a decent salary—a partner. But all Rodney wants to do is hang out with his friends and play ball, music, or video games.' These are surface issues; they don't represent what is really going on down deep for Chelsea and Rodney.

"Let's take a look at Chelsea's core fears—her fear buttons. Chelsea feels trapped, helpless, powerless, and controlled. She is afraid that she can't do anything to change her situation or to get what she wants unless she manages to get Rodney up and going. In reaction to her buttons getting pushed, she criticizes or judges Rodney. She aggressively instructs him to take the lead in the marriage. Chelsea's hope is that if Rodney asserts himself relationally, not only will she feel like she has a true partner in the marriage, but she will also feel less trapped and burdened. In other words, she will experience freedom. When none of these coping reactions work, she runs to get away. This is why she is pressing hard for a divorce. She wants to get away and find freedom!

"The dance continues when Rodney's fear buttons get pushed. When Chelsea aggressively criticizes, judges, or attempts to light a fire under him, he feels like he is inadequate, doesn't measure up, and isn't good enough. Basically, he feels like a failure, which is one of his core fears. He first reacts—or tries to cope—by defending himself. He will attempt to explain or rationalize his behavior or lack of it, or he will go into fix-it mode by making halfhearted attempts to do what she wants. But he is not doing these things for her; they are attempts to keep himself from feeling like a failure.

"When these approaches don't work, Rodney becomes passive-aggressive. He becomes lazy, stubborn, and irresponsible. It makes sense. His fear of failure is so intense that it paralyzes him, so he shuts down. The way he abdicates responsibility to Chelsea and lacks ambition feels safe to him—*there's no risk of failure if he doesn't do anything.* When Chelsea gets ramped up and comes after him, ultimately, Rodney is trying to appease her and restore the peace so he doesn't feel like such a failure."

Pam enjoyed watching the couple's reactions while Greg sketched out their unique dance on the whiteboard. Rodney's eyebrows would rise, and he'd glance over at his wife. She looked resistant, but even her mouth dropped open a time or two.

"But Rodney's coping reactions drive Chelsea crazy and push her buttons again. Chelsea feels *more* trapped and helpless. The burden around her neck feels so intense that she runs away to escape her powerlessness. I'm guessing that when Chelsea feels trapped, she reacts by being rebellious and by doing self-destructive things, but she ends up hurting herself more than anyone else. This again pushes Rodney's fear button: feeling inadequate. Talk about feeling like a failure as a husband. When he feels these things so intensely, he shuts down and withdraws.

"The outcome relationally is that both of their hearts close up and they disconnect. Then you have two people in a marriage who feel completely alone. And loneliness is the kiss of death to a marriage."

"Honey, that's exactly what we do!" Rodney blurted. Excited, he turned to Greg and said, "We totally do that. If I didn't know better, I'd think you guys had hidden cameras in our house."

Pam had to hide her smile at the look Chelsea shot her husband. The young woman looked as if she wanted to strangle Rodney. Obviously Greg was on track with these two.

Bob took the opportunity to interject a little humor. "We do have hidden cameras in your house," he said with a twinkle in his eye. He looked at the others. "Actually, we have them in all of your homes. . . . We've been watching you guys for weeks!"

"What's amazing about seeing Rod and Chelsea's dance up on the whiteboard," Becca said, "is that I can see what we do as well.

Our fear buttons are a bit different, but we dance just as much as they do."

"Yeah, we break-dance," said Ryan drily.

Bob grew more serious. "One of the most powerful things about actually seeing your Fear Dance is that you can begin to see that the very things you do in reaction to your fear buttons getting pushed, in turn, trigger your partner's buttons. The arrows on the board demonstrate the endless cycle in which you can get yourselves stuck. Remember, no one person is to blame for a Fear Dance, but rather both partners help create this crazy battle cycle, which ends any feelings of safety you may have had in the relationship.

"Each individual not only has his or her own fears and reactions, but in a marriage these feelings and reactions tend to play off one another so quickly and intensely that marriage partners often feel absolutely stuck—and not just stuck, but sucked under by their marriage relationship.

"You may remember watching old movies or television shows where someone falls into quicksand. The natural response is to fight, flail, and try to swim in an attempt to keep from sinking, but these coping reactions that come so naturally actually make things worse and cause the victim to sink even more quickly.

"Can you see how far this flailing, clinging, grasping, pushing, and biting of the relational Fear Dance is from the flowing, beautiful movement of two ballroom dancers? The things you do in response to your buttons being pushed seem like they will help for the moment and perhaps recreate safety, but instead, your natural reactions set in motion a cycle that spins round and round and actually ends up feeling far less safe.

"Now let's try to determine what it is you want to experience most in your marriage. These are usually the opposite of the buttons or fears we just named. For instance, the opposite of feeling trapped is freedom; the opposite of failure is success; the opposite of feeling helpless is having power; the opposite of inadequacy is competence. These are our deepest heart's cries. It's like James 4:1 says: "What causes fights and quarrels among you? Don't they come from your desires that battle within you?" Isn't that verse amazing? It's our deepest wants and desires that cause fights and quarrels. When we can discover and claim these, we then know how to break the cycle of the Fear Dance and move toward a new dance—the dance of love for which we were created." Bob looked at Rodney again. "What is it you want most, Rodney?"

"To feel accepted for who I am." He started to read from the worksheet he had completed earlier: "To feel successful as a husband and a father; to feel competent or adequate; understanding; respect; peacefulness; and approval."

"And how about you, Chelsea?"

She read from her list too. "I want a partnership with Rodney; I want some power/control over my life; support; passion; to feel valued and appreciated; and freedom."

"So you see, Chelsea," Bob encouraged, "no one can judge you for feeling desperate and wanting to get out of this swampy quicksand that is literally sucking the life out of you. You're feeling trapped and helpless, but divorce may not make that frustration go away. The risk is that you'll walk away with the same fear buttons, and the next person will unknowingly push them too. You will just create a new dance. Most people haven't figured this out yet. It is not until you identify your fear buttons and what it is you deeply want and then start to communicate and share in a safe place that you'll find the freedom you desire."

Everyone was ready for a break. Bob and Greg suggested that everyone stretch their legs and maybe get something to eat or drink before reconvening for the midafternoon session. Pam was only too happy to comply. What a lot of food for thought they'd all been given!

❁ ❁ ❁

As the others filed out, Chelsea remained, pondering all that had been said.

She looked up when Bob spoke, surprised to find him still in the room. "Is it that marriage takes the life out of you, Chelsea, or is it that *doing marriage the way you have done it* takes the life out of you?"

She thought about it a moment and then answered, "After what we've just seen, I would have to say it's the way I've been doing it—the Fear Dance really has crippled us. But I still want to say it's probably both."

"Tell me about that."

"I'm afraid that I'll work on new dance steps and we'll be dancing more smoothly, but I'll still be miserable. I don't have the energy to relearn. I don't want to dance with Rodney, that's all. I am such an independent person and—and I got married so young. . . ." She felt her eyes fill with tears. "I just have so much regret in my life. I'm so unhappy."

"You must be wondering how marriage and happiness can possibly be packaged together when you and Rodney seem so mismatched. I am hearing you say they can't possibly work together. I think you'll be especially interested in what we'll talk about next."

A TALK WITH THE DOCTORS
Your Fear Dance

When a couple accurately identifies their Fear Dance, it becomes clear that the same fears and reactions appear in almost every conflict, no matter what the topic. When you have a moment, think of a specific conflict or situation that often plays out in your home. Sketch out your Fear Dance using the Fear Dance test in appendix A.

Ten people sat around the small counseling room at the Bradford House: two counselors, eight hurting individuals, and four marriages in great distress. All eight clients were tense, but Victoria knew one was especially frustrated. Charles *hated* meetings, particularly the kind where people sit around hashing things out in detail—what he would consider *ad nauseam*. He was a man of action—a former trial attorney with Callaway, Templeton, and Amsinger in Dallas, Texas—and was now retired, which didn't help his attitude toward group meetings any. He made it known that he had already endured more business and litigation meetings than he had ever cared to. Although he had agreed to come, Victoria was concerned about her husband's ability to have faith in their two counselors, both younger than himself.

During the midafternoon break, Charles had expressed to Victoria that he found the other couples much too eager to emote and dump their family trash for everyone to see. "That minister seemed to be the only one who clammed up," he said. Without a doubt, if Charles could think of a better way—any way—to repair the brokenness in their marriage, he would be doing it right now.

Victoria glanced over at the man who still adored her as much as he had when she was in her early twenties. She'd doted on him and received his affections all those years ago, but now at age fifty-six, she felt continents away. His love for her was like dead-wood—but not from a lack of desire. They shared a mutual admiration for one another, but their passion was gone. How had it come to this?

Charles hadn't been ready to retire; still, he had left the firm as an image of success. Victoria's husband had enjoyed all the accolades and appreciation, but now he was left with emptiness. She knew his dreams were past; he had accomplished all he set out to do. Instead of dreaming new dreams, he only looked forward to more losses such as the ones he'd suffered recently. First their grandson, then Charles's profession, his health, and now possibly their marriage. . . . He wasn't as young as he felt, and though his recent heart attack had been minor, it had shaken him up. His partner in the firm hadn't been so lucky. Victoria remembered how upset Charles was when his colleague Phil died instantly on the subway in a foreign city while away on business for the firm.

After all these years—all these losses—Victoria's husband finally wanted to share life with her. But she had grown independent during so many years of his long hours at the office or in court. Now she wanted to do her own thing. So . . . that's why they were here. Before she could talk herself out of it, she spoke aloud. "Could Charles and I work next?"

❁ ❁ ❁

Rodney thought the stately older woman stood out like a tropical flower blooming against acres of dry grass. Here was someone who was making a break for freedom but not without first counting the cost. Sad, yet alive, Victoria's large eyes danced, full of expectation. The bright yellows and oranges of her pretty floral blouse stood in contrast to her lovely, dark skin.

"Charles, you seem to have some hesitation about joining a group such as this," Greg commented.

Charles nodded but did not speak.

Greg took care to validate Charles's successful career and acknowledge his marriage. "From what I understand, you've seen some good years and some bad. Having been married thirty-two years . . . thirty-two years is good," he said, nodding. "You still have the better half of your marriage to go. But you said something that struck a chord in me. And I haven't been able to let it go. You said that perhaps it is too late for your marriage. Did I remember that right?"

Charles sat tall and erect, but his true feelings were betrayed by the drawn look about his eyes. He straightened and replied, "Dr. Smalley, we are failing; we are traveling down a one-way street, going in the wrong direction. And I don't know how to stop the car." Rodney could almost picture the man approaching the bench in a court of law.

"It sounds like you're feeling pretty hopeless," Greg said. "Not only did you do everything you knew to be a success professionally and in your home life, but you also believed all that should have been sufficient." He role-played for a moment: "'I'm doing all the things that should make this a great marriage; in fact, until recently I believed we did have a good, strong marriage. But the fact that we are here, in light of all this, means *something* has gone terribly wrong. I want to identify what it is.' Is this accurate?"

"Precisely. Furthermore . . ." A long pause followed, and Charles got a bit choked up. Rodney busied himself with a sketch of Greg, taking only momentary glances in Charles's direction. "My wife recently asked, 'Why did you marry me?'" It was then Rodney saw that the distinguished-looking lawyer was visibly shaken.

Greg waited for his client to regain composure before continuing.

"I know this is tough. I hope you won't hold back. Let me ask you something. What is it about that question that so rocked your world? It sounds very similar to the rhetorical question we often ask, 'Why even get married?' Something about Victoria's question is unnerving to you—very disturbing—and I can't quite get my mind around what it is."

"It is an accusation that came out of nowhere," Charles replied. "It puts into question our whole marriage; everything I know to be true about our life together has been put in jeopardy." Surely, this Southern gent hadn't planned on disclosing quite this much information so soon. Rodney was impressed at the connection Greg had so quickly created—as if the counselor knew exactly where Charles was coming from.

The retired attorney went on to describe his pride in his family and profession, his beautiful wife, their successful kids. From his perspective, it all looked good. As if they had actually pulled off being married "happily ever after." He had always believed they were doing great. But then again, maybe not.

"Charles," Greg commented, "I get that Victoria's question felt like it came out of left field and that it seemed to put into question everything you knew to be true. But I wonder how her question impacted you personally?"

A deep breath of air was drawn into this client's chest before an answer came. "It makes me feel powerless, like there's nothing I can do to convince my wife of how good she's got it. I've tried . . . and clearly she is not happy about our life together. If the reason we married isn't clear by now—" Charles's shoulders drooped, and his long arms stretched out—"I don't know what we have left."

Greg continued, "Charles, I get that you are typically very convincing, but right now, when it matters most, I hear that you may be feeling helpless. I suspect that Victoria's question pushed your fear button of feeling powerless. Can you see that?"

Charles agreed.

"Let's start by acknowledging the fact that your button got pushed. Here's why: When your button gets pushed, you always have the option to ask yourself, *What am I doing to push my own button?* You see, sometimes our perception is what actually triggers a button. Let's take a closer look at that.

"It sounds like part of what is going on inside of you is that for all these years, marriage made good sense. But now you're not so sure anymore."

Charles stole a look at his wife.

"Why get married? Why stay married?" Greg asked. "What harm is there in living separated? It sure sounds better than fighting all the time. These kinds of rhetorical questions are familiar to most of us; society is asking them every day. But these are not rhetorical to you. This topic is not open for debate in your mind, and therefore a question of 'Why get married?' feels like a threat to all you know to be true. Since we're here, I suggest we take a closer look at your perception of the question. How's that sound?"

Murmurs of curiosity came from the group. Rodney could tell Charles felt miserable, but he seemed open to what Greg had to say.

"Okay, I'm listening," Charles said.

"Most of us look to the same sources as everyone else for information on how marriages are supposed to work, and there aren't many good models out there to help us find a better way. In fact, we rarely even question the wisdom of what we are being told. Divorce rates among professed Christians are just as terrible as those for nonbelievers.

"For many people," Greg continued, "the primary purpose of marriage is finding happiness. But when happiness is the goal, the normal ups and downs and challenges of life can pose serious danger to the relationship. When things go bad in our marriages—when they don't live up to our hopes and expectations and when there are periods of dissatisfaction—the commitment to stay together becomes strained. People often think things like, *This isn't what I wanted; I didn't sign up for this; I've fallen out of love with him [or her]; There is something wrong with my spouse; We must be incompatible; We have grown apart;* or *We've fallen out of love.* The dissatisfaction or unhappiness then becomes a potential justification to end the marriage or enter into unloving behavior. It never dawns on most of us to ask whether or not we might have been sold the wrong bill of goods and whether we might be trying to arrive at our chosen destination on a road that is taking us in the wrong direction.

"Charles, I'm wondering what it said to you when Victoria asked, 'Why did you marry me?'"

"Well, it put into question the validity of our whole marriage . . . as if somehow the whole thing was merely a farce. That the very foundation of our relationship was never really there in her mind as it had been in mine. That maybe I had been fooling myself all these years . . . and she hadn't been completely honest with me." Charles was obviously trying to maintain his upright and controlled posture, but his composure seemed to be on the verge of collapse.

Greg reflected back what he'd heard Charles say, then he pressed in a little deeper. "Somehow, the fact that your wife is questioning or having some doubt is literally challenging your whole sense of being. It seems to have upset everything you knew to be true or what you expected to be true."

Charles gave his affirmation, while keeping a stony expression.

"When you said, 'I can't believe I'm here,' it was like acknowledging another piece of evidence for the jury that somehow you are guilty of an accusation: 'I'm a failure, and I didn't even know it. I never suspected such a thing.' You feel helpless or powerless to change things. Victoria's question has in a way defined you, and you are going to fight it.

"It sounds like you have had a certain amount of pride in your marriage, your family, and the way you were structuring things. You were like, 'Hey, we're doing this pretty well, this is successful.' And this whole business in the last couple of years has really challenged that whole perception."

Charles replied with a curt "That's correct." Rodney could see that even though Charles appreciated Greg's approach, he was still wary.

"I'm guessing that for a couple who's been married thirty-two years, loyalty is a strong quality of yours. I can imagine that you felt betrayed by Victoria's question. I'm not sure in what context she asked it. But when she dared to voice her dissatisfaction or unhappiness, it felt like a threat. You haven't felt safe since."

Greg checked with Charles to see if he was on track. With his hands folded loosely in his lap, the older man was doing a good job hiding any fear.

The counselor pressed on. "I'd like to do as much looking forward as looking back. So let's set your marriage, as you know it, over here for just a little while so we can reframe your situation a bit—look at it from another angle." Greg tapped on an end table next to his chair. "When Erin and I got married—"

Just then Ryan's cell phone rang. He quietly excused himself, but Becca wasn't so graceful in her show of exasperation. "I'm sorry, Greg. My husband is responsible for saving the world!" She threw one long leg over the other and swung her foot in double time.

Greg calmly continued his story. "When Erin and I got married, we brought numerous myths and happily-ever-after fantasies into our marriage. I remember several that now seem pretty ridiculous, but back then we both believed they would happen. Listen to some of these: 'The honeymoon will last forever and we'll have great sex every night' or 'Greg might be a little rough around the edges, but he'll change over time.' Yeah, right! How about this one: 'Erin will make me whole—she will complete me!' We actually believed these fantasies.

"Basically, Erin and I thought everything was going to be perfect. Before our wedding, we had no idea where we were going to live or what we'd do for money. But we knew that everything would work out. We had *love* . . . so we'd survive.

"I'm sure my father-in-law was somewhat skeptical when I asked Erin to marry me. The poor man probably felt like another father whose daughter brought her fiancé home for the first time. . . .

"After dinner the mother told her husband to find out about the young man. The father invited the fiancé to his study for a talk.

" 'So what are your plans?' the father asked the young man.

" 'I am a seminary student,' he replied.

" 'A seminary student. Hmmm,' the father said. 'Admirable, but what will you do to provide a nice house for my daughter to live in?'

" 'I will study,' the young man replied, 'and God will provide for us.'

" 'And how will you buy her a beautiful engagement ring, such as she deserves?' the father asked.

" 'I will concentrate on my studies,' the young man replied. 'God will provide for us.'

" 'And children?' asked the father. 'How will you support children?'

" 'Don't worry, sir, God will provide,' replied the fiancé.

"The conversation proceeded like this, and each time the father questioned, the young idealist insisted that God would provide.

"Later, the mother asked, 'How did it go, honey?'

"The father answered, 'He has no job and no plans, and he thinks I'm God.' "

The group laughed at the punch line. Greg gave one of his characteristic big smiles.

"Did anyone else think this way?" he asked. "Our society is full of myths and fantasies like these. But perhaps the most problematic myth we hear is this: If you are not happy with your marriage, you may have married the wrong person.

"A marriage is in big trouble when *happiness* is the goal. If happiness or finding your soul mate is the objective, this is a huge setup for failure—or at least years of frustration. This is such a setup, because what happens when you're not happy? What does the absence of happiness mean? It makes you wonder whether you may have married the wrong person or if there is something wrong with you or your mate.

"An alternative to the happily-ever-after fantasy is to see marriage as a journey. The truth is that happiness is nice, but marriage is more about choosing a journeying partner than finding your soul mate. What's great about having a journey perspective is that a journey contains both the good and the bad. It contains the mountaintop experiences and the valleys. So if you make your goal about journeying together instead of about happiness, you allow the marriage to contain both the happy times and the painful times, without seeing the negatives as problematic. Both are expected and accepted." Greg looked at Charles. "Does this fit for you?"

"I've believed just about every myth you mentioned at one time or another."

"Me, too," chimed in Rodney. "Especially the one about getting great sex every night! I didn't know these were myths—I just thought they were nature's cruel trick to get us hitched."

The group was taken aback by Rodney's humor. Once young and "in love," they had all bought into happily-ever-after myths. Laughter filled the room.

"Let's take this journey metaphor deeper." Greg stood and walked over to a whiteboard. "If you look at the decision to marry as actually the choosing of a journey partner with the goal of growing into a more perfect representation of the man and woman you were both created to become, then the evaluation of your marriage takes on a different slant. From this perspective, marriage becomes a series of three simultaneous journeys, each with its own objectives and responsibilities."

While finishing his thought, he motioned for Bob to toss him a dry-erase marker, and he started making notes on the board.

"The three journeys are . . ."

1. My Journey
2. My Spouse's Journey
3. The Marriage Journey

He took a deep, comical sniff of the marker and made a face without skipping a beat. Rodney had come to like Greg a lot.

A TALK WITH THE DOCTORS

Three Journeys

All three journeys—my journey, my spouse's journey, and the marriage journey—need to be attended to. If we ignore any one of the three, the entire system is thrown out of whack. Early on in my marriage, I mainly focused on my marriage and on Erin. But I rarely, if ever, thought about *my* journey.

I'm sure you're wondering what "my journey" is. If I am a follower of Jesus Christ, my personal journey is to become the person God created and called me to be. In other words, my goal is to be conformed to the image of Christ. The key, however, is that I'm 100 percent responsible and accountable for how well I handle this calling during my lifetime.

In terms of Erin's journey, since my wife is a follower of Jesus Christ, her personal journey is similar to mine—to become like Christ. She, too, is fully responsible and accountable for how well she conforms to the image of Christ. I am not responsible for Erin's journey. However, I have the opportunity to come alongside my wife. If I choose to do so, I can love, encourage, and assist her on her journey. My direct participation in her journey, however, is always at her invitation and discretion.

In addition to our personal journeys, we have a marriage journey. As a Christian couple, we have the opportunity to create a marriage that honors the Lord. It's a place where we share his love. This is something that ultimately can only be created together; therefore, the responsibility is shared, and we will each be accountable for how well we did our part to make our marriage one that pleases God.

As we've talked about many of the myths we believe as we walk into marriage, we wonder what some of yours were (or are).

- What are some of your happily-ever-after fantasies?
- What do you expect should and shouldn't happen in marriage?
- What are the standards and ideals you have for your marriage?
- Do you have any rose-colored beliefs about marriage?
- What did you assume would happen in your marriage?
- What do you hope and wish will take place in your marriage?

"What do you think of this idea about having a separate journey from your wife, Charles?"

"We *are* very separate right now. We don't even communicate."

"That is not exactly what I mean."

"I'm not following you, Greg," came Charles's sharp reply.

"Marriage isn't about finding someone to complete us or make us whole, or having a honeymoon that lasts forever. The purpose of marriage isn't even about happiness. It's not about great sex—"

"Well . . . that wouldn't hurt," Bob joked.

"You're preachin' to the choir," Greg agreed with a chuckle. He continued, "The answer to 'Why get married?' is the journey. Charles, it's about you and Victoria experiencing the highs and lows of life *together*. It's about wiping away the tears streaming down your faces as you encounter deep joys and sorrows. It's about doing life together—growing, learning, living, and loving *together*. Two complete people on their own personal journeys more fully becoming the man and woman they were created to be, while simultaneously living in and creating a great relationship for sharing the journey. That's the secret. I believe Victoria's question about why you married her is not so much a statement of regret as it is a question about the journey itself.

"Your marriage certainly does have hope. In fact, it has tons of hope—even when your wife is asking some really hard questions. It's a grave mistake to assume at any age that there is something wrong with your spouse or that you both have changed so much that you are no longer compatible." Greg's gaze shifted to Victoria so she, too, was part of the dialogue.

A TALK WITH THE DOCTORS

The Marriage Journey

This marriage journey is highly unpredictable, which makes it one of continual adventure and discovery.

Let's take a look at the biblical story of the Exodus as a metaphor of your marriage. The story of the Promised Land journey begins when the family of Jacob moved to Goshen. It was a great time for them at first. They lived in peace and stability. Their families grew. Their flocks multiplied.

The early months and years of marriage can be like that. Unfortunately, along the way we find ourselves surprised at how different the actual experience is from what we had expected and hoped for. Just as a new Egyptian leader arose and forced the Israelites into slavery, at some point in marriage, a large percentage of us find ourselves faced with a very different life from the one we started out with. We become disappointed and discouraged. While marriage has the potential of being one of life's greatest experiences, finding the way to that promise, and figuring out how to keep it once you have it, can be extremely challenging.

The average couple starts off their marriage with great expectations, only to discover that at some point their marriage feels more like being trapped in slavery. It may be slavery characterized by turmoil and misery, or it may simply be disappointing and boring, but either way it is a far cry from what they had hoped for.

❄ ❄ ❄

Oh, Victoria knew her version of slavery all right. She knew exactly how she'd gotten there. Her naive ideas about being in love and her bright visions of paradise led her straight toward the pyramids of her handsome beau, Charles Templeton. He was kind, witty, intelligent, and on the road to success. He was precisely right. Her mother had been so proud of her catch and said, "Victoria—" she had given her an English name purposely so that her daughter would never be discriminated against in print—"child, do not let this good man slip through your fingers."

Victoria didn't need much help identifying how stuck she had become . . . or how she had settled into her own private slavery. Life had been happy and full with the four kids, their agendas, social engagements, her committee meetings, the club. She could share life with everyone but Charles, it seemed; but that's just how marriage was, she figured. Her friends had their own dramas in their marriages too—those who were still married. It seemed that husbands either took off with younger women, lost themselves in their hobbies, or got more needy.

Victoria figured that men like Charles started wanting more affirmation and nurturing in midlife just about the time their wives were ready to enjoy freedom from the rigors of daily housekeeping and mothering. She had looked forward to having an empty nest—her kids weren't far away, and she took full advantage of playing with the grandbabies. This was her season of life. If only she could be free.

It was Bob who spoke this time. "For you, Charles and Victoria, your discovery of slavery doesn't appear to have happened at the same time. I wonder, Victoria, if you may have started feeling the shackles long before Charles had any idea you were struggling, but because you tend to be quiet and you kept smiling, he didn't really know how you felt. Perhaps there have been several defining moments."

"Yes, thank you for that important insight, Bob," Greg said. "As terrible as the present reality often is, many people stay in slavery much longer than they need to because even though it's miserable, it is familiar. Only when the couple is willing to risk leaving the familiarity of Egypt can they open up to the possibility of finding a new, more satisfying marriage."

Victoria's thoughts began to stray. How many times had it happened? The sensation of suffocating, with a clenching grip that would come over her. Panic would settle in, and in the night hours she wouldn't be able to reason with her fragmented thoughts. She had to get away. Wriggling free from her sleeping husband's embrace, she would slowly slip out of bed and pull the covers back into place so he wouldn't feel the chill of her absence. Too many times to count, Victoria had stood panting by the bed in the cool night, fighting back anxiety and an irrational strangling feeling. The night terrors seemed to grow more intense, threatening to disclose fears secret even to herself.

She had become haunted by her new incessant need for freedom. While she filled her glass with water in the silence of the night, she ached to get in the car and drive away, but she had nowhere to go. Maybe she could take a bath. No, Charles would wake up and interrogate her for her erratic behavior. Then the lecture would come, and she would end up crawling back into bed feeling ridiculous.

Night after night Victoria had crept out of bed, praying that her husband wouldn't realize she was gone. She had tried to talk with Charles, but she would always say things so poorly that the conversation would immediately go off course and more damage would be incurred before she could stop the momentum of their miscommunication. Charles insisted that he loved her, yet . . . somehow, it always became her problem. She would then apologize in hopes of bringing the pointless dialogue to a close as quickly as possible. The sooner he was appeased, the sooner she could get some space.

This same drama had played itself out in one form or another for weeks, whether it was her gasping for air at night or stifling her thoughts during the day. Often people blame their spouses for letting the marriage die, but she wondered if she was at fault. Victoria was, after all, the one who seemed to be changing. She had already gone through "the change" and wondered if perhaps all this flurry of claustrophobic emotion was merely another chapter of hormonal flux. How could she possibly make it logical for him to understand when she herself couldn't make sense of it?

Without explanation, she had moved into their daughter's old room while Charles was away on a short trip. She knew he would be terribly upset when he returned. But she had to do something before she went entirely mad.

Yes, Victoria knew what it meant to live in slavery. She had been living like a fugitive for far too long.

Victoria snapped out of her reverie. She'd missed a few words of what Greg was saying. She wasn't going to let that happen again.

"Most couples discover that when they leave Egypt they don't find themselves in the Promised Land. Instead, they enter the wilderness. At that point it is easy for them to assume they have made a mistake. They usually want to return to the familiarity of Egypt, but in reality the wilderness is a critical part of the journey to the Promised Land. The wilderness is where couples learn the knowledge and skills necessary to take them to the marital Promised Land so they can successfully live there for a lifetime.

"Our goal is to help you identify your own version of slavery in Egypt—both how you're stuck and how you got there—and then to walk with you through the wilderness in order to gain the knowledge and learn the skills necessary to find your own version of the Promised Land and make a permanent home there."

Victoria wondered why Charles resisted her freedom so. She knew he feared what he didn't understand, and he didn't understand what she couldn't explain. She didn't plan to leave him; her need for space and her own identity was simply a coming home to herself, not a going away. If only she could explain that she was so much more than he knew, so much more to love if he would embrace all of her and not just the parts he acknowledged. If only he could grant her freedom and bless her in her desire to reach out more broadly to the world. Yes, she loved to be in her husband's arms, in his library, in his life; but there was a world out there to discover. She had invited him to come too. But he was so resistant. On the few occasions they had ventured out since his retirement, Victoria felt as if she were dragging around a corpse—only 'Charles the Contrary' wasn't dead, he could still argue! Her sense of wonder, curiosity, and passion was being reawakened . . . and Charles wanted to know what was for dinner.

". . . And what keeps us in the cycle of slavery?" Greg was asking.

"Fear," Rodney offered matter-of-factly.

"Yes. Fear," Greg said. "The Israelites were caught between the misery of slavery and the uncertainty of being free. After all, they had been slaves for 430 years! In that time, they had become completely dependent on the Egyptians and had grown used to being slaves. They were stuck. Being a slave had become routine— it felt safe and normal. Although they didn't like it, it was what they knew. Slavery kept them alive. Slavery defined them.

"Through the Exodus they were rescued from slavery and led out of Egypt and into freedom. However, when they were led into the wilderness and a life of unknowns, they were instantly struck with a host of fears, and the fear of one touched the fear of another until they were ready to forgo the hope of the Promised Land and return to slavery. They longed to return to Egypt and avoid an uncertain future.

"How is this sitting with you, Charles and Victoria? I believe you are right now in a wilderness experience."

Charles spoke up. "At first I thought it was all my fault. But everything is changing. Victoria's dreams and desires are not the same as they used to be. All of a sudden she wants to be alone. She shuts down and gets silent when I try to talk to her. She wants to run around all the time. She's not the woman I married . . . unless she's been this way all along and has led me to believe differently all these years. What am I to do? I guess if this describes the wilderness, then I'm there. My future is by all means uncertain. And yes, sir, I'll be the first to admit I'm scared."

Victoria marveled at how nothing about her husband's demeanor gave any indication that he was scared. He shifted and stroked his silvering goatee with long fingers. But his words were true.

"Charles, even though this may go unstated, you seem to bounce back and forth between two places," Greg said. "One is this: 'I am a failure and really I have been deceiving myself all these years.' The other is, 'Actually, I was doing okay, and the problem is with Victoria.' Although you haven't said that outright, it seems like you can't determine which of the two it is. So you are left bouncing back and forth between one of those two options trying to find the verdict.

"It seems to me that you are spending a lot of energy trying to determine whose fault it is. 'Is it my fault, or is it hers?' Part of you thinks maybe it is your fault, but then you reason, 'I did everything right, therefore it couldn't be—it has to be hers. . . . Yet I care about her, and I hate to blame and point the finger at her.' You are caught in an undeniable quandary."

"I see how I'm stuck, and I'm trying to figure out what I need to change to get unstuck." Charles was growing impatient, his wife noticed. He stretched out his long frame and crossed his ankles.

"This battle going on inside is ripping you apart," Greg said. "You've worked hard to figure this thing out, yet it's getting the best of you. And I don't think you can ever be successful in finding out whose fault it is. In fact, trying to find whose fault it is, is a huge waste of time." He paused and smiled. "I am confident that after thirty-two years you have both contributed quite significantly. Furthermore, I don't think trying to change is going to be anything more than an exercise in frustration for you, Charles.

"We'll come back to this. For now I'm going to ask you to merely consider what we've been saying. I believe the topics we'll be discussing will shed light on your situation. As well, you'll find yourself in the others' stories.

"We do know one thing for certain: 'Happily ever after' doesn't work. We can't just say 'I do,' and then check in twenty or thirty years later. Change is inevitable. That is what makes marriage an adventure. Allow yourself to sit with your questions without needing an immediate answer. It will come."

❂ ❂ ❂

On the way to dinner, Victoria watched as Greg stopped to chat with Charles, who was standing alone on the balcony. Charles looked as if he was taking a moment to reflect back over the day. There sure was a lot to consider. Victoria marveled again at how Greg so readily made her husband feel comfortable. Yet she could see in her husband's face an expression of dread. Knowing the whole night still lay ahead, as well as three more days of uncertainty, would do this to her man. Just like their marriage, which turned out to be unpredictable and thus made Charles nervous, this must be sheer torture for him. He most certainly was having an "in the wilderness" experience—and he looked utterly alone.

"Charles?" Greg inquired as he approached. Then looking up

at the thin, black gentleman several inches above six feet, he asked, "Will you be joining us for dinner?"

The stately gentleman didn't move a muscle but continued to look far off in the distance. Reluctantly, he nodded slowly and after a pause turned toward the therapist.

"Dr. Smalley," came his unhurried reply, his voice low and deep, "what am I supposed to do now?"

"For tonight?"

"Yes, sir. I don't—you see, I'm not—sharing a room with my wife." His voice cracked with emotion. "She doesn't want to be with me."

Victoria's heart tightened. She didn't want to eavesdrop, yet her love for this man wouldn't let her step away.

"I hear what you're saying," Greg said kindly. "What you're feeling is not at all unusual. We find that the anxiety level on this first night often remains at an all-time high, because you have laid yourselves out emotionally without anything yet being resolved." He stood next to Charles quietly for a moment, leaning against the railing of the balcony while looking out at the moonlit sky. The sound of crickets chirping filled the pause. "All we've done so far is set up our next few days together and hear your stories . . . so it still feels undone and really messy."

Charles nodded slightly but remained silent. His legs were locked at the knees, and his arms were crossed tightly across his chest as if he might buckle at any moment.

"One thing I've noticed about myself, Charles, is that after the first day, I feel like a complete failure . . . no kidding . . . I'm not certain of how things are going to come together. . . . I don't feel like I've been at all helpful yet, and I don't know how God is going to restore these relationships. So tonight I'll spend time praying and releasing my anxiety and my sense of failure to him. Then tomorrow morning I'll be ready to go."

Victoria could hear voices, laughter, and the clinking of crystal in the dining hall above.

"You're free to take a drive or relax in the sitting room or whatever you might need to do to take good care of yourself," Greg told her husband. "I would encourage you to quietly wait with your heart open, curious about what tomorrow might bring. In these moments of wondering, I like to read and meditate on Psalm 23." He pointed toward the dining room. "Will you walk with me?"

Victoria relaxed as the two men walked back into the building. She could see that Greg and Bob were comfortable leaving their clients in the care of God and each other. They knew, as did she, that the Holy Spirit was the ultimate counselor and guide.

A TALK WITH THE DOCTORS

Steps Away from the Fear Dance

The LORD said, "I have indeed seen the misery of my people in Egypt. I have heard them crying out because of their slave drivers, and I am concerned about their suffering. So I have come down to rescue them from the hand of the Egyptians and to bring them up out of that land into a good and spacious land, a land flowing with milk and honey. . . . So now, go. I am sending you to Pharaoh to bring my people the Israelites out of Egypt." (Exodus 3:7-8, 10)

The Israelites' journey to the Promised Land, which was described to Charles and Victoria, serves as a backdrop for the journey to the Promised Land in marriage. After working with thousands of couples and individuals, we have found that there are four main steps that help us move from feeling stuck and unsafe to the safe, open, and connected marriage we want. On page 137 is a model of how these steps work.

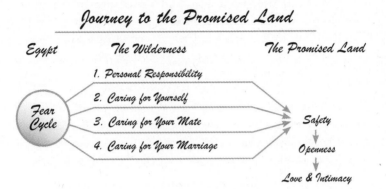

Journey to the Promised Land

| Egypt | The Wilderness | The Promised Land |

1. Personal Responsibility
2. Caring for Yourself
3. Caring for Your Mate
4. Caring for Your Marriage

Fear Cycle

Safety
↓
Openness
↓
Love & Intimacy

Notice that the first two steps, personal responsibility and caring for yourself, deal exclusively with the individual. When our buttons get pushed and we find ourselves in the middle of a Fear Dance, the place we can start to break out of this frustrating cycle is with ourselves. God has given us the power to break the dance, but it requires that we focus on ourselves first and foremost. As you will notice, the work that is done in the next several chapters all deals with the individual. Oftentimes couples in the Intensive say, "We came here to learn how to strengthen our marriage, and you want to keep focusing on us as individuals." Exactly! That is music to our ears. We don't do this to frustrate people, nor are we avoiding the marital issues. We simply believe that a great marriage requires two healthy individuals. We don't know how to help a marriage unless we start with the individuals. This is why the essence of the first two steps is about our personal journey—becoming the men and women God created us to be. Remember, we are 100 percent responsible for our own journey.

Once we have two people who have taken responsibility for their own well-being and are taking great care of themselves, we can move on to the third step. This next step—caring for our mate—deals with our opportunity to come alongside our mate as they deal with their journey—

becoming the man or woman God created them to be. This is when we learn to be a great helpmate. As our mate's assistant, we can learn to love, honor, cherish, support, and encourage our spouse on their journey. What an amazing opportunity.

Now that two healthy people are assisting one another, the foundation is set for building a marital relationship that both people can be thrilled with. The fourth step, caring for your marriage, will help you learn how to be a team with your spouse and how to find win-win solutions to your problems.

MONDAY, 8:00 P.M.

Following a delicious meal of lasagna, freshly made bread, a variety of olives, fresh veggies, salad, and a sumptuous dessert, Victoria saw Charles excuse himself. Quietly she rose and followed.

Charles let himself into the ornate great room, went to the grand piano, and sat silently with the lid closed. Notes had once rolled from his fingertips, but not tonight.

Coming up behind him, she said softly, "Charles?"

Without turning he asked, "Who will you be after your search for whatever it is you are looking for is over, Victoria?"

"Me. Still me."

"While you're getting this all figured out, what am *I* supposed to do?"

She rubbed his back. "Oh, Charles. Find something you love too."

"I already know what I love."

"I'm not referring to me. I mean, yes. I love you too. You know I do."

He turned. His eyes held doubt and pain.

"Oh, darling."

He sighed. "V. You don't belong out there." He made a wide

sweeping gesture. "You need to be home. How can we share this journey if you're not with me?"

"I was only gone for three weeks."

"That's too long, Victoria."

She had so much to say in light of today's session but knew there was no way to win this argument. The verdict had been read. Victoria let her hands drop to her sides and walked out of the room.

She hated silence, and yet it was the only place where she seemed to have sufficient space to breathe. Being married to an attorney meant that she always had to prove her case. Words filled up her world and came back to punish her. She could never say it right.

❂ ❂ ❂

Pam was experiencing pangs of guilt for not feeling worse about her husband's lack of appetite and his need to leave dinner early because of a ferocious headache. He was dozing now. The day had been stressful for him, and in times like these his migraines raged out of control and he needed darkness and silence. At home she would busy herself with keeping the kids quiet and doing chores around the house, but here she wasn't quite sure what she should do. Sitting in the chair next to the bed, she held her Precious Moments cross-stitch in her lap. Typically, making rows of tiny Xs across the pattern brought relaxation, but tonight she was restless. Todd's breathing was heavy and slow now.

Preacher could be outspoken, but even after all these years, Pam had never gotten accustomed to it. She wanted to be well but didn't know how to accomplish it in the midst of all her roles: pastor's wife, mother, sister, daughter. Her whole life had been spent trying to keep the peace. She could totally relate to poor Charles feeling like a failure in his marriage after all those years. She couldn't, however, imagine it all happening in one day as it had for him. Her failure came as no surprise; she'd never been able to please Preacher or fulfill his expectations.

Pam loved everything she was learning here at the Intensive and was beginning to see how profound these truths were . . . for the other couples. It seemed rather impossible for her to ever be "thrilled" with her own marriage. Truth be known, she couldn't imagine being thrilled with her marriage because, frankly, she couldn't name a single thing in life that she was thrilled about. Perhaps the real problem was that she was stuck in survival mode and didn't feel much of anything.

Pam marveled that her husband had agreed to come. God was still in the business of working miracles . . . in spite of her own weak faith. It wasn't that she didn't trust God's power—she was just too depressed to hope much. It was hard to pray, but she loved God. "Father, thank you for this first miracle. Do you think we could have another?" She and Todd hadn't started their work yet. They would be the first couple in the hot seat in the morning. Just the thought of it made her want to devour a whole chocolate cake.

She felt accepted in this group. They didn't *really* know her, but with them she was just another person. They expected her to have issues. It was quite freeing, actually. Yet as soon as she closed the door to her room, the old dark substance of her life waited there to drag her under its murky tide. At home she had no escape, but tonight she had no children, no cleaning, no Bible study—just a grand Victorian house waiting to be explored. And the best part was the snack bar stocked with sweet comfort foods.

Trying not to think about how furious Preacher might be with her for leaving the room unannounced, Pam left him a note and closed the door in slow motion. Soundless. As soon as she felt it meet the doorjamb, Pam scrambled down the hallway, her face flushed with excitement. She would get a little snack first and then see if anyone else was out and about. If not, she'd be happy to indulge in watching a video. After taking a handful of homemade chocolate chip cookies and stuffing one into her mouth, she shoved the other five into the large pocket on the front of her over-size red cardigan. She made her way into the lobby and through the entrance into the great room.

There she heard muffled voices, so instead of turning the corner, she backtracked quietly to the oval dining room to enjoy her cookies with a glass of milk. Divine. She perched on a velvet lounge chair and admired the ornately carved sideboard and gilded mirror while nibbling two more cookies. Regal floral arrangements with magnolias and twisting vines decorated the entry. In the midst of all this Victorian fanciness, she felt like a cocklebur in Queen Anne's pantaloons. She ate another cookie, creamy with butter and melted chunks of milk chocolate. Mmm, delicious. This was precisely the reason she loved food. All her cares seemed to go away. She wondered if Victoria Templeton would like to share a cookie and a cup of tea.

At dinner Pam had seen the lovely woman looking right at her. She couldn't decipher what she was thinking, but she saw pity cross her face—not the "sorry" kind of pity, but an understanding kind. Just before Victoria left the dining area, she had invited Pam to stop by her room sometime.

Perhaps tonight. Pam wondered about Victoria's story and this *knowing* they shared between them. Could it be loneliness, depression? Surely not. The love of a child? Pam knew then that she wanted to talk to her about it—to learn of the pain she recognized in her own reflection. Sweeping the crumbs from her mouth, her decision was made. Calm, yet terrified, she trudged up the wide, circular stairs to the bedrooms located on the second story of the Bradford House.

Halfway up, Pam stopped with the sinking feeling that Charles may have accompanied his wife up to her room, but she caught her breath and continued on. By the time she made it to the landing, Pam's chest was heaving. Goodness, she was out of shape. It was a good thing their room was on the ground floor. Pam's fears were allayed when over the balcony railing she spotted the man in question standing near the fireplace, with his back toward her. She had an urge to call out to him and give a little wave from way up there, but she was on a mission.

Which room had Victoria told her? Pam lingered as long as she dared without Charles sensing that he was being watched and then located Victoria's door a few paces farther down the hall. Pam stopped short of the suite door, trying to breathe calmly. As a pastor's wife, she shouldn't be this afraid of speaking to another woman. *But this is not just any other woman.* She forced herself to take the final steps to the door and knock.

The door opened slightly. "Yes?" Victoria's voice was supple, like an alto saxophone.

"I—um, I'm sorry. I don't want to bother you." Pam's voice was tight and shaky in comparison.

Now that she was standing backlit by the soft light, Victoria's presence was imposing. She was taller than Pam anticipated, stately with an ageless beauty. Having just changed from her silk top and light wool twill slacks, she was a different woman. Her head was now wrapped in a soft turban. Her long, traditional gown of vibrant blues and golds hung beautifully on her frame.

The long fingers on her extended hand and wrist were adorned with jewelry from another time, another place. Standing before Pam was a woman who, in spite of her pain, knew who she was, and this identity had little to do with her husband's profession. She was an expression of prosperity—spiritually, physically, emotionally—and Pam felt terribly self-conscious just then. Her faltering boldness disappeared entirely, and she could hardly hold her gaze.

"Why, girl, aren't you going to come in?"

Pam's lips parted. She looked up at Victoria. All of a sudden she felt different, disconnected; the intimacies they shared didn't bind them together after all. But there was no turning back now. How did she get herself into these situations? Awkwardly Pam stepped in, tripping slightly on the lip of the carpet.

Victoria gazed at Pam steadily. "You're the pastor's wife, aren't you?"

"Uh-huh." She squirmed in spite of the calm in Victoria's voice.

"My husband . . . can say harsh things," Pam stammered. "I hope he didn't offend you tonight at dinner."

"Not at all, not at all." Victoria coaxed her guest to come over and take a seat.

Pam forgot all about asking Victoria for tea or about sharing her cookies. "Your room is lovely . . . and your gown is beautiful too. I've never seen anything like it."

"Why, thank you."

At Pam's self-conscious attempt to start conversation, the older woman took her cue and shared a recent portion of her story. Victoria Templeton had just returned from a monthlong sojourn in Kenya, where she had done a mission trip with the church. She proceeded to share with Pam about her travels.

". . . It took another two years to pull it off, but with the help of several other women friends I gathered the courage to tell Charles of my desire to go."

She told of how she had planned to work hard and hold orphan babies and feed hungry children, but how she never could have anticipated that she would find her soul in the heart of her grandmother's birthplace. Their music was hers, their dance was hers, their colors—it all had awakened something deep inside. . . . Here the middle-aged woman grew quiet. "And Charles would hear of none of it when I returned home. . . . Dear, I had no intention of carrying on. I don't know what came over me. It's just so good to be known. Tell me your story."

Pam had immediately felt at ease once Victoria started talking, but now she didn't know where to begin. She didn't know how much time had passed, but surely it was late. Panic set in. "I-I-I'm sorry, but I really must be going. My husband has been feeling ill. But I do hope we can talk again."

"I do too." With that, Victoria rose gracefully from the English chair where she had been sitting. Seeing her guest to the door, Victoria stopped and folded Pam into a warm embrace. "Thank you, sister. Your visit has been a gift."

As she closed the door behind herself, Pam's eyes blurred with tears. Their brief time together had been intimate even though they didn't get to the part she had come for . . . and Victoria said her visit had been a gift. A gift! Not the burden she was accustomed to being.

She made her way down the staircase and out to the front entrance steps of the Bradford House. There she sat down in the dark stillness of the outdoors. The cool night air tingled on her skin, and she was grateful for her sweater. Her mind lingered over each detail of Victoria's conversation, while she fingered in her pocket for a cookie. Out of habit, she raised one to her lips. It was then that she realized she felt quite full and put it back.

✿ ✿ ✿

When Becca awoke, her skin was clammy. Everything was dark and disorienting. As her eyes began to adjust, the branches of a maple tree outside her bedroom came into focus, and she discovered that she was on her hands and knees in the middle of the bed. She sat back shaking. What a terrible nightmare.

She had looked up and seen the wavy, sneering image of Bob after he pushed her off the high dive. Deeper and deeper she sank. Floundering, she couldn't fight her way to the top. She was drowning.

Just when she was ready to give up, a set of big, strong arms locked around her and pulled her through the watery depths to safety. She was too weak to hang on, but the man carried her and laid her down on the side of the pool where others lay drenched and shivering too. A mass rescue had just taken place. She didn't know exactly who had pulled her to safety, but she had lain there in his arms, like a little child held tightly by a parent after a frightening experience.

Dreams were so weird. When her mind reoriented itself, she remembered: Bob had been very careful yesterday and hadn't pushed at all—she had just been so freaked out about everything, and somehow her fears must have tangled themselves into her psyche.

Just then Becca remembered the rest of her dream. She had felt safe for only a moment before experiencing a sickening wave of terror wash over her. Tearing herself away from her rescuer, she raced down the line of wet, coughing bodies at the edge of the pool looking for Ryan. Frantic, she searched the bodies, then the water. Where was he? Before she'd awakened, her night terror was being played out in full body motion. On hands and knees, she had patted and searched for her husband in the bed.

Wide awake now, terror washed over her again after finding a cold, tightly made bed on his side. Her dream fuzzed into reality, and panic made her stomach wrench. Where and with whom was he spending the night? Groping for the clock, she saw it was 3:00 a.m.

Throwing herself onto the bed, she held her head while her mind raced back over the events of the evening. *Think.* Ryan had been at dinner, talking with Rodney and the butler. She had told him she was coming up to the room. . . . She had showered and fallen into bed exhausted. They had agreed to share a room for the four days they were in Branson. But there was no sign that he'd entered the room. She checked the bathroom. His toothbrush was dry, the towels all neatly folded. A wave of acid welled up from her belly, and she dry-heaved into the toilet.

Dear God in heaven . . . Was he killed on the highway somewhere? Her stomach clenched tight. The rental car. She ran to the window to search the parking lot—it was still where it had been parked earlier in the day. That was the right car, wasn't it? She felt a surge of relief but knew he could still be doing any number of things. In pink satin pajamas, she raced down the hall to the circular stairs and looked over the banister to see if he had fallen asleep near the fireplace. The formal sitting room was empty. *Think, Becca.*

She had left her packet of papers downstairs in the counseling room with all the pertinent information and the emergency phone number to call. "I've got to call. I've got to call. I've got to call," she mumbled while bounding down the broad, mahogany staircase, through the hall, and to the next flight of narrow stairs. With her pulse crashing in her ears, she rounded the corner—and there, sprawled out with his head hanging off the side of a couch, was Ryan—fully dressed, badly rumpled, and fast asleep. She collapsed into a nearby chair.

She should have known. This was Dr. Stuart, who worked any hour of the day or night and could sleep in half-hour segments whenever and wherever he needed to.

The sight of him unraveled her nerves. He was so beautiful. She couldn't conceive of never watching him sleep again. It had been only a month, and she had missed him desperately. She wanted to pull him in, to forget this horrible nightmare. He needed to be in bed with her where he belonged, where she could hold him close and melt into his body.

Becca allowed herself to indulge in only a few seconds of desire before her emotions took a vicious spin. *Look what he's done to me! Again!* she wanted to scream into the dark. His body represented only a memory—something that *was* hers, once, but no more. What was that commitment she was supposed to make to herself? She'd thrust her heart into Ryan's hands, and he'd recklessly tossed her, broken her. And now a part of her lay bleeding on the floor.

Her ribs could have cracked with the intensity of the pain slamming in her chest. Everything hurt, even the roots of her hair. It hurt too much. She wanted to slit her wrists. Life was ebbing from her like the tide going out to the ocean. She sat in the dark room, which was lit only by the cracks of light coming in from the streetlamp outside. Rocking back and forth . . . rocking, rocking, rocking.

Looking around the room, she imagined the people sitting there the day before. She could sense that feeling from her dream of being held by those strong arms, and she began to relax a little. *Jesus?* Her rocking slowed, and sanity began to return. All this was beyond her comprehension. She didn't understand, but slowly, slowly, she wasn't afraid anymore. Down in the center of her being, she felt it . . . a sense of . . . what was it? Safety.

Becca sat in the dark, wrapped in the growing sense that she was going to live. Life was no longer draining from her, and after a bit she could remember some of the discussions from the day before. She looked again at Ryan, with his face scrunched into the fabric of the couch, and she felt deep remorse. Where was he with all this?

She had peeked at his notes while he was out on break. Her husband seemed to be getting this stuff in his head. Her fear was that he was too intelligent for his own good and that he would process things mentally but remain unchanged in his heart. She remembered how he had stormed out that afternoon. What if she left Branson radically changed in both heart and soul, and he left anxious to see what's-her-name? She couldn't go there. *Jesus, help me!*

A pile of blankets was stacked in a corner of the room for guests to use during the day. Becca went over and unfolded one to cover the man she loved and wanted for her own. None of this made sense. She had been betrayed not once, not twice, but too many times to count. How could she possibly have feelings for this man? Maybe she was as whacked as he claimed she was.

Right now she was too tired to figure it out. That was Bob and Greg's job. With a renewed sense of peace, she ascended the stairs and returned to her bed.

❖ ❖ ❖

The Bradford House silently slept on. A mere two hours after Becca had returned to her room, across the hall in a mass of tangled sheets and twisted nightgown, Chelsea groaned and rolled over while trying to calculate how many hours of sleep she might have gotten. Sleep had been a foreign concept recently. How many months had it been since she'd actually slept without using one of the wide variety of over-the-counter sleeping pills? She flexed her toes and gave the blankets a kick to loosen their grip.

She and Rodney had had another fight the night before. She knew he meant well and was merely anxious to dig in. But the mix of his terrible timing and her intolerance for anything he did at this point had proven lethal. Even though she could reason through what had happened—and why—after Greg diagrammed their Fear Dance, in the telling moment, she'd been mean and distant to Rodney.

She couldn't help telling herself that everything was going too slowly. She didn't have time for Greg and Bob's stories. She needed some answers now—today. Rodney was excited by what he'd heard, but she had fidgeted all day yesterday. Chelsea wasn't sure how she'd make it through another day. She didn't want a detailed set of instructions on how she needed to change; she wanted "the four guaranteed steps to freedom" or "the seven habits for highly effective divorces."

She yanked off her blanket—did everything have to be so constrictive? When she hurled it to the floor, she was reminded of Jack. He loved to throw all his blankets and stuffed animals out of his crib. It felt pretty good actually—Chelsea wished she had several more things to chuck across the room.

The image of her little ones lingered, and she felt a tug of guilt. She'd been so caught up in her own issues, the kids hadn't crossed her mind. It was because they were being watched "ever so carefully." No worries there. She hoped they were being good for their grandmother and wouldn't say anything inappropriate while they were there. Hannah had picked up a few choice words in the past couple of months.

Chelsea sat up and glanced at the clock. It was way too early to call her mother, and she dreaded the task. She didn't know what to say when she did call. Mother had paid for the Couples Intensive and would want a detailed report. The pompous woman still did not know the half of her daughter's problems. But she was supportive in trying to salvage whatever was left—if for no other reason than to save face among her friends.

We're now in day two with several other whacked marriages, Mother, and we haven't made a whole lot of progress on our own. No, that would never be adequate for Claudia Rouse. It was no wonder Chelsea was one to always set her expectations too high. Nothing short of her very best would ever suffice for Mother.

Chelsea learned early on the pressures of being a perfectionist, and when others didn't deliver the same care for detail, whether in work, play, or relationships, she was often disappointed. When things were not well defined or moving as quickly as she wanted, she grew anxious.

Except for her brief stint of rebellion when she'd met Rodney, Chelsea had chained herself to the image her mother needed— demanded. Mother still didn't know about her tattoo or her belly-button ring. She was the golden child, which meant it was her job to please her parents, her employer, her neighbors, God. . . . She couldn't believe how stupid she'd been to get sucked into that fling with Duncan, the new accountant at the firm. *What an idiot!*

Burying her head under the pillow, she remembered her session notes from the day before and how she needed to be curious rather than judgmental. Perhaps she should just pause and not judge the "progress thing" either . . . and the three journeys actually made good sense. She *did* want a separate journey from Rod— that was the whole reason she wanted a divorce. She knew that wasn't what Bob and Greg had in mind, but she couldn't fathom herself and Rod ever walking independently, and *in stride*. What if he never picked up and started walking? She felt as if she had been dragging him for the last few years. How do you share a journey with someone who's always several paces—several *years*—behind?

She threw the pillow against the wall with a vengeance. How could they ever get in step? Maybe they really hadn't made a lick of progress since they'd arrived.

Chelsea could hardly stand being with herself, she was in such a foul mood. She had to do something. Pulling herself free from the bedding, her balance was off just enough that when bailing out of bed, she stubbed her pinky toe on the leg of the dresser. What followed was a trail of curses and a wild dance that outperformed any temper tantrum she'd ever witnessed. Was the day really going to go like this?

Five minutes later she had brushed her teeth, raked her hair back into a ponytail, and thrown on a T-shirt, old sweats, and her good running shoes. Bursting through the bedroom door, she almost stumbled over Rodney, who was slumped on the floor in the hallway. Did he have to look so injured? He must have been sitting there waiting for her to come out—too afraid to come in. He'd probably heard all the racket and cussing and chickened out. She had picked a winner, all right.

He wasn't the person she wanted to see just then, and Chelsea exploded. "Where have you been? Wait, don't tell me." She didn't even want to know where he had spent the night. The door slammed shut behind her. "When did you plan on getting cleaned up?" His sloppy appearance and the fact that he would wear the same clothes two days in a row infuriated her.

Without waiting for a response, she ordered her husband to get cleaned up while she was out. She would need the bathroom when she got back from her run. "And pick up your mess when you're done."

"Oh, and Rodney?" She popped her head back around the corner. "Check in with the kids. Hannah has been sick." She knew he'd be a comfort for the kids and would appease her mother with good news of their trip thus far.

She bounded down the steps and hit the ground running. With a surge of adrenaline, she took off at a quick, steady pace.

Running had always been her least damaging way of releasing anger and frustration. She could turn off her feelings and focus on her performance. Checking her watch, she took a pulse.

The sun wasn't warm enough yet to burn through the early morning mist. Down a quiet street, up hills and down; by the time Chelsea took a right turn ten minutes later, she was just warming up. This was when her muscles loosened and her breathing became regular. Typically, she would start feeling the break-through about now, but the feeling didn't come today. Packing a load of guilt and responsibility made her chest feel heavy and unresponsive to her gasps for air. Anger. She wanted to strike out and really hurt somebody. Her eyes blurred with tears. The upcoming street turned to the north and led to a path through a cathedral of trees. Around the turn and up a light hill, she soon found herself on a private wooded trail.

A creek coursed through the bottom of a shallow gulley, and the woods were filled with sounds of the skitterings of squirrels and other creatures. But Chelsea was unaware of her surroundings. Bent at the waist, she gulped for air. As her lungs filled, her eyes overflowed with tears. Before she knew what had come over her, she was weeping bitterly, her body racked with sobs.

Years had passed since she'd last cried. Life didn't afford time to be that vulnerable. Chelsea had railed against God but never grieved or repented. Why should she be sorry? The young woman had given him her all—had gone beyond the call of duty—given 110 percent. And what did he do? God had let her down—didn't keep up his end. No! She would not beat herself up with guilt. Freedom, that's what she needed.

Flushed and shaken from such a total breakdown, Chelsea found a nearby log on which to perch. All she wanted was to be happy; was that too much to ask? The wind started to pick up. She was mad about everything, including the whole happily-ever-after thing. So her dream of being happy was just a fantasy? She wasn't ready to let it go. There had to be something better, at least an easier way.

Wait. They did talk about an easier way, didn't they?

The weather was growing worse. The leaves blew upside down, signaling the coming rain.

Perhaps she never really did believe a white knight would come and take her away. What was she thinking? She had no knight, no dwarfs . . . she didn't even have any friends. Having been so driven to succeed, she spoke in tones that left a ragged trail of regret. *No one likes me—the real me,* she confessed to herself, perhaps for the first time. "I may seem confident and witty, but *I* don't even like me," she said out loud.

Thunder rumbled in the distance, and soon big fat drops of rain were splatting on her face. Her good, hard cry awarded some sense of relief, but now her head ached, her nose was all stuffy, and the rain was . . . ow! The rain was coming hard and stung her bare arms. Her shuffle became a jog. She hadn't worn rain gear, and her sweats were quickly becoming weights, heavy with dampness. Pulling at her soggy shirt, she retraced her steps back through the forest, went down the small side street, made a turn, and then connected back to the main road.

Just then she saw Ryan, who had also apparently been out for a morning run. He saw her too, doubled back, and minutes later fell into step with her. The rain was now coming down in a straight sheet of water, ripping through the branches of the trees along the road.

"It's a bit wet to be out, don't you think?" he called out.

Chelsea was not in the mood for humor, and she certainly wasn't excited about having company. But at least the rain coursing down her face hid any sign of her recent breakdown. She conceded to running with Ryan—seeing as how there wasn't much of a choice. A familiar face, though a much wetter version than she remembered, was a welcome companion in the cold rain.

Just then a car splashed through a puddle and slopped debris and fallen leaves on the left side of her fellow jogger. Ryan let loose a string of colorful curses. Chelsea smiled. She figured this kind of thing didn't happen often for prestigious physicians jogging along the boardwalk in Southern California.

Halting beside him, she couldn't help laughing at the sight. With no dignity left, the handsome doctor was a soggy, muddy mess. There was nothing he could do but shake it off and continue. She took the opportunity to wipe a sheet of water from her forehead. Ryan lifted his shirt to wipe his face.

Mmm. Chelsea looked away after catching a glimpse of his smooth stomach. He obviously had no inhibition about displaying his attractive build. She figured if it weren't so chilly, he would have taken his shirt off altogether.

He smiled resignedly and brushed ineffectively at his shorts before setting off again at a slower pace. He glanced back just once to see if she was ready to fall into place at his side. Ryan was obviously comfortable with women. *He is an ob-gyn, for goodness' sake. Ooh. How could you be married to a man who . . .* She would leave that one alone.

Soon they were in step and making good progress in spite of the downpour. After a half mile or so, Ryan broke into Chelsea's wandering thoughts. "So how are you taking to this whole shrink-wrapped package deal? Are you feeling processed yet?"

She tried not to show her surprise at his witty question. He'd asked it in jest—not cocky as she would have anticipated. Instead of putting her on the defensive, it opened up some lighthearted conversation. He was actually quite funny, if bitingly sarcastic. That must have been the anger peeking through.

Nothing she had seen prior to this moment would have given her any clue that Ryan could be fun. But after running next to him for a few miles, the old longing for a companion who could not only stay in step but make her laugh again began to nag at her heart.

"You're looking a bit miserable there, scout. You okay?" he asked over the clamor of the rain.

"I hope they have a method of processing other than dehydration, 'cause I'm pretty much soaked to the bone. I'll have to start all over again."

"Oh, no. Not that again. We'll be here another few days while Bob convinces you to stay. Here, you can hop on and piggyback," he said with a flirtatious grin.

"Are you mocking me?" A surge of rage coursed through her. "Ryan, I was ready to split yesterday, okay? At least I was honest about where I'm at—that I'm scared spitless of this process!"

He ran on, unfazed by her comeback. Without warning, he sped ahead a few paces then turned and continued jogging in reverse. "Chelsea, I'm sorry. I'm not mocking. You totally did all my work for me yesterday. Can't you see? You played out my whole scenario about wanting to leave. We are both pretty much in the same place."

"No, we're not!" It was no wonder his wife, Becca, came unglued. This man was infuriating.

"I don't mean that our situations are the same; it's just that we both want out. Don't you see the irony? We both want a divorce, right? So where do we go? To a Couples Intensive! Either we're being lassoed by some divine roper, or we've just stumbled into the branding corral on our own."

He broke out laughing at the absurdity of it all.

Ryan's laughter entirely transformed his face; his smile was incredible with his perfect teeth. More than that, it was genuine. Up to this point Chelsea hadn't seen anything true about Ryan. The conceited physician from Newport Beach had shown nothing but walls of pretense. During his and Becca's work the day before, Chelsea had despised him for his sexual exploits, his obvious weaknesses, and his seeming lack of concern for his wife.

The syncopated slapping of their shoes against the pavement and the rhythm of breathing was all that could be heard for another mile or two. Then out of nowhere Ryan said, "So you were totally honest about where you are at, huh?"

"Yep."

"So when are you going to share about the part where you left Rodney for another man?"

Caught off guard, Chelsea almost tripped. Quickly, she regained her composure, hoping he hadn't noticed. She refused to respond to his blunt inquiry. Picking up the pace, she ran several strides in front of him to make her point.

What a jerk! She shook water from her hands. A good physical workout was proving impossible when her world was being drenched and shaken from one moment to the next. She was in peak physical shape, but she was now breathing hard. She slowed to a walk, and Ryan caught up, until he was within earshot of his running partner.

Just when she was about to spout off something hateful in her own defense, Ryan gently asked, "Chelsea, why didn't you say anything about your affair yesterday? I mean, we're all laying ourselves bare in there. You're not holding out on us, are you?"

She stopped and turned with an icy glare. "It's none of your business."

"Hey, I'm sorry if I spoke out of turn." He held his hands up in surrender before letting them rest on his narrow hips, while he danced from one foot to the other in the middle of the road to keep his muscular legs from cramping after more than an hour of running. The Bradford House would come into view around the next curve. "I'm your assistant in this process, remember?"

Still livid, she continued walking in long, stretching strides.

"Okay, look," he said, jogging to catch up. "I shouldn't have jumped to conclusions. It just seemed . . . so obvious."

Yet another standstill. "What do you mean?" She couldn't believe this.

He shrugged, "I don't know."

Chelsea might as well have heard Ryan's thoughts. She was

painfully aware that her husband didn't exactly look like her match, and her cover was blown. *What now?*

"We better hustle up," Ryan said matter-of-factly. "The morning will be starting soon . . . and it wouldn't look good for the *two of us* to show up late." A grin pulled at the corners of his mouth.

9

TUESDAY, 7:00 A.M.

Rain pelted the windows, and thunder clapped. Outside, the tulips bent their heads toward the ground. There was nothing quite like a Missouri thunderstorm. Pam Davis loved the smell of rain—a rare treat for those living in Arizona. Snuggled down between the blankets, she listened to the steady drumming of rain. Like a crackling fire or the breathing of a sleeping baby, its steady rhythm was mesmerizing. At 7 a.m. the room was still dark, and the thought of getting up seemed out of the question. She stretched her foot to investigate the other side of the bed. Empty.

Preacher must have gotten up early to study his Bible and pray. She felt a stab of guilt. Her husband's dedication to the spiritual disciplines always made her feel like she came up short in God's eyes. Still, she was sure God loved being there with her, his child, while she enjoyed his rain and the lovely gift of this room. Mothers knew these things. Her prayer consisted of a mere, "Thank you!"

Stretching her arms to the ceiling, she studied the delicate curves of her fingers and wrists. In spite of all her domestic chores, her nails, which were naturally strong and perfectly shaped, were the envy of women who had to pay a fortune for theirs to look like this. She felt smug and then a little guilty about how Becca had let out a holler when she broke one of her acrylics while pulling out her chair at the dining room table.

Pam had beautiful hands and petite feet, size five and a half. She loved shoes, even though she presently owned only three pairs: old canvas tennis shoes, a nice brown church pair, and black pumps. Pam liked purses, too, but she was content to admire the ones other women carried. Changing purses was not at all practical—especially not with all the stuff she had to carry. She owned a brown one, and she'd use it until its handle broke or the bottom fell out—which was entirely likely to happen with everything she lugged around. Her purse seemed to get bigger at the same rate as her dress size.

Not wanting to think about the bulky form belonging to her under the covers, she daydreamed about all the lovely spring colors of handbags and shoes she had seen in the storefront windows of the airport. She especially liked a lime green one with rhinestones and a big silver buckle. Wouldn't Preacher just have a fit?

Aromas of fresh coffee, Belgian waffles, and sausage wafted up from the kitchen below. Her stomach growled for breakfast. Pam was always hungry, and this was such a special treat!

She got up and checked her blood sugar level with a quick pinprick on the end of her pointer finger. It wasn't as if she was obese, just undeniably thick, and . . . okay, unattractive in the bedroom. Her old terry-cloth robe had become her best friend, helping to hide her self-consciousness until the lights were off. Why was her husband so adamant about her losing weight anyway? "It'll make you feel better," he insisted.

"I'm just a little plump," was always her reply. "I've had three kids, for goodness' sake." She knew her diabetes and the extra weight around her middle were the result of a poor diet and lack of exercise. She also knew he'd be critical, no matter which reply she gave.

"No, Pam. You're fat."

"Todd," she'd reply, wounded.

He never seemed to mind her extra pounds when he pulled her to himself each night.

Her life was lived for him. She wanted to make her husband happy, but her best was never enough. Her friend Janine and several of the church ladies had surprised Pam with a makeover and a new outfit for her birthday. Wouldn't that be a nice surprise for Preacher, they had thought. She wanted to be happy and beautiful. All those women on reality TV shows seemed so changed and empowered by their makeovers . . . but Pam just felt foolish.

She hadn't always been this way. Valedictorian of her class, her mind had been sharp and inquisitive; but to Todd, she was merely a preacher's wife and the mother of his children. She loved these roles, but that wasn't all there was to Pam. There was much more—dreams unrealized, talents undeveloped . . . all selfish endeavors when there was serving to do.

Some women put on makeup in the mornings, but Pam did full-blown reconstruction each day by tacking a happy face firmly in place for her family and the church. This meant never getting too close to anyone, because she needed the buffer during the day to get life in order. She never knew when she'd slip into another bout of depression—she needed time and space to work through that, too. What would the church think of their preacher if they knew his wife was a zombie?

Pam freshened up and threw on a denim jumper minutes before hurrying down to the dining room, where she was greeted with smiles from the others. Her husband looked up from his plate and gave her a once-over. In a single, sweeping glance, he took inventory of her plate and gave her a dismissive look.

Pam knew she was the thorn in the side of his righteousness. Ah, but the food was yummy. The warmth of tea and the apple-cinnamon muffins, the sausage and eggs, and the company of the others helped her forget the man sitting beside her.

❂ ❂ ❂

Breakfast at the Bradford House seemed especially satisfying on a gray morning such as this one, and the guests remained subdued and quiet while they made their way toward the counseling room.

After living in the Midwest the majority of his life, Rodney didn't mind rain; in fact, he kind of liked it, except for on the days when he had games planned outside for the kids. The Missouri spring rain wasn't cold, but the air felt damp and made for good snuggling weather, especially in this dim, cozy atmosphere. He grew moody knowing there would be no snuggling for him today. Thoughts like these made him miss his kids.

Rodney thought the other guests looked tired. Maybe, like him, they had had a restless night. By the time Greg and Bob arrived, several had already started to settle in, taking blankets to wrap up in and warm cups of coffee to sip. The counselors' entrance crashed the sleepy mood of the morning when they burst in out of the rain, shaking the water from their umbrellas and coats. Rodney got such a kick out of these guys. Greg gave Bob an extra little sprinkle baptism, "just for good measure."

"Hey, guys," Greg said, hanging his rain jacket and umbrella on the coat tree.

Just then Chelsea rounded the corner into the counseling room, decked in an Old Navy hooded sweater, yoga pants, bare feet, and a wet head. The sight of her slipping quietly into her seat between the others who had already gotten settled made Rodney's heart ache. Rodney couldn't help but notice that she didn't look in his direction but rather made brief eye contact with Ryan, who looked fully put together, before turning her notebook to a clean page. *Ouch.*

Greg settled into his chair and made light conversation while Bob arranged his stuff for the day. There had been some flooding across a bridge that had made the two counselors, who commuted together, late. Greg got out his notebook and an unused paper clip. Rodney wondered what kinds of sculptures Greg would create today. They had discovered that while Greg did therapy, he twisted paper clips into "art." He seemed to be particular about his paper clips. They were all plastic coated. Rodney imagined that by the end of the four-day Intensive, there would be a pile of multicolored figures on the end table next to Greg's chair.

"Good morning," Bob said warmly, once he was settled. As he had done yesterday morning, he started out the day's session by ceremoniously taking off his shoes with the effect of a Mister Rogers moment.

Rodney sighed. If only this were a Mister Rogers moment instead of the battleground for his marriage. The first day had been messy, with plenty of problems exposed but few resolved. Had they gone through the worst of it, or was there more to come before it started getting better?

As if on cue, Bob answered his question. "Once you're able to see how you're stuck, the rest of the time we'll focus on how to break out of the Fear Dance. But until you are able to clearly see where you're stuck in the spin cycle, it's hard to effectively help you find an alternative."

Rodney had learned where and how badly he was stuck. Maybe there was hope yet.

"First, we want to invite God's presence here with us and ask for his leading. While we're praying, notice whether your heart is feeling more open or closed," Bob instructed. "Wherever you are right now is fine, but it's good to be aware. When our lives and emotions are in turmoil, praying can sometimes be hard, but it can also be revealing."

While Bob led the group in prayer, Rodney found great comfort in resting in the care of God. It felt so good to relax there for a moment.

"We like to check in at the beginning of each day to see how everyone is doing. This gives us all a chance to be aware of what is going on with each other," Bob said.

Greg started the check-in by sharing where he was at person-ally. He shared that he was doing okay but was a little tired because his three-year-old, Garrison, had decided to come to his and Erin's bed during the night and proceeded to run races in his sleep till dawn. Greg quipped that none of the bruises were serious and they'd all be gone in a few days.

Bob leaned way back and crossed his hands across his middle, saying he was in a good place. He went home tired last night and made it a point to get some needed rest.

Charles said he had gotten little sleep and woke up frustrated and anxious.

Victoria was hopeful and rested. She felt the teaching the day before had been empowering.

Chelsea reported that her jog had given her time for reflection on her expectation to be "happy." Rodney's heart skipped a beat as he wondered how that involved—or didn't involve—him.

When it was Rodney's turn, he admitted to the group that he was in the doghouse after starting a big fight with Chelsea. "The information here is great," he said. "Now I know what stuff looks like. We just don't know what to do with it. We blew up at each other last night. Honestly, I'm more concerned now than ever." After last night he wasn't about to try to keep track of Chelsea. Competent, independent, and self-sufficient, she made being her partner miserable—maybe impossible.

Ryan said he didn't know how he felt. Rodney scowled at how great the young doctor looked in his trendy eyeglasses and casual yet expensive-looking clothes.

Becca, by nature of appearance, seemed to be saying, "Hey, everyone, I'm here, but I don't want you to know who I really am." Yet today her makeup was shades lighter and her clothes muted. She wore pale pink jeans with a snug white top and fuzzy slippers. She told the group she had experienced a major breakthrough with the teaching on safety and trust as a result of her horrendous night. "I don't know what this means for the future," she said, while pulling her sleek hair up into a messy twist and fastening it with a clip. "But in this moment I feel more secure and less insanely freaked out than I have for months."

Todd was suffering the aftermath of a migraine. He criticized the Couples Intensive for not being as biblically based as it should be.

Pam was simply anxious to get started. She looked grateful that Bob and Greg were fine with the fact that she didn't have much to say.

"Thanks, everybody," Bob said. "Yesterday we got a good look at how our buttons get triggered and spin us into our dance. Everybody sees it and nobody enjoys it, yet most of us can't figure out how to make it stop. The good news is that even though it takes two to tango—and to do the Fear Dance—it takes only one person to end the madness."

There were lots of affirmative nods and gestures, but not from Rodney. Angry, he rubbed his hand across his face and turned back to sketching in the margin of his notes. If he could have ended the madness on his own, didn't they think he would have done it by now? He began to wonder if they were just wasting good time and money here. Chelsea sure didn't seem any closer to wanting to move back home. He only half listened as Greg went on.

"After working with thousands of couples and individuals, our clinical team has found four main steps that help couples move from feeling stuck and unprotected to experiencing safe, open, connected marriages—the kind most people only dream about."

At that, Rodney perked up. Yeah, he had some dreams all right. But they were only that—dreams. He didn't see how they could ever become reality.

Greg and Bob both expressed that they were looking forward to sharing the steps with the group, confident that each person would be able to feel an immediate shift, even after simply embracing the very first step—taking full personal responsibility for their thoughts, feelings, and actions. The counselors assured the group that a greater sense of personal power and safety in the marriage was just around the corner.

Rodney sighed. If only he could believe it . . .

❂ ❂ ❂

Pam could see her husband's hackles go up whenever Bob or Greg used counseling lingo. The preacher had agreed to come to the Intensive only as a last resort. He was brought up believing counseling was not in the will of God—that the Bible was given for correction and reproof and was sufficient for every human need—without any additional sources, philosophies, or teachings. Psychological terms such as *codependency* angered him.

She sensed that her husband was preparing for battle, knowing the two of them would be working first that morning. He rubbed small circles on both sides of his forehead. She was positive his migraines were linked to emotional stress, though he would never admit it.

Bob asked if Todd and Pam were ready to work. She noticed that her husband nodded at the same time she did, but a slightly awkward moment followed when neither one of them spoke. Pam looked over at Preacher with a questioning glance, and he nodded for her to speak first. That was her cue. She obediently turned to Bob and said, "I'm sorry, I don't know where to begin."

"Why don't you tell us, from your own perspective, a bit about what's been going on with you and Todd."

The fear rising up within Pam stood in sharp contrast to the ever-present smile she tried to keep pasted on her face. "I guess I have a lot of fear about therapy." She gave a nervous giggle and apologized again. She couldn't tuck her arms tightly enough around her waist to feel secure. But she was determined to see this through, so she pressed on and expressed how much she wanted to please God and her husband by being a good mother and wife . . .

how life in the parsonage was lonely and demanding. She felt a shiver of shame and the urge to be sick.

Pam loved her family beyond reason, but she often wondered: If she loved them so much, why this depression, this angst? It wasn't just the stress of the ministry. If so, there would be hope of recovering. It was deeper, more threatening—a vacuum of crushing loneliness.

With considerable effort, Pam regained her inner composure and crossed her hands in her lap. It helped to focus on the light as it prismed through the beaded fringe dangling from the edge of the lamp shade near Greg. Shaking now, Pam shared that no matter how hard she tried, she never felt that she could hit the mark. Sometimes she felt as if Todd was unfairly hard on her, but then he would encourage her to stay on the path God had laid before her. "Preacher is helpful in pointing out the ways I'm not measuring up to the standard of a dedicated Christian woman."

The preacher was a tough man to please, she admitted, afraid to look at him as she said so. His face rarely conveyed much beyond disinterest, impatience, or scorn. The only time he showed passion was behind the pulpit. He seemingly underwent a personality change each week when he stepped across the threshold of the church sanctuary. Pam adored him in those hours. He was the only pastor she'd sat under for twenty-one years. His animated voice boomed and his eyes flashed when he exegeted Scripture. In the presence of God, he wept down on his knees, beating his fist into the floor.

The preacher she loved; it was her husband she struggled with. He had a thing with tradition and control. Her gaze shifted. The knowing look on Bob's face revealed he recognized this about Todd too. "I want to live a disciplined life of service, but I just don't have it in me. I want to give up." She had no doubt, however, that calling it quits wasn't an option.

The more she spoke, the more desperate the emotions welling up inside her became, until she finally burst out, "I hate my life . . .

and I hate myself!" She couldn't contain herself any longer. Pam began sobbing uncontrollably.

❂ ❂ ❂

Rodney turned to the counselors like a child would to a parent after a little brother had fallen off his bike. Pam needed help.

After a pause, Bob spoke with extreme gentleness. "I know you're really hurting, Pam, and that matters a great deal to us. Thank you for letting us know your heart. Your tears are welcome here."

All but one in the room seemed moved by Pam's pain and feelings of hopelessness. Todd had his hands locked in place over his kneecaps, his back and arms stiff. His mouth was held in a hard, straight line. Rodney hated criticism and couldn't stand the thought of sharing any portion of his life—not even a few days—with a man who could make his wife hate life and even herself.

"Todd, I'm interested in how all this looks from your perspective." Bob was about to give his client the opportunity to share his own view of what was causing the problem without prejudging him based on his wife's pain. Rodney couldn't believe it.

Todd's hard exterior remained unchanged. He crossed one leg over the other and stated calmly that even though he understood this was a Couples Intensive, his purpose for being here was quite different from that of all the others. "My marriage is fine. My wife and children, however, need help. And I want to know what I can do."

Pam's head hung in shame.

Bob appeared unimpressed. "Your marriage is fine, based on what? You don't look fine." Bob put his stocking feet up on the side of the couch where Chelsea was sitting.

Todd stiffened. "What? You think that just because my wife is blubbering again and can't cope with life, that means my marriage has a problem?" Todd's face grew red and his already loud voice rose a notch. "Can't you see she has a problem?" When he pointed at his wife, she shrank into the couch. Dogmatically, he boomed, "I am committed to: one, being faithful to God; two, being faithful to my marriage; and three, being faithful to my family. This is not a marriage problem, Bob. Pam has a personal problem. I thought you'd be able to see that by now. And on top of that, it's a spiritual problem." He clasped his hands again as if his three-point sermon had come to a close.

Bob's quiet voice stood in marked contrast to Todd's. "How does Pam feel about that? You think it's fine, but you obviously don't give a rip about how she feels."

Todd looked as if he'd been slapped. "How dare you suggest that I don't care about my wife? Why do you think I came? Because I want to sit here and listen to all your psychobabble?" He leaned forward. "Let me tell you something. I am here because I care and I know she needs help. Whenever she's not moping, she is eating herself into oblivion."

"Come on, Todd." Bob didn't back down in his approach, even though his physical posture remained relaxed and unintimidating. "Pam doesn't appear to think the marriage is going all that great. In fact, she looks terrified." He turned and looked at Pam, who was still cowering on the couch. "When I said that you didn't care about how she feels, I was referring to her feelings about the marriage. I think she genuinely loves you, but she's not feeling too good right now about being married to you. She looks too frightened to even speak the truth about it."

Rodney watched as Victoria shook her head slightly and said under her breath, "Sweet Jesus." Her eyes rested on Pam before looking away from the woman's obvious pain.

The tension in the room was thick while Bob and the preacher faced off. Yet even though Bob was directly confrontational, Rodney could sense his compassion.

"Todd, you seem so angry," Bob said.

"I am angry. I resent your implications." Todd's voice was stone cold.

"Are you saying that you've only gotten angry since you've been here?"

"No. I'm not." He blinked hard over his contacts. The preacher looked as if he was being cornered. Rodney noticed that he wasn't the only one in the room who grimaced.

"My point is not to make you look bad," Bob continued gently, "or to suggest that what is going on is your fault. But from what I see here, neither of you is very happy at the moment. It sounds as if you are experiencing a lot of ongoing frustration as you attempt to live out a faithful life by serving God and your family. They, too, seem to be having a hard time. And your wife seems especially desperate and scared. About life . . . and you."

"Is she afraid of me, or just of her own inability to be a good Christian wife and servant of Christ?"

"You could ask her."

Todd looked as if he wasn't sure what to do.

More to himself than to the others in the room, Todd began to quietly recite a passage of Scripture that he had memorized and, Rodney suspected, had used many times. "The ear that heareth the reproof of life abideth among the wise. He that refuseth instruction despiseth his own soul: but he that heareth reproof getteth understanding. The fear of the LORD is the instruction of wisdom—" (Proverbs 15:31-33, KJV).

Bob broke in. "Do you not want to know your wife's answer?"

"It's not that I don't want to know, I was just thinking about how fear and respect go hand in hand and that a certain amount of fear is good for all of us."

"But, Todd, do you want her to be afraid of you?"

"No, not really." He paused before looking at his wife. Abruptly, he turned and asked Pam if she was afraid of him. She looked as if a giant spotlight had just been turned on her face. She floundered, not knowing how to answer. It was evident she was frightened of her husband, but she appeared to struggle with what she believed to be the real problem: her lack of faith and discipline.

Rodney was relieved when Bob came to her rescue. "Pam, don't try to answer everything all at once. My question now is, do you feel emotionally safe with Todd? Do you feel as if you can trust him to carefully and tenderly handle your heart and emotions?"

Pam began to sob again and whispered a distinct, "No." After a few moments she looked at Todd and said, "You get so angry and stern. I'm always afraid I'm going to be in trouble. I feel like I'm a huge, complete disappointment to you . . . and I sometimes just want—" she sniffed—"want it to be over."

Rod could hear that she meant more than just the marriage. Was Pam suicidal? A sick feeling grabbed at his stomach.

After allowing for a pause, Bob leaned toward the couple. "Todd, I understand that you've been in a shepherding role for a long time. And your first reaction to pain is to help fix it. Notice, I said *reaction*. Where else have we used the word *reaction*?"

"In the Fear Dance."

"Yeah, and many of the things we do are merely an attempt to cope with stuff that is going on in and around us—things we don't deal with well. It may feel easier and more righteous to stuff our own feelings while tending to others' pains and sorrows. But as we've been talking yesterday and today, I've seen some things that are touching awfully close to your heart. I don't think I see a healthy, vibrant pastor with a troubled wife. Instead, I'm seeing a lot of anger. Do you sense that too?"

"There are times I get angry, yes." He withdrew a small bottle of Tylenol from his shirt pocket, popped several into his mouth, and swallowed them dry. "And I do tend to have a temper. But I've learned to ask God to help me keep it in check. Mostly I feel frustrated."

"How many of you realize that frustration is merely expectations that have not been met?" Bob gave his listeners a moment to ponder what he'd just said. "We create a picture in our mind of the way we want things to go and then get frustrated when they don't turn out that way. Often this makes us angry. We generally don't realize how attached we are to the pictures we create in our heads. And how we can even get mad at reality when it doesn't match our fantasy, as if we actually should have been in control."

Pam revealed how concerned she was that Todd was so often moody and temperamental at home, yet she defended him at the same time. "He needs a lot of time to himself." She described his typical day of meditation, prayer, and preparation for sermons and the classes he taught. "He has to study and deal with very difficult relational issues. His calling is demanding. I accept the fact that his attention must be directed toward the parishioners."

"What happens if you or the kids need to interrupt your husband?" asked Greg.

"He gets very put out . . . and yells. We've all learned to tread lightly, and the girls have learned to need a lot more of me and less of him. . . . All of us accept it . . . except our son, Zach."

Todd tipped his head to the side and closely observed his thumbnail.

Pam jammed her hands into the pockets of her dress. Her words came out haltingly. "Our oldest child especially needs his dad's attention. I think that's part of the reason he started acting out. But that didn't work either." Pam flushed with exasperation and went on to explain that when their youth pastor had discovered Zach in a compromising situation with the deacon's daughter, their family started to unravel.

Todd turned to look at his wife with an incredulous expression. "Are you saying Zachary's behavior is my fault, Pam?" She froze.

Bob stepped in. "I can see your anger welling up again, Todd. What's going on right now emotionally?"

"How dare she imply that our son's sin is somehow my fault!"

"I wonder if you'd be willing to take a moment to figure out what it is about that suggestion that triggered such a big reaction," Bob replied in a disarming tone. "How does all that feel inside of you right now?"

A grueling silence followed, heightened by the rain pounding outside. Thunder crashed, making everyone jump. Rodney, who tried to avoid conflict at all costs, bit and chewed at his cuticles.

Todd must have heard the question, but he didn't respond immediately. The minutes ticked by. Each of the guests sat with bated breath to see what this time bomb of a man might do. His usually controlled expression was disturbed while he seethed. He rubbed his clenched fist while staring at the floor. One thing was certain in Rodney's mind: Pastor Todd Davis would have detonated in another environment. It appeared that he was pondering whether to go out and destroy something or stay here and bring down the house.

"It feels terrible! I hate being put on the spot! And I feel like at any minute I'm going to explode and do some serious damage."

Pam, who had been cowering, now expressed shock at Todd's ability to assess and articulate his anger. Like a marionette being pulled up by its strings, she drew herself up and took in a breath as if she was going to speak. She paused as if momentarily lost in thought. Then she seemed to snap back to the moment, and her words flooded out. "I want him to admit that he is partly responsible for what is going on with our son. Is that too much to ask? Sure, Zach has made his own choices, but now he's totally cut off from his father . . . and me." Her chin began to quiver. "Our son . . . he needs us." She couldn't hold back the tears, and she mopped at them with her sleeve.

Bob didn't address Pam right away but instead remained focused on Todd. "If I could share something that might actually give you some relief now and in the future and would in no way contradict the Word of God, would you be interested?" He didn't wait for an answer. "In fact, I'm only encouraging you to hear me out. If you don't like it or you disagree with it, you can toss it."

Todd nodded slightly while holding his head between his hands.

"I want to share with you how we see anger working in people's lives." Bob went on to explain that even though anger is a common emotion in relationships, it is usually misunderstood. Few people realize that anger is a secondary emotion, which means it is purposeful and goal directed. "What I mean is this: Behind almost all expressions of anger lie vulnerable feelings like fear, hurt, sadness, powerlessness, etc. We often choose anger to hide these primary feelings in order to avoid something or to attain something else. We may want to avoid getting emotionally close, getting hurt, having someone see that we are frightened or feeling vulnerable. On the other hand, we may use anger to get our children to behave, to make our employees work harder, or to remind our spouse how much we dislike it when they are late. Todd, did you ever see the movie *The Wizard of Oz*?"

"I did."

"Do you remember when Dorothy, the Scarecrow, the Tin Man, and the Cowardly Lion finally make it to Oz? They are granted an audience with the Wizard so that each of them can make their individual petition for help. As they enter the Wizard's chamber for the first time, do you remember how he presents himself?"

"Yeah. 'I am Oz, the Great and Powerful,'" Todd said in a deep voice, imitating the character in the movie.

"Exactly. He presents himself as an angry, loud, imposing figure, surrounded by bursts of flames and flashing lights. Then Dorothy tells the Wizard why they are there and what they hope he can do for them. The Wizard sends them away on a quest—something they have to do before he will help them. They set out, successfully melt the Wicked Witch, and return to Oz with her broom as proof. When they reenter the Wizard's chamber, how does he present himself this time?"

"The same as before."

"Yes. Big, booming voice with all the smoke and flames. Now after all they have gone through, Dorothy begins to get upset. But her dog, Toto, runs over to a little booth off to the side and pulls back a curtain. Behind the curtain is a very average-looking man who is frantically pulling levers and shouting into a microphone. It becomes instantly obvious that this man is the 'Wizard' and that the big, frightening image is nothing more than an illusion.

"The startled Wizard realizes that Dorothy and company can now see him. He tries to close the curtain, nervously pulls on the levers that promote his angry illusion, and shouts into the microphone, 'Pay no attention to the man behind the curtain!' Dorothy immediately sees the deception, marches over, and pulls open the curtain. The Wizard stops what he is doing as Dorothy confronts him. She yells at him, 'You are a very bad man!' He pauses and humbly responds, 'Oh, no, my dear. I'm a very good man. I'm just a very bad wizard!'

"The man was hiding behind his big, scary, angry wizard facade. He didn't want anyone to know that he was really just a regular guy—vulnerable and afraid to be truly known. Todd, this is exactly how people typically use anger. Either we try to hide our vulnerability and fears behind a show of power, or we use anger to intimidate people into doing what we want them to do. Either way it's dishonest or manipulative, or both.

"I'm suggesting that underneath your anger lies some other feeling that came first. I'm thinking it's one that makes you feel extremely vulnerable . . . one that you'd rather not acknowledge even to yourself, let alone anyone else. Those feelings tend to be the buttons that trigger our fear cycle. I'm suggesting that when you get angry, you become the Wizard. And just like him, you're probably not a bad man, just a bad wizard."

By this point, Todd's fury had subsided, though his breath was still coming in short gasps. Slowly, he nodded his head.

Rodney wondered if the preacher really got what Bob was saying or if he just wanted the focus to turn elsewhere.

Greg stepped in then and led the group through this new idea of acknowledging and putting anger to work in a healthy manner rather than allowing it to damage and destroy our relationships.

A TALK WITH THE DOCTORS

Anger

We can learn how we use anger by asking ourselves two questions:

- What am I trying to accomplish with my anger?
- What am I hoping will occur if I get angry?

The answer will frequently reveal what we are really trying to accomplish so we can examine whether we are pleased with the way it has been working for us. Remember, the fact that we hide behind our anger does not mean that we are a bad person, but merely a "bad wizard," hiding the truth about how we feel and who we are for fear of what will happen if we are truly "seen."

Like Todd, most people do not realize that there are deeper feelings underneath their angry display. We are often unable to face the truth of how vulnerable and powerless we feel when experiencing fear, hurt, and sadness. We often unconsciously choose anger instead. We may even believe that anger is our natural response, because the interval between the vulnerable feeling and the anger is so short it's as if the first, true feeling didn't even occur.

Once we are able to see that we *choose* anger as a response, we become empowered. We are no longer helpless victims of our emotions or circumstances. Instead, we can decide how we prefer to respond. If we don't like the decision we made or the consequences that followed, we have the option to choose differently next time.

We also now have the opportunity to understand ourselves better by taking the time to examine *why* we chose anger as our response. We can extend a little grace to ourselves by exploring our behavior and motives without judging ourselves. This personal grace makes it easier to recognize our deeper feelings underneath the anger, without the fear of being judged as bad or wrong for having those feelings. We often discover things about ourselves that we didn't even realize were true. We may have never realized before that under our anger we felt hurt when our spouse belittled us, or we were afraid that they had the affair because we were not good-looking enough or not a good enough lover, etc.

We can also discover the things in our past that taught us to react with anger. Perhaps we felt hurt when our spouse said we were stupid because it felt like the pain we experienced when our father called us stupid. And then, after this continued over the years, we began to fear that we just might be stupid or inadequate or worthless. We all have our own stories. The more aware we are of our deeper feelings and the reasons we choose to act the way we do, the more we are able to feel understanding and compassionate toward ourselves.

When we treat ourselves well—with understanding, kindness, and an absence of self-judgment, we can more easily relate openly and honestly with others. Personal integrity comes from acting in ways that are honest and true, so sharing our true feelings leads to a greater feeling of personal integrity.

Another common drawback to choosing anger as a response is that people will generally respond to the emotion we show rather than the deeper emotion we feel. For example, our spouse does something that we feel hurt by, but instead of showing our hurt, we get angry. What our spouse sees is our anger. They will generally respond to the anger by getting defensive or angry in return.

Most of us don't like someone getting defensive or angry toward us when we are feeling hurt. We would prefer that they care about how we feel and respond by being caring, understanding, sensitive, and/or apologetic. However, they often won't even realize that we are feeling hurt, because all they see is that we are angry. So the likelihood of receiving a satisfying response is remote. Sharing our deeper, underlying, honest feelings makes us vulnerable, yes, but it also creates the possibility of having our emotions understood and cared for. Isn't that what we all yearn for?

10

Chelsea had grown accustomed to Rodney's comical expressions; still, this was a new one. He looked like Mr. Potato Head as he made a beeline for the restroom. She realized how accustomed her husband, just a big kid himself, had grown to the schedule of young children. Rodney had commented earlier that he couldn't believe the other guys could sit drinking coffee and sodas for a couple of hours without intermission.

The group was now animated and talkative during their breaks. Even though this was only the second day, they had spent enough "real" time together for the clumsy apprehension to wear off. Each gave the others grace whenever they needed to be alone, which for Chelsea was much of the time. She saw now that Todd needed some solo minutes as he made his way toward the door. He went outside to stand under the awning and watch the rain. If he hadn't beat her to it, she'd have chosen that spot; the cool, fresh air was exhilarating. Charles and Rodney eventually poked their heads out too and asked if they could join him. Soon she overheard all three men in a lively discussion about bluegrass music. Yes, the group had definitely relaxed since the first session yesterday morning.

Chelsea left Becca and Ryan talking quietly with their heads together, recapping their notes from the last session. She marveled at how Becca could stand being in her husband's presence after the layers of betrayal she'd suffered as a result of his actions. Becca grated on her nerves, but maybe there was a reason she acted the way she did. Chelsea didn't want to think any more about that. She pushed back her own guilty conscience. She knew she would have to come clean with her own husband sooner or later.

Chelsea decided to run upstairs for a quick getaway before the group reconvened in a few minutes. She must focus on holding things together. She'd have to check in on the kids. She wondered if little Hannah was sleeping well at night. Did Jack have his Popsicle-stick project finished for preschool? The car would be ticketed if it wasn't moved on street-sweeping day; Rodney had forgotten to get a sitter for the fish; the office had left a message. . . .

❊ ❊ ❊

"You know, I've been thinking about what happened when you were talking to Todd and Pam," said Rodney after they had all returned to their places after the break. "In our marriage, I'm more like Pam, and Chelsea is a lot like Todd."

Chelsea frowned. She wanted to argue in protest, but on second thought bit her lip.

Rodney persisted. "Why can't she just love me the way I am? I understand the Fear Dance stuff, but I don't think we can make this deal work. Because, like Pam, no matter what I do, it's never good enough for Chelsea. She's always upset with me and tries to get me to do or be something else. My wife will never be okay with the way I am. Maybe her buttons are getting pushed, but what if she just wants to dance with someone else? It would be understandable, because I'm terrible at dancing, both literally and figuratively. But I can't become someone else."

Chelsea really didn't feel like being part of this dialogue and was relieved that it just involved Rodney.

"Do you want to . . . become someone else?" Greg asked with surprising seriousness. He was already at work on a new paper-clip sculpture. His collection was growing quite impressive.

"No. I mean, I like who I am . . . and what I do," Rodney acknowledged, sounding for a moment like a frustrated teenager. "I don't want to change."

"Rodney, how do you really feel about yourself, overall?" Greg pressed a little. "What do you see when you look in the mirror— how do you feel about yourself as that man?"

Rodney shrugged and ran his hand over his smooth head. "There are things . . . about me . . . that I like a lot."

"Such as . . . ?" Greg prodded.

"I know how to get the good stuff out of life. I'm into beautiful sunsets, babies, a great guitar riff . . . you know, the simple things."

"That's really awesome." Greg paused. "But I keep sensing there's a big *but* still hanging out there."

"Hey, no fat jokes!" Rodney shot back in jest. That was her husband, always the comedian. He flashed a jaunty smile at Greg, catching the counselor and other guests so off guard that everyone burst out laughing at his comeback.

Greg seized the opportunity. "Well, now that you mention it, how do you feel about that?"

"What, being overweight?" Rod asked, sounding a little surprised.

Greg nodded.

He glanced down at his middle. "I hate it! I'm into sports and love to play hard, but instead of having the body of an athlete, I get the Pillsbury Doughboy model. A lot of it is my fault and I feel bad about it. I don't take care of my body, and yet in my job I encourage kids to be active and fit."

"So why is that?"

Yeah, why is that? Chelsea didn't know how many times she had asked the same question.

"I don't know. . . . I just feel so de-motivated. I mean, what's the point, anyway? No matter what I do, my wife's not going to be happy."

Bob jumped in. "Rodney, what are you feeling right now?"

"Look, I feel ripped off, okay?"

"And why do you feel that way?"

"I told you. Because no matter what I do, it's never enough for her." He was getting irritable.

"So if Chelsea would just really love and accept you for who you are . . ." Bob let his words trail off.

"That would be awesome! I would be a happy man."

"And how would you feel about yourself?"

"Whole . . . complete . . . like my life was worth something."

Oh, for crying out loud—now who's being dramatic? Chelsea thought.

"Rod, how did Chelsea get so much power?" Bob asked.

"What do you mean?"

"It sounds like you're saying that the way you feel about yourself—your worth, your success, and even your motivation in life—is largely dependent on how Chelsea feels about you and the way she acts. That's a lot of power."

Chelsea watched as Rodney's round face contorted comically into several different expressions while he attempted to understand what Bob was getting at. It was hard not to laugh.

"How often do you feel powerless?"

"In many ways, almost always," Rodney replied.

"I'm not surprised. You've given Chelsea a tremendous amount of power to determine how you feel about who you are. 'If she would just love me and accept me, then I could feel good enough, lovable, adequate, etc.' Rod, why are those things dependent on Chelsea?"

It was true. Rodney was letting her love and acceptance, or lack of it, control his life.

Bob was still speaking. "Of course, the way she feels about you matters greatly. But you've got troubles, and who do you see holding the key to solving those problems in your life and marriage?"

"Chelsea?" Rodney was beginning to see Bob's point.

"So unless Chelsea does this, that, or the other thing, you're . . ."

"Stuck."

"Exactly. And powerless to do much about it. Unless, of course, you can change or control your wife. What do you think? You up for it?"

"What, changing or controlling Chelsea? I don't think so!"

Bob smiled in response to his client's emphatic answer. "So the only important question at this point is this: Are you ready for an alternative? Don't answer too quickly, because sometimes we continue looking for the magic angle—the right words, behavior, or circumstances—that finally causes our spouse to act and feel just the way we want them to so we can feel great."

"No, I hate feeling this way. Give me an alternative."

Bob warned Rodney that he might not like the answer. "One of my colleagues, Dr. Bob Burbee, calls this 'the best marriage advice no one wants to hear.' The alternative is to take full personal responsibility for one's own feelings, actions, and responses. Actually, personal responsibility is the first step that will take a person out of the fear cycle toward a great marriage."

Bob went on to explain that they also call personal responsibility "the power of one" because it is the key to personal empowerment. On the other hand, when a person allows his well-being, emotions, and behavior to be dependent on others, it keeps him in a place of disempowerment. "When others are blamed for how we feel or respond, they are essentially given the power to determine our worth, identity, adequacy, lovability, etc., or how we should act or respond. Like, 'I couldn't help myself because you . . .' or 'If you had just . . . then I would have . . .' But the Bible speaks to the contrary. It says we will each be held fully accountable before the Lord for what we do or don't do, whether we like it or not.

"The good news is that accepting personal responsibility for one's feelings and actions actually empowers each individual in the marriage or family to have the authority and ultimate control to become all God has called them to be. Who you are and how you act are no longer determined by anyone but God and you. Remember, this is what we call your personal journey—the responsibility to realize your God-given destiny and to follow the path God has called you to. No one else is to blame, but there is also no one else to have to wait for or be dependent on. The responsibility to be conformed to his image is 100 percent yours."

"Rodney, did you notice how strong your emotions were a few minutes ago?" Greg asked.

RODNEY'S FEARS
Failure
Inadequacy
Not measuring up
Not being good enough

CHELSEA REACTS
Criticism
Judgment
Anger/escalation
Running/fleeing
Rebellion
Ambition
Pursuing status
Self-focus

RODNEY AND CHELSEA'S FEAR DANCE

RODNEY REACTS
Being defensive
Going into fix-it mode
Being passive-aggressive
Keeping the peace
Abdicating to Chelsea
Lack of ambition
Withdrawing/shutting down

CHELSEA'S FEARS
Being trapped/helpless
Being powerless/controlled
Being taken advantage of
Being judged

"Yeah, I got a little upset, and then I went back to what I usually feel: hopeless."

"Can you see how your fear buttons got pushed?" Greg pointed to the chart hanging on the wall that had Rodney and Chelsea's Fear Dance mapped out. "What button or buttons just got pushed?"

He looked at his list of fears on the hand-drawn chart. "Wow, all of them! I felt inadequate, like I don't measure up, and that I'm simply not good enough. I guess I am a total failure." Rodney was noticeably struck by the revelation.

"And how did you react?" Bob asked as he got up and walked over to the chart.

Rodney studied the chart and said, "First I got defensive, then I began to shut down and feel defeated."

"And where did you focus your attention while looking for a solution?" Bob asked, as he pointed toward Chelsea's reactions on the chart.

"You're right. I was thinking about how different things would be and how much better I'd feel if Chelsea would just blah, blah, blah. But truthfully—" he caught her eye—"I *would* feel better if she would do those things."

"I get that, Rod, but how much control do you have over what she does or doesn't do?"

"Not much," Rodney said. When he saw Bob raise his eyebrows and open his eyes wide he amended, "Okay, none."

Bob pushed up his glasses and went on. "Now that's not to say you can't attempt to manipulate or control her to do what you want. But even if you succeed, what does that make you?"

"I don't know," he replied with a shrug.

"It makes you manipulative and controlling. And most people don't feel too good about themselves knowing deep down that they are being manipulative and controlling. It really takes a bite out of your feelings of personal integrity, or feeling good about the kind of man you see staring back at you in the mirror."

Now this was a first. Chelsea had never heard anyone address her husband about being manipulative or controlling before.

"So, you wanna see the alternative?"

"Sure."

"This will probably not come as a surprise at this stage of the game," Bob said as he took a marker and drew a diagonal line from the upper left-hand corner of the chart to the lower right-hand corner. "Notice how the line equally separates the diagram. On one half are Chelsea's fears and reactions, and on the other half are yours. Which of these things can you control?"

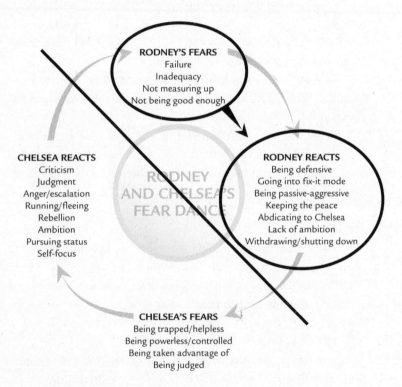

RODNEY'S FEARS
Failure
Inadequacy
Not measuring up
Not being good enough

CHELSEA REACTS
Criticism
Judgment
Anger/escalation
Running/fleeing
Rebellion
Ambition
Pursuing status
Self-focus

RODNEY
AND CHELSEA'S
FEAR DANCE

RODNEY REACTS
Being defensive
Going into fix-it mode
Being passive-aggressive
Keeping the peace
Abdicating to Chelsea
Lack of ambition
Withdrawing/shutting down

CHELSEA'S FEARS
Being trapped/helpless
Being powerless/controlled
Being taken advantage of
Being judged

"My side."

"Yes, sir. And when your buttons have been pushed, where have you historically looked to find relief?"

"I almost always look to her side, figuring if she would just do something or if she would just stop doing something . . . then everything would be great."

Bob grew serious for a moment. He looked around to make sure he had everyone's attention. Then he said slowly, "*Personal responsibility* takes place when your buttons get pushed and you have an emotional reaction, yet you *stay focused on your side of the equation*. You must take responsibility for your feelings and fears, as well as responsibility for your reactions.

CHOOSE TO RESPOND

RODNEY'S FEARS
Failure
Inadequacy
Not measuring up
Not being good enough

CREATE SPACE

CHELSEA REACTS
Criticism
Judgment
Anger/escalation
Running/fleeing
Rebellion
Ambition
Pursuing status
Self-focus

RODNEY AND CHELSEA'S FEAR DANCE

RESPONDS
RODNEY ~~REACTS~~
Being defensive
Going into fix-it mode
Being passive-aggressive
Keeping the peace
Abdicating to Chelsea
Lack of ambition
Withdrawing/shutting down

CHELSEA'S FEARS
Being trapped/helpless
Being powerless/controlled
Being taken advantage of
Being judged

"There are two great options there. First, you can attempt to create a little space between your button getting pushed and your reaction. That way you can move from a knee-jerk reaction to something you think through and choose. Then it becomes a *response* rather than a *reaction*. This first option allows you more say in becoming a person you can feel good about being. It gives you time to even ask the old WWJD question—What would Jesus do?—if, like me, you want to be increasingly conformed to the image of Christ.

"The second option is to focus on understanding your buttons: why and how they got there. Usually this takes us back to the earlier years of our lives, to where some early hurts or disappointments occurred, or where the messages got written on our heart. For example, you react strongly to feeling like you're not good enough or that you don't measure up. Did you ever feel that way, or hear that message, before meeting Chelsea?"

Bob sat down while Rodney considered the question.

"Boy, did I ever."

Chelsea knew her husband would be hit with a flood of emotions as he thought back on his childhood.

"My dad was a cranky old man and never seemed happy about anything or anyone. Except . . . my brother, for some reason. I've never been able to understand that, either, because my brother was always getting into trouble, and I was the good kid. But for whatever reason, my dad loved my brother. No matter how bad he was, Dad either made an excuse for him or got over being upset real quick."

Rodney had rolled up a scrap of paper and was now chewing on it.

"But with me it was different. He never said the words, 'Why can't you be more like your brother?' but I could see it in his eyes. He had an unspoken pride in my brother, yet he always seemed uninterested in me—and even disgusted at times. All I ever wanted was for my dad to be proud of me, too." Tears welled up in the big man's eyes. "I loved my dad, even though he was so hard on us. I just don't know why he didn't love me."

It was evident that the pain in his heart went deep, and as Rodney allowed himself to feel it, he could no longer speak. He covered his face with his large hands and wept softly . . . and alone. Chelsea couldn't meet him in this place. For the first time, she recognized how similar her husband's feelings from the past were to his feelings with her. Did he see it too?

At some point along the way, she had started to treat him much as his father had. He loved her, so why didn't she love him in return? No wonder he continually asked, "What's wrong with me? Why can't you love me?" She had never seen her husband weep as he was weeping now. Still, she felt numb.

The room remained quiet. The others appeared to be profoundly impacted by the depth of Rodney's pain. Todd seemed especially struck by Rodney's outpouring of emotion, even though he was undeniably uncomfortable with the situation. Chelsea, of course, knew firsthand the story of Rodney's strained relationship with his father. She'd even seen him cry about it once before. But something was different this time. She wasn't sure what it was or what to make of it, but she did care about him, and it hurt her to see her husband hurting like that. She reached over and cautiously placed a hand on his shoulder. Instantly, he pulled away.

After a few moments Greg asked, "What's going on for you right now, Rodney?"

He drew a shaky breath and honked into a tissue before answering. "I began to think about how painful it was to want my dad's love and how I've never really understood why he didn't give it to me. Then I realized how much those feelings are like the feelings I have with Chelsea now."

With the back of his hand, he wiped new tears away. "When she reached out to me just now, I wanted to feel her love wrap around me and hold me." Rodney looked over at Chelsea. "But I knew she would hate that, so I pulled away." Big tears slid down his face. "It makes my heart feel like it is being torn apart."

Bob kept his gaze squarely on Rodney while seeming to avoid eye contact with Chelsea. She wondered briefly about his motive.

"Rodney, those are some intense feelings. I wonder if you are seeing how much that stuff with your dad is affecting the intensity of your feelings with Chelsea and how that old stuff affects how you react today."

"I think I can."

"So here is the opportunity. Clearly, it would feel good if Chelsea was able to love you like you've always wanted to be loved. The problem in the long run, however, is that you'd stay just as dependent, powerless, and potentially abandoned as you are right now. I suggest that instead of focusing on what you want from Chelsea right now, you could stay focused on what is going on inside you emotionally, asking where it comes from and what you can do to make a difference. Notice that the focus is on *you* and *your* needs, and what *you* can do to make things better.

"I realize that you cannot make things perfect on your own, and you cannot create a great relationship with Chelsea unless she participates. But I'm confident that there are lots of things you can do—things you are not doing now, choices you aren't even aware of yet—that could make life significantly better for you personally."

It all made sense to Chelsea. She didn't know yet what to do with it, but she liked where this was going.

Bob went on. "The man you are, Rodney—how you live your life and conduct your relationships—is determined by you only, under the guidance of the Holy Spirit. Notice also that the power we've been talking about is not power over others; it is merely power over your personal well-being and the kind of person you are. Nobody else has control over that any longer. Another benefit to taking this much personal responsibility is that it leads to true peace and serenity. Are you familiar with the Serenity Prayer?"

Rodney was nodding, and as Chelsea looked around, she saw everyone else doing the same. "Can anyone recite the prayer?"

Pam sat forward and proclaimed, "God, grant me the serenity

to accept the things I cannot change, the courage to change the things I can, and the wisdom to know the difference."

Chelsea was startled by her boldness.

"I used it while teaching a Sunday school class for third graders," she said with a shy smile. She looked embarrassed by the sudden attention turned her way.

"Thank you, Pam. The key to serenity, or peace, is putting your efforts and energy into trying to control things that only you can control, like yourself, for instance. You sacrifice your peace when you try to control things that you cannot, like your spouse, your children, and the rest of the world."

❂ ❂ ❂

Victoria had watched the others throughout the session. The men were somewhat hard to read, but she was especially tuned in to the women. Pam had sat attentively, seeming to take in every detail. Victoria wondered what could possibly be going on in Chelsea's head while watching her husband go through such deep emotional work. She thought she saw an expression of relief, more than anything, on the young woman's face. On the other side of the room, Becca appeared unusually quiet, as if she'd been so transfixed with Rodney's work that she'd momentarily forgotten about her appearance.

No sooner had this thought entered Victoria's mind than Becca bounced into action. "Honestly, Bob? Right now, serenity is about the last thing I've got. I have no peace . . . and it's not my fault, nor my responsibility. Yesterday I wanted a faithful husband. But right now, I want revenge!" She threw her body into a different position. "Ryan and . . . what's-her-name ruined my life!"

Either the barometric pressure had everyone on edge or they were in the thick of dealing with core issues. Tension began to rise again. Bob remained quiet and unmoved.

At Bob's silence, Becca squirmed a little. "Well, they did. They ruined my life," she said sulkily.

"Becca, I get that Ryan betrayed you, your trust, and your marriage. I can hear loud and clear that you are very angry and hurt. I can see that your heart is broken, and I understand that you're scared out of your mind that you may never be able to trust him again. But I'm having a hard time with the 'he ruined my life' part."

Becca could wind up tighter and more quickly than anyone Victoria had ever met. Livid, she glared back at Bob. Stabbing her finger toward her husband, she yelled, "I didn't choose to be married to an adulterer. I didn't choose to have my life torn apart. I didn't choose this, Bob! And Ryan *does* control my life. He owns it all—he pays for it all. With all you've been saying, are you insinuating that I'm responsible for this?"

Bob slowly shook his head. "When I'm talking about personal responsibility, I'm in no way saying that you are responsible for any of Ryan's choices, behaviors, or feelings. But right now you are talking and acting like a helpless victim."

"But I *am* a victim." Becca blinked back tears. "I've lost *everything*. Nothing is left in my control."

"Your world has been totally rocked, and I know this took you to places you never in a million years imagined you would go," the counselor said. "I'm confident you would have never chosen this option if you had been given a choice." Bob's voice softened a bit. "I'm so sorry to say this, but you weren't given a choice. So now the only relevant question is, what are you going to do with it? This is where your responsibility lies. This is also where you'll find some power.

"You couldn't control what Ryan did, and you can't control what he will do tomorrow. Could he cheat again? You bet! Trying to control him will only make you crazy and will always leave you feeling vulnerable. No matter how good you get at it, he is always only one act of his will away from breaking your heart."

In spite of her relative calm in the previous couple of hours, Becca's insecurities now boiled back to the surface with a vengeance. She threw off her fuzzy slippers, and her pad of paper went flying as she flung herself against the back of the couch. Grabbing a pillow, she held on to it for dear life. She didn't scream, but it looked as if she wanted to. Victoria was increasingly aware that this poor child had huge issues to overcome.

"Am I supposed to say, 'Thanks for the insight, B-o-b,' now that I know how messed up I really am?"

Bob calmly folded his hands behind his head and leaned farther back without regard to her furious outburst. "You do, in fact, have a lot of say about what you do in response. Becca, you have say over who you are and whether your responses to life are ones you can feel good about: being a woman you feel good about seeing in the mirror . . . having nothing to do with how you look on the outside, and everything to do with who you are on the inside—your character.

"And please understand that we are not encouraging you to be a doormat, putting up with anything that Ryan, or anyone else, dishes out. There are boundaries that can and need to be set about caring for the temple of the Holy Spirit: that invaluable part of who you are. Remember we talked about the key to trust as being able to trust yourself in the face of being hurt. It may be that the most loving thing you could do is to set a boundary with Ryan. We need to talk about that more, but for now we're simply focusing on how you take care of your own temple before talking about how to respond when others are dishonoring your temple."

It seemed as if Becca had just taken two steps forward and five back, but Victoria was beginning to recognize the depth of her pain. Her lack of full understanding in a couple of key areas was creating a profound feeling of vulnerability. She began to hope that this process would lead to God's healing.

"Let me ask you this, Becca. Like with Rod, I want to know

where your power has gone. You do feel powerless, don't you?" Bob asked.

Her face pinched in resentment. "More than I have ever felt in my entire life. Every time I try to relax and just trust him for a few moments, I begin to panic."

A TALK WITH THE DOCTORS

Personal Responsibility

When couples come in for marriage counseling, they are especially prone to want to point the finger and talk about their partner instead of themselves, just as Ryan and Becca did. Many people seem to keep a running list of the things their partner needs to change so that the marriage can heal. Often, both spouses will go on at length to convince the therapist that their partner is the problem, and if only we could change that person, things would get better. What people don't realize is that this approach leaves them totally disempowered and only makes things worse.

I have no real ability to control the thoughts, feelings, and behaviors of another person, and any attempt to do so is manipulation. *When I am convinced that the solution to our relationship problems or my personal problems depends on my partner changing, I become disempowered.* My ability to achieve my goal is not within my own power to control. To the extent that I make my well-being dependent on my partner's changing, I give both my personal responsibility and my personal power to them.

When Becca learns to take personal responsibility, she will regain personal power and will no longer be at Ryan's mercy. Let's go back to when Ryan talked about jumping through all those hoops. One way of understanding codependency is this: It is the belief that, in a relationship, a person is not only helpful in meeting the other's needs, but they are actually responsible for meeting those needs. This dependence on another encourages us to be manipulative, controlling, and demanding in order to get our needs met. Being manipulative, controlling, or demanding results in the loss of integrity, self-respect, and personal power. Such strategies also trigger more fears and reactions in our spouse.

❁ ❁ ❁

Chelsea was intrigued at the way Rodney's issues had resonated with Becca. Maybe this group counseling was worth something, after all.

After talking a bit more with Becca, Greg said he wanted to bring their discussion on personal responsibility full circle. He explained how this was a pivotal point for each of them, and since they had been working on the Fear Dance diagram with Rodney and Chelsea, he asked if they might pick back up where they had left off.

"Chelsea, we talked from Rodney's point of view on this, but did you know that when you take personal responsibility, you become powerful and are no longer at his mercy?"

That was an odd twist. "What do you mean, 'at his mercy'?"

"You no longer need to feel responsible for his well-being. After all, you can't do anything to change or control his well-being, right? God doesn't even do that. The more we come to embrace this fact, the freer we all become. We are born responsible for ourselves; we will die responsible for ourselves. And so will our spouses. Being married doesn't change this."

Chelsea had to think about that for a moment. "So Rodney is responsible for his health, how he eats, and whether or not he worships God. But what about the day-to-day stuff? Like who's going to clean the bathroom, balance the checkbook, get the kids to the doctor . . . pay the bills?"

"That is a great question. Those are essential responsibilities, and we see how you have felt almost completely alone in taking care of them. But notice how the focus shifted from personal responsibility—being accountable for your own well-being and being the person you were created to be—to the question of who is responsible for getting important things done.

"For your marriage to be great and everyone to be thrilled, the division of labor has to be handled to everyone's satisfaction. But that is an issue of teamwork, not personal responsibility. We will address teamwork thoroughly later on, and unless you are thrilled with the outcome, we've failed. But in order to become a great team, the players need to get themselves in order first. Personal responsibility is the essential first step."

"You know," Bob said, "even before we develop a well-entrenched Fear Dance, we are engaged in developing a 'system' in our marriage. This system includes increasingly well-defined roles, responsibilities, rules, expectations, etc., and often operates without our being aware of it. The system helps us find ways to accomplish our goals and objectives—again, even when they are unconscious. For instance, it sounds like your early years of marriage were not much different from mine."

He turned his attention toward her husband. "Rodney, you invited Chelsea to join you in your laid-back lifestyle. You kicked back, smoked some weed, played the banjo . . . both of you living pretty loose without much responsibility. Is that right?"

Rodney nodded.

"You have gotten used to that role, while Chelsea began to feel more and more inclined to step up and move this thing forward. Especially after the kids came along, she naturally took on the caregiving role. It started off as genuine caring, and it sounds as if it worked for both of you initially. Both of you generally liked the feel of the system in the beginning. Is that right, Chelsea?"

"I suppose," she said, propping her chin on her fist.

"But I'm guessing there came a point when it stopped feeling good," Bob continued. "It was at that point when it stopped being a *gift* of caring and started being care*taking.* Care*taking,*" he said more slowly. "Do you hear the difference? Caretaking is actually *taking* in the guise of caring. It looks like caring on the outside, but it is actually more about taking, or getting what you feel you need to be secure. Doesn't it feel much safer just getting things done rather than waiting for Rodney to pull his share of the weight? You've convinced yourself, with Rodney's help, that he's not reliable. On the surface it looks like you are caring for him, but really what you are trying to do is get yourself, and the kids, to an okay place. It's easy to reason, 'When I hold everything together, I can be okay.'"

"I'd say you guys have quite a system going," Greg added, bending and stretching out a paper clip for a new sculpture. "It works for Rodney because he doesn't have to face his fear of failure or inadequacy, and it works for Chelsea because she doesn't have to face her fear of feeling powerless. A match made in heaven."

"Yuck!" was Chelsea's only response. This whole way of looking at things made her feel as if she'd just taken a sip of sour milk.

"I think what I want you to really focus on is how this system is working for you two," Bob continued. "My guess is that parts of it aren't working anymore, but there are ways in which it still 'functions.' Here lies the problem: Chelsea, you are exhausted—finished—but Rodney, there are parts of the system you don't want to let go of. You are still struggling to hold on because apparently you don't know what to do if you let go."

"Yeah." Rodney looked reflective for a moment. "I do like it when Chelsea steps up and holds the family together. I just don't want her to stop loving me because of it."

"And how does this make you feel about yourself?"

Rodney wrinkled his high forehead. Chelsea thought that with his head shaved clean, his exaggerated expressions were so pronounced, it was as if he were shouting through a bullhorn. "Looking at it this way, I feel like a wuss, like a scared little kid."

Just then Greg's paper clip sprang out of his hands and landed in Rodney's lap. "Oops!" Greg cracked up. Chelsea knew Greg was laughing at himself, and his laughter gave the rest of them freedom to have a little comic relief.

Bob joined in. "He has these paper-clip sculptures all over the place, and I can never find one still intact because he uses mine, too!"

With a smug grin, Greg countered without missing a beat, "We sell them on eBay, actually. That's how we fund your snacks."

Getting back to the matter at hand, Bob said, "We are never codependent without reward. There's a reason the system continues.

"Chelsea, it seems you have made a hefty investment in a male puppet, because it gave you the opportunity to be the nurturer and therefore you can have it all together. If you could just love him enough, encourage him, take care of him, whatever, until he comes into his own, then it would be evident that you pulled it off. 'Chelsea really made a difference.' 'Chelsea is really significant.' Something like that. It's a great strategy."

That didn't sit so well with her. "I don't want that job anymore." She needed to think about what he was saying. Something about it sounded right, but if she had wanted Rodney to make her feel significant before, she didn't anymore.

"Yeah. One of the interesting things about codependency is that it usually starts off feeling warm and cozy, but after a little while it begins to feel crowded, disappointing, and lonely. And usually one person gets there before the other. In this case, Chelsea, you want out of the system, and Rodney would be more content if you stayed.

"The future can look awfully daunting. Even under the best of circumstances, this life we lead can be pretty overwhelming. If you've got some difficult stuff in your background, it makes it hard to find solid ground sometimes—a place to stand and make good sense out of things—and to know what, when, where, and how you can trust anything.

"Intimacy—if you are being open with your hearts and feelings and if you are caring about each other—is risky business. Reality is, there are plenty of ways people can get hurt. Yet the thought of not being intimate is worse because you'll just sort of die alone.

"So you are left in a quandary. Either you must go into the realm of your fears and uncertainties, face them together, and figure out how to conquer them—or avoid your fear without looking at it in the face. But then you will still be trapped in it and have to live in it alone. Being afraid is one thing, but telling yourself it is not okay to feel afraid makes it hard to live in your skin.

"Chelsea, you actually have a strong husband who is afraid to tell you what is going on for him because he's afraid you can't handle it. He's not afraid *he* can't handle it; he's afraid *you* can't handle it. Part of the reason is that you haven't been able to be honest with yourself and make it okay to be afraid. If you make it okay, you can start working with that. The first step is to say, 'Okay, now that I'm all right with the fact that I am afraid, I can ask what my options are here and what I am needing and what I can do.'"

Chelsea tried to let all that sink in. She was beginning to see how she had tricked herself into thinking that her caretaking role built up her own self-worth and value—how much she demanded control and how disempowered she had become by all her self-made rules. She was about the least free person she knew, other than her mother. She could see how similar her story was to that of the unlikable Todd, as well as being like Becca's demands that her husband jump through hoops to prove his love. They were all trapped and angered by their own martyrdom and manipulations.

Never would she have guessed that this was all based in fear—the fear of failing or not measuring up. For years she'd been trying to please her mother, whose voice constantly whispered in the back of her mind. Could she allow things to be as messy as they actually were? Could she be okay without trying to shove things into compartments so they made sense? This was so overwhelming she'd have to stay with it for a while. Her tears had turned on that morning, and she couldn't seem to stop them now.

Bob had nudged her even further, saying she and Rodney could actually offer one another comfort and strength while trying to get it all figured out. She had always found Rodney's fear pathetic, but now she was being faced with her own. Honestly, she would much rather deal with his. She didn't like all the rules being changed. Her old patterns seemed much safer—but the fact remained: They weren't working anymore. She couldn't go back. She was on the other side of Egypt now. Freedom sounded scary. She was facing the unknown—without guarantees, without a filing cabinet filled with records and receipts—only the big Red Sea. It would take a miracle.

Chelsea's entrance back into the counseling room after lunch was quiet. This was the last place she wanted to be and the last thing she wanted to do. Surely Bob would be along soon. She had seen him headed this way. She stretched while rehearsing what she wanted to say. The words weren't forming right and most likely would come spilling out in a big pile. Nearly as nervous as she imagined she'd be if she were turning herself in for a crime, she knew how Eve must have felt when she ran and hid in the bushes. Chelsea would much rather have hidden than face up to her recent choices.

But she was ready to do it—to come clean, to make her confession for a crime she had committed against God as well as against her family and community. The impact of it made her perspire.

Scuffing her tennis shoe on the floor, she looked down at the path it left in the carpet. Ryan had caught her eye just before the lunch break and made a quick tip of his head toward Bob, a reminder that she had some business to attend to. As livid as she'd been at his comment out in the rain, he was right. She'd been holding out—on the group, on Rod, on herself, and on God. And it would only bring more pain and disillusionment if she remained silent. She'd come here to get help and to come clean.

A tear splashed on her tennis shoe. She'd rehearsed it a hundred times. "Dr. Paul, I—"

Just then Bob entered the room . . . and Becca waltzed in right behind him. "There you are, Bob!" She placed a hand on her hip. "I've been looking all over for you." She stepped right past Chelsea and began to relay to the counselor how impossible a time she was having and asked if she could "work" next.

He agreed, oblivious to Chelsea's unspoken request. Chelsea's stomach sank. She couldn't believe what had just happened! All her empathy for Becca dissipated, as did her resolve to let her story be known.

❂ ❂ ❂

A few moments later, all eight clients and the two counselors were reassembled for the afternoon session. Becca thought they looked tired but willing to make every minute count. Without any preliminaries, she launched into her most pressing quandary.

When she'd finished, Bob responded, "An affair is always devastating, but after hearing your story, Becca, I feel like you have been remarkably undone by Ryan's choices. I know he has worked a big number on you and has said lots of mean things—not to mention the affair itself—and I'm taking all those things into consideration. But right now, in this moment, it seems as if you are desperately clinging to the hope of keeping him, almost as if you'll disappear if he goes away. It's almost like your very identity is somehow tied to him. And if he was taken from the picture, you would be left with nothing . . . or something you want to deny or perhaps keep hidden. Does any of that feel as if it fits?"

Becca's mind flipped through its channels and landed

momentarily on the mall at Fashion Island. How she would love to escape to the comfort of a department store right about now and lose herself in browsing through the new spring fashions. . . . She nervously tapped her acrylic nails on the end table next to her chair. "I don't know."

Bob bit his lower lip and appeared to think for a moment. "Is it possible that this whole ordeal has held such power over you because it touched something from your past that you felt like you had either dealt with or buried, and the affair has somehow brought it back to life?"

"I . . . I don't really know. You mean like my parents getting divorced?"

"No, I think it might be something more internal—having more to do with the core of who you are. Is there anything about *you* that frightens you? Has there been anything in this upheaval that has caused you to question yourself?"

She couldn't believe how much she had entrusted Bob with the day before, but because it had all been about Ryan, it had been relatively safe. Now she was under the spotlight, and she felt her facade melting. She did the only thing she knew to do—throw Bob off course.

It was time to pull her snug sweater off over her head, which she did with great fanfare, leaving her in a blue tank top. Bob remained relaxed in his semireclined position. Affecting a bored, slightly sulky expression, Becca stated her case. "I've already been through all that questioning about whether it was my fault." She tucked a section of hair behind her ear and sniffed loudly.

"Yes, and was there any time in your past when you felt that way?"

"That something was my fault? Not that I know of. Maybe I'm in denial and I just don't know it." She curled up in a ball around a pillow from the couch.

She was afraid her mask was tilting.

"Would you say you have any baggage from your past?"

She laughed and noticed that she sounded a bit hysterical. "Are you really going to make me go back to my childhood, Bob? My childhood doesn't even count as *baggage*—that's way too fancy a term. To have baggage you would have to have a suitcase to put it in. My past was so messed up there was no suitcase; it was more like a pile of trash."

Her mask slipped a bit more.

"It was just bad, okay?" She clamped her eyes shut, trying to ignore the memory of all the nights when, as a little girl, she'd felt desperate and alone. "I was abused in every way possible. Maybe I believed my husband wouldn't do that to me. Yeah, I have other issues, but all that awful stuff he did is not it. So if someone starts to abuse me, I am basically unfazed. Try to hurt me. You can't. I guess Ryan's behavior sounds a ton worse to you than it felt to me. It really means nothing." She shrugged and sat up straight again, holding her head high. "No, that's not what ruined my life."

She waited for a condescending reaction from the others, which was sure to come after such a confession, but it never came. Instead, hardly anyone dared to breathe. Victoria's eyes were closed, and she kind of hummed, "Come on, girl, tell the doctor all about it."

"Becca, I'm staying right with you," Bob assured her. "You have dismissed people you feel are lower than refuse. You're right: They can't hurt you anymore. You left that world and found yourself a new one. And when some traces of bad human behavior show up, you can dismiss them, too. But not this."

He pulled himself to a more upright position. "You were a tough kid. You shouldn't have survived, but you did." Bob spoke directly but with marked tenderness. "You look dainty, but you're tough. Still, the truth remains. As a child you deserved to be loved and cared for. You should have been able to count on the grown-ups entrusted to take care of you; you were an innocent little girl, just like your own two little girls now. You needed to be protected and kept safe, and the people you counted on betrayed you.

"It almost sounds like you were able to figure out how to deal with the abuse, but there was some other part of the betrayal that got you. Maybe in some way you felt abandoned or lied to, and that was the most terrifying of all. Does any of that sound right?"

Becca definitely remembered how she felt—the heaviness in her body, the unending hours of darkness, the dank, putrid smells that filled her nostrils. . . . Following her father's abandonment, her mama started drinking and spending time with boyfriends, who came and went and used not only her mama but pretty Becca, too. Isolation was both her protection and her punishment. And then . . . the ultimate abandonment.

Her mama couldn't stay, and her only daughter must not have been worth carrying along. Social services found her in the woodshed. She believed for years that when Mama was able to, she would come back for her. She waited and waited. Maybe Mama went to a special hospital to get better. She knew Mama would come. She made plans for that day. But it never came. Pretty Becca had been bounced from one foster home to another until she could escape the system and live on her own.

". . . I could handle Ryan being selfish or mean. I didn't care if he was self-absorbed through medical school. I could even handle him being unfaithful or making stupid mistakes. I could handle that. We'd work through it. I only asked that he *tell the truth*. But he just kept lying. And I got more and more frightened. And his leaving me . . ."

Up to this point she had managed not to convey any emotion. Now she broke down. What did it matter if her dignity was gone? Her body shuddered with sobs. "I panic, I go crazy. I want him to be near me. I've begged him not to leave me." The same surge of panic from the middle of the night grabbed at her stomach. "That's why I ask him to do stuff. When he's doing things for me—even if he's mad, he's still with me."

"Can you tell me about the lying?"

She knew Bob was trying hard to understand the connection,

as if he was certain it would make sense as soon as all the pieces came together. "What is it about your husband's lying that is more terrifying than his cheating on you? It gets you so worked up and in a panic that it's almost impossible for you to function. Almost like you can't think of anything else."

❍ ❍ ❍

Rodney wondered if Ryan ever really noticed the fervor with which his wife rocked back and forth as she was now, grasping the sofa pillow tightly as if it could ease her pain. How long had she been doing that? He glanced around the room. Victoria and Pam were crying now too.

"That is exactly what it is like," Becca was saying in response to Bob's question. "It's like I get crazy inside . . . frantic! Bob, my husband has looked me in the eye and sworn he was telling the truth, all the while *still lying*! It's like he's not there, and I want to nail his shoes to the ground until he comes clean. It's like I can't breathe unless he is honest."

"Becca, what goes on in your head in those moments? What kind of thoughts are you having, and what are you saying to yourself?"

"I'm frantically trying to figure out if he is telling the truth. All these conflicting voices are screaming at the same time: 'He's lying, can't you see?' 'No, you have to give him the benefit of the doubt. Just because he's lied to you in the past, you can't assume he's lying now.' 'Yes, he is.' 'What kind of a Christian wife are you anyway? You need to let the Lord protect you and be your strength.' 'What's wrong with you, are you going to let him do that to you again?' And on and on."

"Again, just like yesterday—it sounds like in those moments you have a hard time knowing what is real," Bob said. "I wonder if it's this feeling that is driving you crazy."

By the look on her face, Rodney could tell Bob had hit it dead center for Becca. She began to talk about the ongoing struggle she had with that as a child. People constantly telling her she was making things up or that it hadn't really happened the way she said it did, the way she was sure she'd seen it. Then there were the parts she admitted that she did make up, and it all kind of blended together. It was completely "crazy-making." Bob asked her how she was able to deal with that, how she was eventually able to escape with such a strong sense of herself—and her sanity.

Becca explained that the older she got, the stronger she became. She was able to see that she was not crazy, no matter what people said. "Though I got shortchanged on the family side of things, God gave me an intelligent mind and a pretty face. I used them both to build my academic career." Once she was safe in college, a whole new world opened up. Becca earned academic scholarships and soon found herself on the dean's list, an outreach team, and the cheerleading squad. She shared how she'd made an oath with herself never to allow another person to make her feel worthless again.

"That's when I met Ryan . . . and it was all working until this stuff started to happen." She picked a feather out of the pillow she was holding. "Do you know, it doesn't even affect me that much if anyone else lies to me. But I let my guard down with Ryan. I let him into my soul." She tucked her chin and began to cry softly. "I wanted so badly to have somebody I could trust . . . just one person I could believe in, who would be honest with me."

It all made sense to Rodney, and the whole room seemed to sigh.

Bob then said, "No wonder you have such a strong reaction to Ryan's lying. That pushes a *huge* button for you. I can't think of anything you've said that could get you spinning into your Fear Dance faster than this.

"And Becca, one of the biggest, most common challenges I see for women in your position is that they are so often caught unaware. Like you said earlier, you believed 'this would never happen to me—he would never do that.' There is nothing more painful than coming face-to-face with the fact that, in spite of your desire to believe your husband was trustworthy, he is not. But this is when healing can begin.

"You actually found a lot of security—even if it was false—in a fantasy that you created. Remember yesterday when we challenged the myth that trust can be earned once and for all? I realize that you've never expected perfection and that this is far from perfection, but can you see how attached you were to the hope that this time things would be different? You really hoped that this relationship with Ryan would be one in which you could keep your feet on the solid ground of truth . . . that you could have one relationship—even if some cruddy stuff was going on—in which you knew what was real.

"You really wanted to believe that it was possible and that you'd found it. To me, Becca, it seems like you wanted it so badly that you are kicking and screaming over having to let it go. What you've come face-to-face with is the reality that there is no way to return to the comfortable fantasy you once believed. From this point forward, you are forced to live with your eyes wide open."

Becca agreed, looking a bit dazed.

Bob got down on the floor and lay his head on one of the other couch cushions, with his hands crossed behind his head. All the others were now sprawled around the room. Rodney thought it felt more like one of his kids' slumber parties than a counseling session. "What starts the conflict raging inside when you think Ryan might be lying?"

"I get these red flags."

"And when these red flags come up, what do you do to try and address them? What are you trying to accomplish?"

"I'm trying to figure out how to get information from him."

"Right. Control. Okay, what are you trying to control?"

"Hmm. Something that I can't. But, Bob—" her eyes took on a haunted look—"that's what I struggle with."

"Hang in here with me. Together we'll figure this out," Bob

encouraged. "It drives you crazy, and it will every single time. What do you try to control?"

"Ryan's behavior."

When he asked her to elaborate on that, the group soon learned just how obsessed a woman can become when she knows her husband is cheating. Rodney hated every minute of it—it was enough to make a person batty. Though he had suspicions about Chelsea, he had left it alone. No way could he see himself acting as manipulative and paranoid as Becca sounded.

Bob addressed the group. "When we focus on someone else and when controlling or changing them is the key to our well-being and security, it leaves us very, very vulnerable. We know there is nothing we can do to truly keep that person from hurting us, and we just stay in that place of being vulnerable."

Greg, having been quiet throughout the entire exchange, spoke up now. "It takes you face-to-face with your helplessness— and you know why? When it comes to Ryan's choices, you *are* helpless. That's the truth. You've gotten yourself paralyzed in this deal to the point that you are ready to walk away from it because you are so scared. You are so scared of losing him that it is almost like you are forcing his hand.

"The good news is that it doesn't have to be that way. By God's grace, you have the ability and the power to make this story different for you. The first step, though, is personal responsibility—realizing that the job of taking care of Becca is yours. As long as your well-being is dependent on Ryan, you are powerless, and that includes your ability to stay grounded and to know what is real. It includes learning how to deal with the reality of your helplessness against others and the tragic decisions they often make.

"It means being personally responsible for your own physical, emotional, spiritual, and mental well-being: your whole self. And it means doing all that well enough that you can stay in close relationships with people who will let you down and still be confident that you'll be okay.

"Taking personal responsibility is the first step, because that is about simply accepting the job. The second step out of the Fear Dance is *doing* the job—what we call self-care: learning how to take good care of yourself physically, emotionally, spiritually, and mentally."

Greg stood and wrote a list on the board.

Step 1: Personal Responsibility
Step 2: Caring for Self
Step 3: Caring for Your Mate
Step 4: Caring for Your Marriage

He circled in red *Step 2: Caring for Self.*

"Becca," Greg said, turning to her and speaking in one of the most gentle tones Rodney had ever heard, "you can't focus on your marriage yet, because you don't know how to care for *you*—you never really have. And if you're like most of the rest of us, you probably didn't even know you were supposed to." He walked back to the group.

"But, Greg, I *do* take care of myself. I keep myself in good shape, I try to eat right, and I generally don't let people get close enough to hurt me . . . except for him," she said, looking over at Ryan with a pained expression on her face.

Bob then asked, "But how about emotionally?"

She thought for a moment. "I take pretty good care of myself emotionally too—at least I thought I did. I just am not dealing well with this situation. Normally I do okay."

"You know, in part I think that may be true. But it seems that this situation with Ryan may have exposed some levels where it may not be true, and I have a hunch that may be what is nailing you here. Would you be open to walking through this a little further to see if I'm right?"

Rodney was glad that Bob took special care to find out if Becca was still up for going further. He hated to think of the pain she was going through. By her expression, Rodney could see she didn't know where Bob was headed, but she seemed willing to hear him out. Rodney couldn't believe the level of trust and intimacy that had been established in just a day and a half.

Bob first reviewed the two commitments they had discussed the day before: One, commit yourself to being trustworthy toward others; and two, become trustworthy to yourself, which includes requiring others to be trustworthy toward you. He pointed out that Ryan and Becca had some major deficits with this principle in their relationship. In fact, it was painfully clear that there wasn't any safety to speak of between them. Ryan kept asking Becca to trust him, but he was in no way trustworthy. Becca, on the other hand, wasn't trustworthy with herself. Granted, she was trying and doing better than she had in the past, but she was still driving herself crazy. Over and over she would extend herself to Ryan—like holding the teddy bear out to him—expecting that he was going to take care of her. But just as when Greg let the bear drop to the floor, this way of relating was not working.

Rodney saw exactly where Bob was going. Along with the others, he had learned that it was Becca's job, not her husband's, to care for her heart. It was Becca's responsibility first and foremost. For Ryan to have access to that very dear and intimate part of her, he needed to show that he deserved that kind of trust. Bob reminded her that she had every right to expect that—a responsibility to require it, actually.

"I want to suggest to you that one of the reasons you are feeling so insecure in the relationship at this point is that you do not trust yourself," Bob said. "As a matter of fact, I would suggest that at this point you probably trust yourself even less than you trust Ryan."

Becca shook her head and tucked her hair behind an ear. "Right now I don't trust him at all. But I do trust myself . . . and God."

"Then why do you keep extending your heart out and saying, 'Please, Ryan, take care of my heart, because I don't know what to do with it'? If you don't trust Ryan, why are you continually trying to hand him your heart? And if you are trying to hand your heart to someone you don't believe is trustworthy, how can you trust yourself? That sounds like miserably poor judgment. Actually, it sounds careless.

"I see that you have made attempts to care for yourself, but I get the impression that your attempts are feeble even by your own estimation. You don't feel confident that Becca is going to take good care of Becca. Or maybe you don't even believe that you *can* at this level."

Bob was pushing hard now, and Rodney felt like he wanted to defend or protect Becca.

As if he could read Rodney's mind, Bob continued, "I am saying this so strongly because you are not alone in this struggle, and it is especially hard for women in our society to feel okay about taking good care of themselves. You've got to hear me loud and clear. Taking good care of yourself is not only a right, it's a responsibility before God. Women in our society are taught from the time they are children that if anyone you care for has a want or need, there is only one acceptable response: yes. Anything else is seen as selfish or self-centered. And nothing could be further from the truth; nothing could be further from the heart of God. Do you remember what Jesus replied when asked what the greatest commandment was?"

"To love God and to love your neighbor," Becca said.

"That's close, but it's not the whole story. He said the first commandment is to love the 'lord your God with all your heart and with all your soul and with all your mind and with all your strength.' In other words, love him with your whole being. Then he went on to say that the second is like it: 'Love your neighbor as yourself.' You were right that the two things he commands are to love God and to love your neighbor. But he is assuming that you are already loving yourself. And by this he does not mean love yourself *more* than others, but love and care for yourself well and then treat others the same as you do yourself. That way everybody is treated well . . . yourself included!

"Becca, do you realize that you are the temple of the Holy Spirit? The Bible says this very clearly in 1 Corinthians, chapter 3. Neither the world nor you yourself appear to fully understand that God said this part of you—" he gestured toward his heart—"is so precious, so priceless, and so valuable that there can be no compromise. This is the part of you that lives in the holy of holies of your personal temple. God ordained you—not Ryan—to be the steward, or caretaker, of your temple.

"How much do you know about the original Old Testament Temple? There was a courtyard where people could mill around . . . and then there was the inner sanctuary . . . and beyond that, the Holy of Holies. And how many people were given access to this very sacred area of the Temple?"

"One," Todd said.

Rodney grinned. Count on the preacher to know the answer to that one.

"Yes," Bob agreed. "Only the high priest could enter the Holy of Holies. And do you know what kind of condition that guy had to be in before he walked in? Anybody know?" Bob answered his own question. "Pure, righteous, holy, and clean. And just in case he wasn't, what did the other religious leaders do? They tied a rope around his ankle so that if he passed out or died in there, they could drag him out by the rope. Only one person could enter this very sacred and holy place.

"Your inner sanctuary, Becca, is just as sacred. You are the temple of the Holy Spirit. Yet most people I know don't have a clue about how precious and sacred this part of their temple is. A lot of us act like our friends and acquaintances are on a tour bus, and we yell, 'Hey, come on in! Take a tour of the holy of holies. Feel free to take a souvenir on your way out!' "

Rodney knew a little bit about the rich symbolism of the Old Testament place of worship, with its precise measurements, its laws of purity, and the special guidelines God set in place to keep it sanctified and holy . . . and he was getting a word picture that would stay with him forever.

Bob went on, "God has very clearly stated that there is a place in you that is so valuable that if anybody else is given access to it—which ideally should be only one person—and if that person has squandered the right to enter, you get to call the shots. You may be willing to give him another chance—or even repeated chances. That's up to you. I just pray that you get a clear vision of what it is you are really dealing with here, Becca."

Rodney could see that Becca was still troubled. He figured this new paradigm was going to take some time to sink in.

"But I'm not a typical person, Bob." Becca was insistent. "Take everything away—my clothes, my car, my house, my life-style, whatever. I enjoy fashion, but in comparison to receiving my husband's love, material things mean nothing to me. I've been so depressed these past few months, I can't even get dressed or brush my hair. This stuff—" she made a sweeping gesture to indicate her expensive clothes, jewelry, and makeup—"brings no happiness. I would give back everything I have, I would stand in front of you today wearing sackcloth, if I could have my husband back."

"That absolutely horrifies me," Bob said. Rodney was surprised at his bluntness. Becca must have been, too, because she was visibly taken aback. But her only reply was, "That's how it is."

"I understand that, but do you know what that says to me? I get how much you love Ryan. I don't see that as being a problem. It's the absence of that same love for yourself—the fact that you would be willing to humiliate yourself, to treat yourself like that—that horrifies me, Becca. There is no way you will ever feel safe with yourself if you treat yourself that way."

"But that's the truth."

"I see that. If you take a good hard look at Becca, what do you see?"

"I don't know."

"I am deeply concerned about this, and I want you to think carefully about it. This is a serious problem. Let me ask it this way: Do you have any sense of what the Lord sees when he looks at you?"

"Not really."

"How does he feel about you?"

"I think he loves me, or I wouldn't be here."

"Okay. Do you have a sense of how deeply he loves you, how passionately?"

"I think I feel that. But Jesus loved me so much he hung on a cross for me, Bob. He literally gave his life for me. Why would I do anything less for my husband?"

"Becca, I'm thankful you love Ryan that much. That's awesome. God loves him that much too. It's you, though, who's missing in this equation, not Ryan. Imagine looking at yourself in the mirror for a moment. What do you see, and how do you feel?"

"I'm okay. Reasonably attractive. I'm a decent person."

"Any imperfections?"

She was mangling another tissue by this point. "Let's not go there, Bob." Her eyes started to glaze over.

"How do you feel about taking care of yourself, especially emotionally?"

"Fine."

"Becca," Greg cut in, "we consider the word *fine* to be an acronym for *f*eelings *i*nside *n*ot *e*xpressed."

"Yeah, that's pretty much how I feel right now," she admitted.

"Becca?" Bob prompted. Rodney could see that Bob needed her to get in touch with her feelings before they could make any progress, and she had walled them up tight. "Tell me about your daughters."

"Thank you. This is something I can actually get right!" Becca looked relieved. "I love my girls more than life itself. I'd do anything for them," she said emphatically.

"Describe for me the first moment you saw them, the moment

each of them was born, when you first held them in your arms. Describe to me what you saw."

"They were beautiful . . . perfect!"

"How did you feel about them?"

"I didn't know I was capable of loving anyone that much."

"Okay, good. Now I want you to take a moment and compare how you feel about the girls with how you feel about *you*. Any difference? How do you feel about taking care of *you* in comparison with taking care of *them*?"

"I *love* taking care of them, even though it's challenging at times. It's my job and they need me. I *tolerate* taking care of me because I have to."

"Are you telling me that you love caring for them because it's your job?"

"No, I love taking care of them because they're awesome!"

"And taking care of you is different because . . . ?"

"There is no comparison between me and the girls. They are precious and beautiful and perfect. They're still innocent and pure. Unlike me. I've been trashed. After a while life just wears the shine off of you, and even if you cover up the blemishes on the outside, it only hides all the disappointment underneath."

"What do you think God sees when he looks at you?"

"He loves me," she said matter-of-factly.

"Do you think he is awed by you?"

That one took little thought. "No. I think he's disappointed in me. I've let him down so many times."

"So you actually think that *you* love *your* daughters more than he loves his."

"They are his daughters."

"So are you. And I'm confident that as much as I love my children, I can't outlove God. And I'm confident that he is passionate about you, to the point of death. Imagine your girls becoming adults and feeling about themselves the way you feel about yourself;

imagine them neglecting themselves emotionally and allowing themselves to be treated poorly. What would that be like for you?"

"I would hate it, and I'd want to talk some sense into them."

"Me, too. I can't bear to see my kids not taking good care of themselves. Sometimes I just want to grab them and say, 'Don't you see how valuable you are? Why won't you take better care of yourself?' And I'm confident that is how God feels about you. But don't take my word for it. You need to check that out for yourself.

"This is what I want you to do," Bob explained. "Tonight, I want you to spend some time taking a look—without trying to change anything—at how you feel about you and how you treat yourself. Ask God how he feels about you. Ask him if he'll let you see yourself through his eyes and if he'll let you experience how he feels about you. Then compare it to what you see and how you feel. Don't try and change anything at this point. Just gather information."

"But I wasn't like this before. When I was in college and before I married Ryan, I was strong. This isn't me!"

"I totally get that you weren't like this, that you were carefree and trusting. Yet in spite of that, you have an amazing opportunity to grow here. All I am saying is give it some thought overnight. I know that there is plenty of work left to do about this, and I am confident that this was a key piece of the puzzle that had to be addressed before we can go much further."

A TALK WITH THE DOCTORS
Self-Worth

In order to live out the greatest commandments, which are to love God and to love others as we love ourselves, we must understand a foundational key. The key to this second commandment is the last part: *as you love yourself.* Why? Because love comes to us from God through our open hearts—hearts available to receive his love and send it on to others. When we do not love ourselves, our hearts are closed toward ourselves, which hinders our relationships with God and others. Our hearts are the key to the entire process. That is why in the greatest commandments we are not commanded to love ourselves. God assumes that we are already doing that job. He created us to love ourselves, but many fail miserably at this job. And the reason is usually found in how we see ourselves and how we perceive our own value.

Do you take good care of yourself physically, emotionally, mentally, and spiritually? Do you think of yourself as valuable? Do you like yourself? Do you accept yourself? Do you forgive yourself? Do you realize that in addition to your relationships with God and others, you have an important relationship with yourself? How do you treat yourself? Do you speak to yourself harshly or kindly? The reason these questions are so critical is because we can't adequately love God or others unless we love ourselves—we love others like we love ourselves.

When you see snapshots of your family, do you like what you see? Or do you look across a row of beautiful smiling faces and critically see yourself and think, *Yuck, is that really me?* If you look at yourself through the camera lens, you may not like what you see. Some of what you see—in your behaviors, in the responses of other people, in the attitudes that you cast out among others—just won't be pretty.

The danger is that you'll run from the ugly stuff and put away the camera. In fact, that's why people avoid developing an honest, objective relationship with themselves in the first place—because they're afraid of what they'll see. But some people dare to look at themselves, and when they do, it yields great results in their relationships—with God, others, and self.

Although it's good for us to look at ourselves through a camera lens, many of us use the wrong lens. Sometimes we use the lens that Hollywood uses when filming aging actors and actresses—the soft-focus lens that blurs the wrinkles. Other times we use a distorted lens, like carnival fun house mirrors, which makes us look uglier or more distorted than we are.

The most objective and true camera lens is God's. As we mentioned, sometimes when you look at yourself through the camera lens, what you see isn't pretty. Or other times it's too rosy. How do we make sure that in seeing ourselves through our camera lens, we are getting an accurate picture? Get God's lens if you want a healthy view of yourself and your relationships. In other words, we have to be willing to look through God's eyes.

It's critical that we get our lens from God. His lens is the most accurate: never portraying you better than you should appear, but always showing the true beauty inside you. This is exactly what Scripture reveals: "The LORD does not look at the things man looks at. Man looks at the outward appearance, but the LORD looks at the heart" (1 Samuel 16:7). God sees us as we really are.

When you have a healthy relationship with God, you are in the best position to see yourself as he sees you, which will result in a healthier relationship with yourself and others. When your relationship with God is out of balance, you can't see yourself properly. We need to echo the prayer of the apostle Paul: "I pray also that the eyes of your heart may be enlightened" (Ephesians 1:18). We need our hearts to see what God sees when he looks at us.

How do you see yourself? Do you see yourself as valuable? precious? priceless? Do you honor yourself? Honor is a way of accurately seeing the immense value of someone made in God's image. God created each of us as a one-of-a-kind person, with unique gifts and personality. He sees us as precious and valuable. When we see ourselves as God sees us, when we recognize and affirm our value, we help create a safe environment that encourages our relationship with ourselves to grow.

But you can't affirm that value if you don't first recognize that we are people of limitless value, made in God's image and worthy of great honor.

Picture yourself as personally autographed by God. Wouldn't you feel thrilled to be seen with someone who bears God's personal autograph? Wouldn't you want to have your picture taken with such a person and hang that picture on a prominent place on your wall? We have God's autograph written on our hearts: "You show that you are a letter from Christ, the result of our ministry, written not with ink but with the Spirit of the living God, not on tablets of stone but on tablets of human hearts" (2 Corinthians 3:3).

We honor ourselves when we see ourselves—and treat ourselves—as incredible gifts from God. Each of us has immeasurable value as a unique, divine creation. Life goes so much better for everyone when we treat ourselves like priceless treasures. Jesus told us, "Where your treasure is, there your heart will be also" (Matthew 6:21). When you consider yourself as a treasure, your heart will follow—and so will your words, and actions. Conversely, if you consider yourself a piece of junk (or worse), your heart, words, and actions will demonstrate that fact. When you do not value yourself, when you do not see yourself as a treasure, hardness of heart sets in. And hardening of the heart is the kiss of death to a relationship—especially with yourself. When someone's heart is hardened toward themselves, they can be described as disconnected, closed down, shut down, numbed to life, detached, indifferent, lifeless, heartless, or emotionally unavailable. Do you feel that way? Do others accuse you of being this way? Again, the danger is that a closed heart disconnects us from relationships with God, others, and ourselves.

If you ever doubt your value, consider what your heavenly Father says to you:

- You may not know me, but I know everything about you (see Psalm 139:1).

- You were made in my image (see Genesis 1:27).
- In me you live and move and have your being (see Acts 17:28).
- You are my offspring (see Acts 17:28).
- I knew you even before you were conceived (see Jeremiah 1:4-5).
- I chose you when I planned creation (see Ephesians 1:4, 11-12).
- You were not a mistake, for all your days are written in my book (see Psalm 139:16).
- I determined the exact time of your birth and where you would live (see Acts 17:26).
- You are fearfully and wonderfully made (see Psalm 139:14).
- I knit you together in your mother's womb (see Psalm 139:13).
- I brought you forth on the day you were born (see Psalm 71:6).
- You are my treasured possession (see Exodus 19:5).

Every man or woman whom God ever created—and that includes you—was made in God's own image. That means you are a person of incredible value, just as much as your children or your spouse or your neighbor or your friend are.

But is there a difference between how you see your children or your friends and how you see yourself? If you have children, picture the moment you first laid eyes on your child. How did you feel about your child? Was he or she the most beautiful and valuable creature on earth? We bet you would do anything to protect and care for that child. Now, what do you think God sees when he looks at you? Is there a difference between how you see your child and what you think God sees when he looks at you? Is there a difference between how you see your son or daughter and how you see yourself? If the answer is yes, you have lost sight of what is true about yourself. It's difficult to fathom the love God must have for you that even if you were the only person on earth, he would have sent his Son to die for you. That's amazing love. And his love for us stems directly from how valuable we are to him.

So, as a person made in the image of God—and therefore people of incredible value—do you deserve to be treated well? Absolutely.

If you have placed your faith in Jesus Christ, then you have been given even greater value, for the blood of Christ has been shed so that you might have eternal life. The apostle Peter says to us: "You know that it was not with perishable things such as silver or gold that you were redeemed from the empty way of life handed down to you from your forefathers, but with the precious blood of Christ, a lamb without blemish or defect. He was chosen before the creation of the world, but was revealed in these last times for your sake" (1 Peter 1:18-20). Would God spill the precious blood of Christ for someone he didn't consider precious?

Beyond that, if you belong to Christ, then even now God is at work within you so that you increasingly mirror the goodness and glory of Christ. Paul says that "we, who with unveiled faces all reflect the Lord's glory, are being transformed into his likeness with ever-increasing glory, which comes from the Lord, who is the Spirit" (2 Corinthians 3:18).

Would you treat Christ poorly? Would you neglect him? Then why would you neglect or treat poorly someone who increasingly mirrors his likeness—someone like yourself?

And it gets even better! Right now, at this very moment, God himself has taken up residence in your physical body. The Bible calls your body the temple of the Holy Spirit, the temple of God (see 1 Corinthians 3:16; 6:19; 2 Corinthians 6:16). You might wonder, does it make any difference to God how we treat his temple? You'd better believe it does! Paul writes to the church, "If anyone destroys God's temple, God will destroy him; for God's temple is sacred, and you are that temple" (1 Corinthians 3:17).

Does that put a different spin on how you see yourself? It should!

We need to see ourselves honestly and objectively. God wants us to develop a healthy relationship with ourselves. We should see ourselves as valuable because God never creates junk. God sees us as so valuable that he would lay down his life just for us. Remember, before you can truly take good care of yourself and experience the honor and privilege of self-care, you must recognize and embrace your value. You will not care for what you do not value, and if you try, it will feel like a chore. Where your treasure is, there will your heart be also.

"Wait!" Rodney couldn't stay quiet another minute. "What about Ryan? He's been sitting here silent through this whole session. When will he have to start taking some responsibility for his actions?"

"Honestly, Rodney," Bob said, "as hard as this is to hear, Ryan may never choose to take responsibility for his actions." All eyes fell on Ryan. "He may shift blame or try to ignore his responsibilities, but he is fully responsible for what he does, whether or not he wants to accept it. He, like all of us, will have to stand before the Lord and make a full account for the decisions he's made, the things he's done, and what he's made of the life God gave him. There is no escaping that."

Whew. Rodney could breathe again.

"But," Bob went on, "you see, here we have been talking about Becca's contribution to her own problem—things she's having a hard time with. Becca, please know that none of this is meant to imply that Ryan's affair was in any way your fault." He looked around at the group. "Let's remember again the three separate journeys: Becca's, Ryan's, and their marriage together. Becca is responsible for her journey. She can experience personally the fullness of life that God desires for her. But it takes two people to make a great marriage. Does this bring clarity to your question? I am not suggesting in the least that she bears any responsibility for Ryan's choice to have an affair. That decision was made on *his* journey.

"No matter what Becca was doing personally or in the relationship, or how it made Ryan feel, he had plenty of options for how to deal with it. He is fully responsible for choosing the option he did. Apparently, neither Ryan nor Becca had any clue about how to deal with their disappointments and frustrations. But they will both be given powerful resources to make healthier choices and to take full responsibility for themselves first, then for their marriage."

Rodney nodded, still on edge, but in deep thought. He found Becca still stunning, still sexy, but his concern for her well-being now surpassed his awareness of her physical beauty. He had caught a glimpse of her childlike heart, and he was as concerned for her as for his little kids at the Boys & Girls Clubs. *This is what Jesus must see,* he thought.

Bob turned back toward Becca and said, "When all is said and done, my prayer is that you will fully understand the inexplicable beauty and preciousness of your heart, so much so that you will never again allow anybody to treat it carelessly—not even yourself."

Becca's blinking no longer held back her tears, and they flooded down her cheeks. She whispered, "I thought I would do just about anything to get Ryan back."

"And . . . ?" Bob prompted.

The lovely doctor's wife thought for what seemed to Rodney like a long time. Finally she spoke, and it looked as if it caused physical pain for her to get the words out. "I think I believed I had no worth of my own. And when Ryan left me, somehow it meant that all my parents had done to me was true, and my dreamy life in the present wasn't real after all."

"That was the hard part of your lesson," Bob said gently. "But what is the rest of the story?"

Becca took a moment to reflect. Then she smiled. "I want to believe what you said about the holy of holies."

A TALK WITH THE DOCTORS

Self-Care

Self-care is the acceptance of personal responsibility leading toward getting filled mentally, physically, spiritually, and emotionally. It is a second pathway out of the Fear Dance, and when exercised it creates more safety in a marriage. It begins with recognizing the truth of who you are—your identity and value in God. The ultimate goal of personal care is the fulfillment of the greatest commandments: Love the Lord your God with all your heart, soul, mind, and strength (an act of giving and receiving, and the ultimate act of self-love), and love your neighbor in the same way you now love yourself. This process enables you to become and remain a full vessel, and then to give from your abundance. Self-care is about wholeness.

We are called to love the Lord with our whole being, but since love comes only from God, we must first be filled with his love. "We love because he first loved us" (1 John 4:19). As we allow ourselves to be filled with God's love, the essence of life, we are truly loving ourselves. Once we are filled with his love, loving him and others becomes a natural outflow.

This pattern of receiving and giving, receiving and giving is the foundation of how God created the world to operate, and thus all human life is based on this.

We run into significant relational problems when we look to other people, rather than God, to be the source of our fulfillment. A healthy, sustainable relationship is one in which two people look to God as their source of fulfillment, actually get full, and then share the blessings with each other and the world.

Taking good care of yourself is *always* in the best interest of all parties involved, because you can't give what you don't have. Receiving and giving are both integral parts of good personal care. If you receive and don't give, what you are hoarding becomes stale and useless. If you give and don't receive, you eventually become empty. Excellent self-care, then, requires finding a healthy balance between giving and receiving. Personal care involves the heart-spirit-mind-body connection:

- Mental self-care involves reading books, being involved in mentally stimulating conversations, and listening to teaching or preaching that challenges your thinking.
- Physical self-care involves exercising, healthy eating, getting enough sleep, and taking time to relax.
- Spiritual self-care involves communion with God, reading the Bible, praying, worshipping, reading Christian books, and having conversations related to your faith with other believers.
- Emotional self-care involves allowing God to love and encourage you, loving yourself, attending to your emotional desires with care and compassion, and speaking to yourself with kindness.

People often avoid personal care because they think it is being selfish. In fact, the opposite is true. The fuller you are, the more you have to give. The more you have to give, the more you are able to serve God and others. There is nothing selfish about that. Jesus says, "I have come that they may have life, and have it to the full" (John 10:10). His desire is for our hearts to be full so that when we give, our love is coming out of the abundance of our hearts instead of from a diminishing reservoir.

The intensity of the afternoon had passed, and the group had enjoyed a pleasant, if subdued, dinner. An ache was forming in Pam's chest, one she had pushed down and refused to acknowledge for nearly twenty years. She had never allowed herself to revisit the dreams, the secret yearnings, that were awakening in her now. For Pam, marriage had been an act of obedience—a pouring out. Rather than feeling wanted or fulfilled as her husband's helpmate, she felt like an old, empty closet. No, she couldn't let her passions awaken now—they would kill her. Only if she refused to feel could she survive.

Pam didn't want to die, as she had blurted out during the session. She just wanted something to change. Desperately. She wanted to feel. By shutting down her feelings, all caring stopped. This eased the pain, but when she stopped caring, she got scared. Wasn't that the last stop? Pam didn't start out locked in the bathroom for hours at a time or wearing size sixteen dresses or binge eating. . . .

A light had sparked when she was with Victoria last night—as if the light had been switched on in the closet. Being in the serene, older woman's presence was like hanging beautiful garments in the dark emptiness. And in the safety of the counseling room, messages were being written on the walls of Pam's heart. She dared to say things she'd kept inside for years. No one there told her to have more faith or pray harder. Unlike her life at the church, she wasn't having to use what little energy she had left to dodge difficult conversations and uncomfortable situations.

She almost believed she could allow her secret passions, which had been quietly tucked away these twenty-one years, to surface when she was with her new friends. Dare she consider her lost yearnings for art, poetry, and friends? This was the "unspoken knowing" she shared with Victoria Templeton, and her visit last night had sparked new hope. Though the door to Pam's heart wasn't fully open yet, it now stood slightly ajar.

Now, on the second evening of the Couples Intensive, Pam sat in a cozy corner on the main floor of the Bradford House, reading a book of poetry she'd found. Her husband entered the room and walked toward her. "What's wrong with you?" He gave an exasperated sigh. "I didn't know where you were. What's this?"

He reached for the book, but she held it out of his reach and told him it was a book of poetry by Emily Dickinson. He said he had expected her to be in the room, pressing his cotton shirt for the next day, when he returned from making a phone call. "Are you sick?"

This didn't feel like love. She felt tired. She tried to answer him thoughtfully, to explain that she was taking the evening to relax and enjoy some time alone.

"Pam—"

"Please," she interrupted. "No more confrontations, not tonight. I'm sorry, but I'm tired, it's late. . . . This isn't about you."

She wasn't playing by the rules. Her words had been delivered in a deadpan voice, with no eye contact. Now she turned toward him, allowing him to see her face. He could probably tell that she'd been crying, but she didn't care.

He studied her for a moment, realization dawning. She could see that something she'd said triggered a response in her husband. The color in his face drained, and he stormed out of the room.

She was shaking now. She stood up and steadied herself with the back of her chair before following her husband. "I'm okay. I really am."

❋ ❋ ❋

Victoria quietly strode up beside Charles, who was standing in front of the large fireplace in the great room. She wanted to reach out and touch her husband's face, or even his sleeve. After sitting in the group all day and watching the others—such as Becca—struggle with their insecurities while courageously confronting their greatest fears, Victoria felt empowered. She, too, could allow some walls of protection to come down. She, too, had been validated in her need to look after herself. Did Charles understand?

More and more she wondered what was going on in her husband's heart. She knew Becca's work had affected him; she had seen the agony reflected on his face during the afternoon session. Their daughter, Ashley, was Becca's age, and Charles would zealously protect her at any cost. But Victoria had seen something else—something more than a typical male's response to a beautiful damsel in distress. She wondered if Becca's work had begun awakening Charles's heart. Group therapy was wonderful in that while listening to others, your own issues had a way of making their way to the surface even more clearly than when working on them directly.

This room was Charles's favorite in the Bradford House, perhaps because it was most similar to his impressive library at home. The host couple had built a fire to take the moist chill out of the great room. Sparks popped and hissed against the backdrop of music playing softly. The room was fragrant with smoky pine.

The individual elements worked together to create an atmosphere where one's defenses easily fell away. Victoria's husband's silence enveloped her, yet it was not altogether uncomfortable. Truth be told, she didn't care for a man who talked too much.

But neither did she want to be the initiator of their reconciliation. Perhaps it was only fair—she had been the one to push away. Or had she? Was it simply for self-preservation that she'd turned inward to tend her wounded soul? All of that didn't really matter now. All she wanted to know was whether this handsome gentleman would move toward her now . . . and if he did, would she be able to handle it?

Victoria knew she needed to be patient. She had been astounded at the great care, patience, and time Greg and Bob had devoted to creating a safe place for her husband to explore his heart. Over the past two days, with delicate yet deliberate strokes, the therapists had gently drawn out issues that had remained tangled and knotted in the sinews of Charles's being for many years. At first, the long pauses during their work made her restless and anxious. How hard it was not to chatter and fill the spaces for Charles as she had done throughout most of their marriage.

Just then Al Green, one of Charles's favorite soul artists, came on the stereo singing "Everything's Gonna Be Alright." A shy smile came over Charles's face, and he turned toward her.

"May I have this dance?" he asked, bowing slightly.

She stiffened involuntarily, but his gentle hold on her wrist was unyielding.

"Charles," she pleaded.

They danced, slowly and clumsily at first. Why could she dance with the best of the African drummers yet lose herself—her strength, her identity—in the embrace of a simple waltz?

He stopped and searched her eyes for the meaning of her resistance. "Relax, V," he said softly. "Move with me. If you don't like this music, we can find something more suitable to your taste."

Everything in her wanted to gravitate toward his body. But

her mind was resistant. His touch felt good, so good. But her new-found independence fought relentlessly. All she could think of was the number of buttons her charming husband was pushing. With her whole heart, she wanted to be kind and not disappoint him. But she feared being sucked in at the cost of losing herself. She didn't feel safe.

"There, now," he said when the song ended, slowly releasing her hand. "Was that so bad?"

Lowering her quivering chin, she fought back tears and darted from the room.

◎ ◎ ◎

As Becca and Ryan returned to their room after dinner, Becca noticed that her husband looked preoccupied. She wondered if the day's sessions had upset him more than he was letting on. Neither had intentionally avoided the other; it was just that they were focused on getting their own fingers out of the door. They hadn't been able to offer each other much in the way of comfort or support. The sessions were intense, leaving them both exhausted.

Ryan slumped on the bed, staring out the window. Perhaps he just didn't know what to do with himself. Her session on her own self-worth offered an incredible breakthrough—though maddening in a sense. She would start processing it tomorrow. For now she would try to cheer Ryan up by reading an article out of her new *Shape* magazine.

Fitness stuff always helped him perk up. She crossed over to the armoire filled with all the brand names, the perfect accessories, gorgeous shoes, and far too many handbags for a six-day trip.

"Look what I have here." She reached for her Marc Jacobs carryall tote. Pushing aside her latest Dooney & Bourke handbag and matching mini satchel—one never knew which bag might be needed on a trip like this—she pulled out a magazine. "I bought this month's edition at the airport." She flipped through the pages to an article on toning. "I'm feeling so flabby. I totally need to get back into my Pilates routine this evening. Look, here it says we need to . . ."

Ryan frowned. He was oblivious to her chatter. She sat on her knees in the middle of the bed. "It says here that . . ."

He still wasn't listening.

"Okay, maybe not." She was stung by his lack of response. She settled back on the bed and began reading silently. Let him stew if he wanted to.

Ryan was silent for a while. He definitely had something else on his mind. Finally he turned his head toward her for the first time. "Becca, what do you think about Todd?"

That was random!

Ryan was still talking. ". . . He really attacked his son's character today . . . and he seems pained by the whole thing. Later he said he may never speak to Zach again. I don't get it."

Becca didn't have the energy to worry about Todd's drama. She wanted to slap Ryan silly for not paying attention to her, but instead she reached for his hand. "I'm sure he's going to be fine. You heard Bob. The preacher has just been a 'bad wizard.' He'll get it figured out." But then again, Ryan's concern for the one person in the group he was repelled by confused her. What was going on?

"It makes you think, doesn't it?" Ryan asked. "Think about why you're acting the way you do . . ."

Her husband had never spoken like this before. Usually she was the one to start conversations about life and what it all meant—not often, certainly, but Becca didn't know how to respond to Ryan's seeming so . . . so . . . vulnerable. Instead of his typical businesslike assurance or playboy come-ons, Ryan was letting her see into his soul for a moment. She was not accustomed to his having doubts.

She tried to change the subject. "Would you like to go shopping or watch a video or something?"

He blinked, took a sip from his water bottle, and was back to normal. "No. I'm gonna shower, check my messages, and find a place to crash. Did you check in with the kids?"

❁ ❁ ❁

Ryan would not sleep in the same room with his soon-to-be ex. He changed into sweats and grabbed a pillow before leaving the room. He motioned to Becca, who was on the phone, and slunk down the stairs to sleep in the counseling room.

Ryan's psyche was on overload, and he needed some space. He rounded the corner. A shot of whiskey would be nice. A warm body would be even nicer. . . .

There sat Todd.

Great. This was definitely not what I had in mind. In fact, the loud-talking minister was about the last person he wanted to see right then. If Ryan thought he could get away with turning on his heel, he would have. But it was too late—Todd had seen him. *Might as well be civil.* "Hey."

"Hi," Todd said flatly, without moving from his catatonic position. The dimly lit lamp cast shadows across the length of the wall, resembling the Washington Monument.

The guy had to be the stiffest person Ryan had ever met. Only a few strands of hair were still glued down with gel; all the others were making a wild break for freedom.

Ryan gathered some blankets, yawned loudly, and stretched, hoping his exaggerated gestures would communicate his intent to sleep without having to embark into full-blown dialogue. He perched at the edge of the couch he wanted to pass out on and shoved his hands into the front pocket of his bulky 49ers sweatshirt. He had kicked up the heat a few notches, but the room was still cool. Todd hadn't seemed to notice.

Ryan sat in silence for a few minutes, fiddling with the cord on the hood of his sweatshirt, tightly winding it around his finger.

Todd didn't move. He just sat and stared straight ahead. He wasn't in the lotus position, so Ryan figured he wasn't meditating; his eyes were open, so he probably wasn't praying.

What could Ryan say to this man who made the hair on the back of his neck stand on end? There had to be something likable about him, or he wouldn't have a congregation, right? Ryan had slept in all sorts of interesting positions and situations while in residence at the hospital, but this was just plain weird. He obviously wasn't going to sleep much, so he figured he might as well discover a redeeming side to the character of Pastor Todd Davis.

He ran over a creative list of inoffensive lead-ins. Right about now, he missed his professional role, which made people automatically sit up and take note. In this group he was just another guy—and one who'd been harshly judged by the person sitting across the room.

"I think maybe your son deserves another chance." *Okay, not so subtle a lead-in.* Ryan gazed at his finger. The cord was wrapped too snugly, and his fingertip was slowly turning purple. "I mean . . . look at me. I've done plenty of stupid, screwup things. I've let people down. But they've always given me another chance."

He let the cord unravel and heard Todd take a deep breath.

"You know nothing about my son."

"Why don't you tell me?"

The dialogue started out a bit rough, but the two men talked into the night. Ryan was shocked to discover Todd's passion for God, his son, his family, and . . . his love for science and how he had always dreamed of one day becoming a microbiologist.

"Really? What happened?"

Todd explained that his parents had fallen on hard times when Todd was finishing high school. Todd had to work in a feed store to help pay the medical bills after his father got sick. A couple of years later, while on his deathbed, Todd's father's final wish was for Todd to promise he'd follow God's call and become a full-time minister like himself. He wanted Todd to take over his church.

Todd's shoulders started to sag for the first time since he'd arrived in Branson. He'd struggled with his loyalty to his father. It meant letting go of his full-ride scholarship to the university. And he knew he could never make his fiancée's dream come true either—he'd planned, someday, to buy her an old Victorian house. "So yes, I've lived with anger all my adult life. I don't think Pam's ever felt called to the ministry . . . and I've been a pretty lousy minister myself. Believe it or not, I think the anger keeps me going."

Now in his forties, his life was half over, his wife was trapped in illness—directly related to her circumstances—and his son hated him. "I was loyal to my father at the expense of my son . . . my family." He sighed so deeply that Ryan was sure this was the first time his night companion had ever shared his secret.

"Man, I don't know what to tell you. Let's talk to Greg about this tomorrow, okay?" Ryan bunched up the pillow and shoved it under his head. "Do you want a blanket? We've got to get some sleep or we'll never make it through tomorrow's session."

"Nah. You go ahead and sleep. I'll leave in another minute or two." Todd reached over to turn off the light.

Finally Ryan could sleep.

But he didn't.

In the silence of the night, he stared at the strange patterns on the ceiling made by the streetlamp outside. Something wasn't right. Ryan just wasn't quite sure what. The way Todd looked tonight was almost too . . . too . . .

Ryan propped himself up on an elbow. "Wait. Todd, how can you live with that kind of anger?"

A long pause followed. Ryan was surprised to realize he was holding his breath as he waited for Todd's answer.

The older man eventually spoke. "Honestly, I've lived with it so long, the question is whether I can live without it." Todd popped several Tylenol capsules into his mouth and swallowed before exiting the darkened room.

❂ ❂ ❂

Today had been the most complicated yet momentous day of Chelsea's life. Even the birth of her children didn't compare to this. It was like she was experiencing the birthing of herself. She was being squeezed and pushed toward a life she couldn't see. Old things were being cut away, allowing new life to take their place.

For the second time that day, she found herself running in a downpour, sobbing. She had tried to choke down some food at dinner, but then Ryan, Mr. I-Treat-My-Wife-Like-Dirt, came into the dining room. When he looked at her with raised eyebrows, she went berserk. He seemed more concerned about *her* marriage than he did his own!

She had excused herself. She was such a loser—no, she hadn't come clean. Numb, she ran out into the rain and kept running.

The first session that morning had worked her over. Every single thing Todd and Pam were dealing with nailed her. For the first time, she recognized that her anger was actually the fear of losing control.

As hard as she tried, she couldn't escape her own judgment. She wanted to believe she was valuable. This stuff was making sense in her head, but there was a war waging inside her. Her worth had always been tied to her performance. And today she'd failed again. Feeling as if she was navigating through an emotional minefield, she'd tried to connect with Bob to tell him her secret. They had been interrupted by Becca. She'd had another opportunity but had chickened out. Forgiveness seemed awfully hard to come by.

As she slowed down to a gentle jog, Chelsea's thoughts turned to the night she'd met Rod. At the time she was seventeen, restless and bored with her neatly arranged honor student–athlete life. On a dare she agreed to go to Daytona Beach with some classmates. She lied to her mother and snuck out for the weekend. Naive as she was, she encountered some shocking things that weekend at the designated party spot—a campsite on the beach.

After getting her fill of partying and foolishness, she wanted to go home but was too proud to call her parents. Instead, she opted for a jog along the water's edge. When she ran toward a man sitting on the jetty, strumming a mandolin, she slowed to hear what he was singing.

"Where you going in such a hurry?" he asked.

She stopped. His voice was kind and not at all like the catcalls of the high school jocks Chelsea had grown accustomed to.

Nothing in the picture seemed to align with the only reality she'd ever known. Rod had no intention of keeping up any appearances, and he didn't seem to mind whether she stayed or continued on with her jog. The twinkle in his eye drew her in.

She had dallied, watching his huge, gentle hands on his instrument. He had a mischievous smile that played on his lips without fully breaking open, which dared her to let down her guard. They ended up sitting cross-legged in his van on worn velvet pillows, drinking organic home brew, getting to know each other, talking into the night. The pungent aroma of incense always took her back to that first night. She'd felt safe and respected. Smells of the ocean . . . crashing of the waves . . . He sang to her. He kissed her nose. And he played with her hair. She would never be the same.

With Rod, she had found a raw and authentic quality about life. He was real, and he had loved the parts of her that no one else even knew existed. People saw what they wanted to see, and Chelsea's family and teachers and coaches wanted a star. Chelsea was spunky and quick, a star athlete, always performing—yet Rodney looked beneath her tough exterior and saw more.

Why had she pushed so hard to the opposite extreme? sucked back into the lie? Having swung out to the polar opposite, she was trying to figure out where she belonged.

She was ashamed at how she had let the world's definition of success lead her so far away from the one man she loved. How dare a bunch of "suits" define her husband's worth! She was sorry for not being safe enough for Rodney to open up and share his heart, for having judged and defined him.

"Jesus, you took all this on your back. I'm sorry. I'm so sorry," she cried out to the sodden sky.

✧ ✧ ✧

With a prompt from Ryan, Rodney had left his dinner half eaten and had gone looking for his wife in the pouring rain. He was worried about her safety in the middle of a thunderstorm, and it was growing darker. Fortunately she hadn't left the main road and was easy to spot.

"Chelsea, come back! What are you doing?" He took off his shirt and wrapped it around his tiny wife, who was shivering violently.

"I don't know, Rod. I just had to get away from everything. I had to. Please don't ask me anything more, okay?"

"Okay. But let's get you inside and dry." He wished there was more he could do to help her. But at least she didn't argue as he led her back to the Bradford House.

Once in their room, Rod changed into dry clothes and went down to the kitchen to get her some hot tea, leaving her to take a hot shower. Because of sheer size alone, he didn't get cold like she did.

He let himself back into the room, finding Chelsea sitting on the bed with her head wrapped in a towel and her robe pulled tightly around her. She pulled her knees up to her chin, accepted the mug of tea he handed her, and sipped the warm liquid.

"Is there anything you want to tell me?" He hoped that he'd given her enough space to feel secure. He put his own mug down and tried not to look anxious. "What made you bolt like that?"

Silence. Chelsea's fingers tightened around her mug.

"Well, it's . . ." She cleared her throat. "It's just that . . ."

She stopped and took a sip of tea. Rod thought she looked a little sick. It was making him nervous.

"Rod . . . I've never told you this—"

Just then a crash of lightning split the sky, and everything went totally black. They both dove for cover.

"That lightning bolt was so close! I'm—I'm scared, Rodney." The thunderstorm raged, and ferocious winds lashed branches against the windows. "How do we know this isn't a tornado or something?" Lightning split the sky, and the thunder sounded like bombs exploding in a war zone.

❁ ❁ ❁

After the worst of it had passed, Chelsea was willing to let Rodney leave her side just long enough to light a candle he said he had seen in the bathroom.

After the initial shock of the severe storm wore off, the two of them held each other and laughed at their fear until their stomachs hurt. It made Chelsea wonder. . . . Could they possibly embrace each other's insecurities, as Bob had suggested? She'd never known how much of her life was driven by fear.

Rodney, the one quiet constant in her life, acted nearly as nervous now as he'd been on their wedding night. Not from the thunderstorm; it had lessened to a steady downpour. He sat holding her by candlelight. She felt his fingers quiver, and she knew he wanted to be with her tonight.

Chelsea pulled the towel off her head and tossed her head gently from side to side, feeling her hair fall down around her shoulders. She was beautiful, and tonight she felt it in the flickering candlelight. To deny it would have been false modesty, and Chelsea had promised herself to live life truthfully. Which meant . . . which meant . . . "Rodney?"

"Hmm?" he said into her shoulder.

"I . . . I've got to tell you something."

Though she had often felt unnoticed by Rodney, she had his full attention now. His vulnerability and his words in the counseling room had touched her deeply. And now his gentle hands . . .

Plenty of doubts still hung in the back of her mind, but their miracle had begun. Their Red Sea was stretching wide before them, and they were stepping out toward its shore, becoming again the companions they both needed and wanted.

But it would all come screeching to a halt when a few syllables formed the words "I've cheated." She couldn't blame him anymore. She couldn't outrun it. She had to face it head-on. The initial fear in Rod's eyes. Then the stricken look, the loss of expression, his innocent face growing drawn and tired, dulled to more pain. Tears. He pulled away.

Dear Father, what have I done? "Rod, I'm so sorry. I'm so, so sorry. I'll leave if you want me to."

"No, Chels. We'll figure this thing out."

13

Each couple seemed anxious to get back to the counseling room for their third day of searching for the missing pieces to their dilemmas. Rodney noticed that whenever Bob and Greg were in the room, everyone seemed to breathe easier. No matter what kind of terrifying scenario was playing itself out, if Bob and Greg were on the scene, it seemed as though everything was going to turn out okay.

Greg looked a bit sleepy but ready to start. "Hey, everybody. As I look around the room this morning, I can see a wide range of emotions—all clear signs of progress being made." *Progress! Is that what he calls it?* fumed Rodney.

Rodney had lain awake most of the night, weeping and fighting the truth of what his wife had shared. He couldn't believe how badly it hurt. In the first couple of days, he had been fascinated by the process Greg and Bob implemented along the way—how their means was itself the message. They created intimacy and often demonstrated the concepts they wanted their clients to learn. And yet . . . what did all this mean for him? Nothing! Right now he was so hurt he couldn't think straight. He had seen and learned so many things, but here they were on day three . . . and after sleeping alone again, the thought dawned on him: This most likely was the reality of the rest of his life.

Twenty minutes before the first light of dawn, he had dressed and gone outside into the dripping fog that wrapped around the Bradford House. A hoot owl had called across the morning stillness. Rodney wanted to pray, but he felt as betrayed by God as he'd been by his wife.

Now, in his opening prayer for the morning session, Greg asked all of them to open up their hearts and earnestly ask the Lord to make his presence known—not to be distant or indifferent but real, close, and present. After his prayer, he said, "I think I'll start the check-in today. I found myself praying a lot for each of you at different times of the night, and I'm excited about what God has in store for us today. Yesterday we spent serious time and energy learning how to take care of ourselves. Today I'm hoping we'll be able to focus on the second major step away from the Fear Dance: how to care for your mate and how best to assist on his or her journey. We have lots of great tools to help you love, encourage, support, honor, and come alongside your mate."

Rodney kind of zoned out as they went around the circle giving their updates. He was having trouble staying engaged, both from lack of sleep and from discouragement. He did note that Bob said something about the third day being especially important for those who felt as though they hadn't made much progress. Well, that sure applied to him and Chelsea.

He perked up a bit when it was Chelsea's turn to share. "Yesterday was quite a day for me," she said. "I had some incredible breakthroughs. Thank you, Becca, for your courage to tell it like it is." She got choked up and reached for a tissue. "I really appreciate everybody here." Rodney was glad she hadn't revealed any more. He was still reeling from her revelation last night; he wasn't ready for everyone to hear about it.

After everyone had shared, Bob addressed the whole group. "Who wants to work first this morning?"

❀ ❀ ❀

Victoria was surprised when Charles spoke up immediately.

"Dr. Smalley, I'd be interested in your help today. Victoria and I need help talking to each other. That is, of course, if Victoria is willing."

"Victoria, are you up for that?" Greg asked her.

"I believe so," she replied. Her scarf was too tight. She should have sat closer to the door.

"Victoria," Greg was saying, "I'm curious: When did things really change for you in the marriage?"

"Six years ago."

"And what happened?"

Victoria hadn't expected Greg to go right for her soul. But this was why they were here. If she was going to learn to swim, she had to get in the water. She quietly cleared her throat and took the plunge. "There was a terrible accident." She stroked her neck while she spoke. "Can you pass me a tissue, please? Thank you. . . . Little Isaac, our grandson, was riding his bicycle one Saturday afternoon and was hit by a car."

Victoria felt Charles grow rigid at hearing his recurring nightmare spoken of aloud.

"Charles became so caught up in his grief, he couldn't comfort me. I had to survive and heal on my own. It was then that we really started to disconnect—especially emotionally."

"Is that when you started becoming so independent?" Bob asked with great tenderness.

For the first time in a long while, Victoria felt she needed to establish physical contact with Charles. She reached out for his hand as if to anchor herself to her lifetime partner. "We were all overcome with grief. Then months of court trials followed.

Someone had to be strong for our son and his wife. Someone had to pray, someone had to hope, someone had to find meaning amid all the turmoil. Charles was undone. I had to set aside my own fears, questions, and anger and stand strong."

"I can't even imagine how terrible that must have been for your family."

She continued. "Charles is quiet by nature anyway, but he grew more and more silent and distant. We just survived one minute at a time, and then I sought out counsel and comfort from others—I had a strong community of women who surrounded me and held me together. I don't know what I would have done without them." Tears welled up, but she blinked them away. "Unlike Charles, I was able to process and grieve. . . . Anyway, here we are six years later. Our personal journeys are separated by a great distance."

"So where are you at in the marriage at this point?" Bob asked.

"I'm afraid that if my husband opens up, his needs will be so overwhelming I'll be bowled over. . . . I can't—I won't—try to fill all the roles and provide for him all the comfort that has been given me by my counselor, pastor, and community over this six-year period. I can't be all that for him, but I feel like he wants me to."

"Am I right in thinking it feels to you that Charles has a heavy door bolted and locked that is keeping a huge vacuum of relational need at bay?"

"Yes, that's it."

"Do you feel as if you have had any access to this part of Charles?"

"No, and I'm not sure I want to."

"Not knowing how to emotionally rally together around the horrible tragedy of your grandson's death has seriously crippled your marriage. I'm afraid that out of grave concern for Charles, as well as the need to protect yourself, you have given him license to remain distant. But at the same time you are hurt and frustrated by it."

"Yes." She continued holding Charles's arm.

"Victoria, how do you feel Charles feels about you?"

"Charles cares deeply for me, even when he can't express it well."

"Do you feel loved by him?"

"I know he loves me."

"I want you to be clear about the difference between 'I *know* he loves me' and 'I *feel* loved.' I hear you saying, 'He loves me,' but do you *feel* loved?"

For the first time, Victoria felt put on the spot. Pulling again at the neckline of her blouse, she whispered, "I don't know. I have never asked or expected my husband to make me feel loved."

"I think that you may be confusing yourself by making that assumption. Let me ask you this: How deeply do you feel Charles cares about your feelings?"

"I am afraid my feelings scare him. I am a strong and passionate person."

"I'd like to go one step further," Bob said. "How deeply do you feel Charles cares about your feelings, thoughts, ideas, and desires?"

Victoria was getting more and more uncomfortable. She was afraid her answer would betray Charles. "I . . . don't know."

He asked several times from different angles, allowing plenty of time for her to process, but this appeared to be a place where Victoria was stuck. She was having a difficult time verbalizing whether or not Charles cared about how she felt.

Finally Bob suggested, "I wonder if you have learned to edit your words before you say them, to the point that you are not only having trouble defining how you feel but also find yourself unable to say it aloud in front of him."

It was Greg's turn to ask a question. "Victoria, have you felt emotionally safe with Charles? In other words, have you felt that he handles your heart and emotions with genuine interest and care? That you can share your deepest feelings with him and feel as if it is extremely safe—that you won't regret it but instead will feel that it has drawn you closer to each other in the end? That your feelings aren't judged, minimized, ignored, or mishandled in any way?"

"No, I haven't. But in fairness to Charles, I don't think he knows how to handle anyone's feelings, including his own."

"Do you have a right to be loved?" Bob asked.

Without a moment's hesitation she responded, "Absolutely."

"Do you have a right to want it?"

"Yes."

"Do you have a right to ask for it?"

She paused. "Yes." She could tell her voice sounded a little more tentative.

"Do you ask for it?"

"No," she replied, dropping her gaze to the floor. "That's hard for me to do. It just doesn't seem . . . right, somehow."

"Wait a moment," Bob cut in. "We just had a fascinating exchange, and I want to play it back for you. Victoria, when I asked if you had a right to be loved, you didn't hesitate. In fact, it was the most animated I've seen you this morning. Emphatically, you said, 'Absolutely.' Then I asked, 'Do you have a right to want it?' Again your answer was a definitive yes. 'Do you have a right to ask for it?' You were a little more shy, but you still said yes. 'Do you ask for it?' 'No.'

"You believe you have a right to be loved and a right to want to be loved, but in the very next breath you said, in essence, 'But if I ask for love, it makes me selfish.'" He paused before continuing, "That makes me question whether you feel you have a right to ask Charles for it. You have placed judgment on it. It sounds like a part of you is convinced that wanting or asking Charles to love you is too selfish . . . yet you will allow yourself to be loved by others."

The proverbial pot had been stirred, and Victoria could not stay seated a second longer. With her shoulders bunched up to her ears, she felt constricted and cornered. "Excuse me for a moment. I need some air." Blinking back tears, she walked over to the door and inhaled deeply. She could sense that behind her no one was moving. Turning back toward the group, her eyes were brimming.

"I don't ever tell Charles's story; I made a promise to protect his privacy." She inhaled deeply through her nose. She looked straight at Charles. He gave a subtle shake of his head. But Victoria pressed on. "I've just realized that though we are on separate journeys, this is where our paths converge. This part of his story is also mine. I just wasn't able to acknowledge it until now."

She drew in a shaky breath. "You see that scar across Charles's left cheek?" No one dared look. "While I was out getting groceries one day, my husband stayed home with our three grandchildren. The kids were all out playing, and little Isaac, three years old, was pealing around the driveway and sidewalks on his tricycle. In the blink of an eye, he rode right out into the street." She covered her face and tried to compose herself and then continued, "Charles ran and threw himself in front of the oncoming car trying to save our precious boy. . . . Our grandbaby died on impact, and Charles was hurt very badly." Her voice cracked, but she grew louder, desperate to get her terrible secret out in the open. "But this—this mark on his face, the scars on his back and shoulder are nothing in comparison to the scar across his heart." More quietly she added, "I don't think his heart will ever beat the same again. No, I—" she bit her bottom lip—"I don't have the right to ask him for more love."

A pained hush fell over the room. Ryan and Becca had locked themselves together in a tight grip. Chelsea and Rodney both had wet cheeks; the only person with dry eyes was Todd—and he was blinking repeatedly.

Greg got up. Leaving the door open for her comfort, he helped Victoria back to the chair where he had been sitting, closest to the door.

Charles sat stock-still in his seat. He stared straight ahead, breathing steadily, giving no sign of any real emotion.

"Charles, are you all right?" Greg asked with great sensitivity.

"I have no doubt of your honor or loyalty toward one another. Nothing needs to change there. What we have here is a breakdown in communication. We will continue when we know your heart is being attended to. We need to be sure everyone is well cared for along the way."

Charles had the most profound look of sadness, Victoria thought. "Thank you. I want to continue."

Bob explained that he would like to come back to Charles in a moment, but he didn't want to leave the place yet where they were dealing with Victoria's heart.

"It sounds to me like your heart has been hurt so profoundly that it has jagged scars too, Victoria," he said. "You've received good care from the outside—from friends and your church—but you have not allowed Charles to see either your pain or your healing. Being the strong matriarch, you've tried to be strong for everyone else—you've focused on helping them heal. Maybe you've felt that this part of your shared space has died, but if there's a little corner that can keep beating, you've got to allow it to live. You don't feel it is okay to ask for love from Charles, and in its absence, you have learned to live without it.

"You knew how to receive love from other sources because you are a survivor—it's in your genes. You come from a line of strong women; you know you've got to live. And even though you don't blame Charles for failing to meet your needs, I'm guessing you're a little frustrated that he hasn't taken initiative for his own healing. Taking all these things into consideration, you most likely have adopted a position that goes something like this: 'If I'm not going to feel loved and cared for by you, fine. But I am not going to cater to what you want, and I'm certainly not going to put out. Furthermore, I am not going to be real clear with you about what I really do want.'"

Bob paused for a moment.

"You are ultimately the judge on this, Victoria. So, as you think about that, what is going on in your mind?"

"I feel exposed but understood." A gentle pause followed.

"Let me ask you something, Charles," Greg said. "What did you make of what we were just talking about?"

Charles was accustomed to weighing his words for impact, and Victoria knew he would not be at all intimidated about taking as much time as he needed to answer. "I became caught up in dealing with my grief and . . . guilt . . . privately." He touched his scar briefly with a long, dark finger. "I thought it was the kindest thing I could do. While trying to protect my wife, I locked her out."

"You got it."

"I haven't tended to her well." His chin dropped slightly. "It's no wonder she doesn't want to be with me. Not only have I let down my grandson and my family, I've let down my wife, too." He closed his eyes and opened his palms. "I want to know what I can do to make it right."

"Mhmm. I hear the depth of your love for your wife and your family. But it's interesting where you went with that. You took what she was saying and turned it into an action step—a fix-it. I'm wondering if, instead, you could focus on her heart?"

Charles folded his arms then. "I don't understand."

"You've had a lot going on, and I don't want to minimize any of it. But in regard to your marriage as a whole—both before and after the accident—you said, 'This is what she needs from me, and this is what I need to do.' You want to do whatever it takes for her to be 'fine.'

"When Victoria is emotional, it appears to make you feel very uneasy. It doesn't look like you know what to do with her heart, much less your own. You've worked hard in your marriage to honor your wife, but have you honored her feelings?"

Bob reached for the little white teddy bear sitting on the end table and held it out, cradled in his hands. "If this is her heart, have you handled it as if it were a priceless, precious work of art? Remember the definition of trustworthiness: When you have access to the part of another human being that is of infinite worth and value, particularly their heart, you demonstrate through word and deed that you fully comprehend how valuable and vulnerable it is, and you treat that person and their heart accordingly."

"Honestly, Dr. Paul, I've never given it much thought. I always attempted to respect Victoria, but I've never thought feelings were that important. Truth is important; reason is important; righteousness is important."

"You are describing the mind: truth, reason, righteousness. But we are talking about the heart," Greg encouraged. "Victoria knows that and feels that. So it doesn't feel to her as if you truly and deeply care about how she feels. Therefore, she *knows* that you love her, but she doesn't *feel* loved.

"While we've been talking, it seems to me this very important part has been missing. I honestly did not get from your earlier description of the marriage any sense of your heart. I didn't hear your words speak of truly caring for her. I know you love her, but what you were primarily talking about was your frustration and disappointment with how hard you tried to do all these things and why it didn't work. You had all the right things in place, and you were handling them fairly well.

"In fact, you've even respected one another's differences, but undeniably, there are walls up that are making you both very lonely . . . with little or no intimacy. Your wife does not feel emotionally safe, and apparently, Charles, neither do you."

"What makes you say that?" Charles asked. Victoria was curious too.

"Do you share your deepest feelings with Victoria?"

"No, I don't share them with anyone."

"Why not?"

"Because there is no reason to talk about those things. It's unnecessary, and I don't see the point."

"Yet you both feel disconnected and unloved. Isn't that true? I've got a hunch the two may be connected."

"Dr. Paul, I want to learn to do a better job of caring for my wife's feelings, because I want her to feel loved. But I can handle my own emotions just fine."

"Charles, how do you really feel about Victoria . . . down deep?"

Charles paused for a moment, during which Victoria pondered their dialogue. Bob was good. He must have known Charles could hold firm with anyone, but when it came to her, he became melted butter. He softened. With all rationale set aside, he said words that brought fresh tears to her eyes. "I love her . . . deeply."

"And what do you want from your marriage? What do you want the experience to be like with Victoria? If we lived in an ideal world, what would you want it to be like?"

"I want to feel close to her again," he said in almost a whisper.

"I believe you. Do you only want it to be a one-way street, with you feeling close to her, but Victoria not feeling close to you?"

"No."

"Okay, so you learn to care for her heart, and she feels great about that and feels deeply loved by you. But she feels shut out of your heart and, therefore, is only able to love you from a distance. That doesn't work well. Real intimacy is an experience where two people with open hearts share who they are with each other. Remember, intimacy is a connecting of hearts. Deep intimacy involves sharing our feelings, hurts, fears, joys, passions, dreams, etc. It may include talking, but it doesn't always have to. The one thing it does always require, however, is openness—and that's the rub.

"The moment you truly open your heart to another person, you become vulnerable. That's what makes it feel so risky. But that's also what makes it compelling and powerful. It is wonderful to be able to feel genuinely loved by another, but it is incredible to be given the opportunity to deeply love and care for another and to be allowed to really know them. Without intending to, I think you may be cheating Victoria out of both."

When Charles turned to look at Victoria, she saw something

she hadn't seen in a long time: the affectionate expression Charles once gave to a vulnerable young girl he'd fallen in love with many years before. Beyond any hidden motive, she could see that he really did want to feel close to her again.

"I don't know what to expect, Dr. Paul. I don't feel much of anything anymore, other than frustrated and depressed."

Bob stroked his beard.

"Your heart has undergone some serious scarring, but more important, I think your heart has been held captive. The good news is Jesus came to set captives free. It says in Isaiah 61:1 that the promised Messiah would come not only to save us but to heal our broken hearts. Rather than doing or fixing or debating, I recommend focusing your time and attention on creating safety together. Instead of trying to pry your heart open, work to become trustworthy and safe with yourself and with her, and she can do likewise. I guarantee that the opening up at that point will be fabulous." He broke into a contagious smile.

Then he added, as if it was an afterthought, "It's interesting to me that both you and Victoria fear the same thing in you, Charles: that somehow your pain and grief is too deep to overcome. I wonder if there's stuff from your past that is complicating things for you—maybe even beliefs you have about feelings. You may want to explore those areas at some point like Rodney did. But for now, let's not worry about those other chambers of your heart. Let's just work on helping you two connect a little easier.

"The first step in being able to effectively communicate with each other in a way that allows your marriage to flourish—" Bob looked right at Charles—"is to take the time to deeply and completely understand both how your wife perceives the situation and how she feels about it. And above all else, *care about* what she is feeling. That is the *care* in caring for your mate. Are you open to really hearing your wife's heart in order to deeply understand how she feels and what has been going on for her?"

"Yes, I am." He looked straight at the counselor as if gathering his courage together and sighed. "Okay, Dr. Paul, teach me how to do this."

"Do you want to know one particularly nasty myth that keeps many people from experiencing the tremendous benefits of effective communication? Somewhere along the way, we have come to believe that real communication occurs when we understand the other person's words. We equate this with accurately noting the words and phrases we hear.

"But in fact, good communication is more than that. In an intimate relationship, emotional communication—or what we call Heart Talk—usually does not occur until each partner understands the feelings that underlie the spoken words. People generally feel more understood, cared for, and connected when their dialogue focuses on their emotions and feelings rather than merely on their words or thoughts.

"Charles, keep in mind that our primary goal as Victoria continues is to truly understand her feelings."

Charles nodded his agreement, and Bob continued, "In this process it is imperative for you to help Victoria express what she is feeling so she will feel understood by you. In order to accomplish this, we need to explain the process of Heart Talk."

A TALK WITH THE DOCTORS

Heart Talk

When two people are in conflict, they often point to their differences as the problem. However, their differences are not the source of their problem. Differences are actually a blessing in a marriage when you know how to deal with them and discover your loved one's unique way of looking at life—the passions and feelings behind his or her perspective. We must go beyond understanding the spoken words to grasping the emotional nugget underlying the words.

To show that you truly care, you must listen for the emotions beneath the words—listen to the other's heart with your heart. There you will find the core of his or her concern. A lot of people remain stuck in the Fear Dance at precisely this point. They tend to use "work" words in order to be productive or "thought" words about their actions, instead of speaking from the heart and talking about their feelings or deepest concerns. They remain stuck until they finally learn to look for the emotional nugget behind the words. They free themselves only when they discover how to go beyond the expressed thoughts and opinions to get to the underlying feelings.

When we work to uncover the emotional nugget, we can finally say to our family member, friend, or partner, "I care how you feel. Your feelings matter to me." And when our loved ones get this message, they will feel deeply cared for. That's when they feel loved. On the other hand, when we don't relay this message, true communication grinds to a halt.

A lot of us struggle with this skill. We tend to think linearly: We cut to the chase, get to the bottom line. We want to solve a problem and complete a task, not deal with emotions. We want only to figure out how to "fix it."

Without listening for and responding to the emotions, however, all the problem solving in the world won't get us to the real problem. Only when we understand the feelings involved can we effectively start the task of problem solving. In addition to trying to "fix" problems, several other things are a complete waste of time if we focus on them during an argument.

Let's take a little quiz. When you find yourself in a conflict with someone, how much of your conversation includes questions such as the following?

- Who is right? Who is wrong?
- Whose fault is this mess? Who's to blame?
- What really happened here?
- How can we solve it or fix the problem?

At least 90 percent of the people who come to us for marital help begin their sessions by asking exactly these questions. They believe that if they can establish who's right and what happened, they will improve their relationship.

But you know what? If that's where they remain stuck, they rarely ever do.

When we focus—at least, as a place to start—on trying to determine who is right and who is wrong, we embark on a totally useless pursuit. Starting anywhere other than attending to the emotions will end in derailment most of the time. When we begin by attempting to figure out who is to blame or what really happened, we succeed only in fueling power struggles and hurtful disagreements.

Heart Talk (aka emotional communication), which is focused on connecting and caring for one's relationships, stands in sharp contrast to Work Talk. Work Talk is something we do at work, wherein we are communicating simply for productivity and reaching a predetermined outcome.

On the other hand, Heart Talk comes down to listening and speaking with hearts open. Here, the focus is on how the person is feeling. We recommend using five simple steps:

- Make safety the first priority.
- Listen to the words the speaker is saying.
- Listen with your heart.
- Reflect back to the speaker what you hear him or her saying.
- Allow the other's emotions to touch you.

(See appendix B for more detailed explanations of these steps and more information about Heart Talk.)

As Bob explained the steps of Heart Talk, Greg diagrammed them on the whiteboard for the group.

HEART TALK
GOAL: Caring, not resolving!

Speaker

1. Focus is on myself.
   · Who am I focused on? Me
2. Talk about my heart—
   feelings, emotions, buttons,
   fears, wants/desires.
   · What am I talking about?
   My feelings

Listener

1. Repeat back what my spouse
   says.
   · No judgment—curiosity
   · Who am I focused on? Them
2. Focus on their heart—
   buttons, feelings, emotions,
   wants, etc.
   · What am I repeating back?
   Their feelings
   · Allow their words to impact
   me—let their feelings touch
   my heart.

KEY: Manage your buttons when they get pushed!

Bob asked, "Victoria, would you share with Charles first?"

She took a breath, her hand gripping the arm of the chair.

"Remember, Charles, your job is to focus on your wife's heart and repeat back what you hear her saying."

Victoria pried her fingers from around the chair and moved toward her husband. She didn't feel at all comfortable with the exercise, but she decided to give it a chance. She and her husband sat face-to-face, about to share their hearts.

Victoria started. "I . . . I've been thinking a lot about this lately. Early in our marriage, I saw myself as your assistant." She looked back at Bob with a need to explain. "That's how women were viewed when we first got married, even those of us who were well educated at some of the best girls' schools available. We were primarily trained to be receptionists, secretaries, and homemakers. For the most part, we looked pretty and held little sway with our husbands' professional decisions. I came through the hippie era and the women's rights movement, but I never got involved with any of it; I was a society girl." She clasped her hands and twisted her wedding ring. "We thought we were above all that."

"Victoria," Greg jumped in, "you're doing great. Go ahead and speak directly to Charles. You may want to give him bite-size pieces so he can repeat back what you share." Then to Charles he said, "Try it. Repeat back what you heard."

Charles looked at her. "So you saw me as the leader, and your role was more about figuring out how to be a follower."

She tilted her head. "To some degree, yes. But when you were away at work, home was my territory. I was the leader there."

She had earned a degree in English literature, and her opinions had always been appreciated by her social committees and her friends. She was well read on a wide variety of topics. She and Charles had spent many evenings reading together, but they rarely shared what they were reading.

". . . I tried to discuss topics with you in the earlier years, but it seemed that you would always retort with something to the effect of, 'You're not saying it correctly, Victoria,' or 'Your opinion is too shortsighted—you can't think that way. . . .' Then the lecture would start. And then I would be silent . . . with you, anyway."

"Charles," Greg inquired, "I'm wondering if some of your buttons just got pushed? You look pretty distant right now."

"Yes."

"Which button got pushed?" Greg prompted.

"I'm feeling like a failure."

"Now that you've identified the feeling, ask yourself what you need in this moment."

Charles thought about it for a few seconds. "I want to know if I've really been a failure all these years."

"Charles, can God provide comfort to you right now?" Greg asked.

"Yes."

"Why don't you quietly take a few minutes with him right now and ask him to join you in comforting yourself. You may also want to ask him what is true about you. Whether you are a failure or not."

Greg addressed the group while Charles closed his eyes. "This is why I wrote at the bottom of the board that the key to Heart Talk is to manage your buttons when they get pushed. As you attempt to do Heart Talk, be aware that your buttons are going to get pushed along the way. No big deal! When your fear buttons get triggered, simply take a few moments and take care of yourself so that your heart remains available to keep caring for your mate. If you don't, your heart will close and the process will shut down. Then both people walk away feeling hurt and frustrated."

"I'd like to try again," Charles said after a few minutes. He turned back to his wife. "V, I think I heard you say that our home was your territory and that you were the leader there. It sounds like you feel hurt that I didn't appreciate your opinions. I hear you saying that you tried to discuss topics in the earlier years, but I would correct you and lecture you." Charles added, "I'm sure that was painful."

Tears welled up in Victoria's eyes.

"Charles, great job of allowing her feelings to touch your heart and impact you," Bob affirmed.

Charles continued, "Can you tell me how that made you feel?"

"It stung. I felt unimportant, so I'd close up. There were plenty of other friends and acquaintances in my life who could appreciate me and my point of view. I resented you at times, but I never really lost my sense of self. My mother had instilled in me a wonderful belief about who I am. But it certainly became harder over the years to acknowledge my value to you."

"I hear you saying that you didn't feel valued by me."

"No . . ." Victoria thought about it. "I felt you valued me in the roles you wanted to see me in."

"It sounds as if you felt I didn't take the time to understand

and care about how you felt. Like this was just the way things were supposed to be."

"Yes."

"You guys are doing a great job," Bob encouraged.

Turning back to Charles, Greg said, "It appears that you have recently discovered that after many years, your wife has some different opinions, tastes, and goals from you. Is that right?"

"Yes."

"Typically, this kind of deal feels threatening—and chances are, you don't know exactly what to do with it. Your first reaction has always been to debate and try to convince your wife that your view is the right one. When that didn't work, you began to resent the differences and pull away.

"I remember when Erin didn't want to share her feelings with me. Looking back now, I understand what was going on. Because I was so disconnected and detached from my heart, I felt incredibly uncomfortable with feelings—hers and mine. I didn't know what to do with feelings in general. So I'd try to make her feel better—happier. I would try to fix the problem by asking all kinds of questions to try to make sense of what she was saying, but it's really difficult to try to use the brain with matters of the heart.

"I would tell her that her feelings didn't make sense. She really loved it when I said that! Finally, I would ignore her feelings or minimize them. Whatever I did, the point was that I didn't know how to deal with heart issues—feelings and emotions. Not only was this killing our marriage, but it caused Erin to disconnect from me—which makes sense. I didn't accept or care for that part of her—a very important part of her. The bottom line was that our hearts were not connecting.

"Charles, it seems that you aren't quite sure what to do with Victoria's heart, so your tendency is to debate and argue with her. Is that true?"

"Yes, I would say that is accurate."

"What would keep you from taking the time to understand

your wife? We are not talking about positions; we are talking about feelings. Somewhere in there, her feelings get run over while you're trolling for facts.

"I am suggesting that when the debate begins, it's much easier to try to determine right or wrong than to listen and feel—especially after spending much of your life in the courtroom. But as soon as that judgment takes place, in that moment, you are not caring about her feelings. Your productivity or problem-solving skills take precedence over feelings, and what gets lost in all this is the heart.

"It's my guess that you are a significant force to contend with. I am certain your personality is every bit as strong as hers. But I'm not too concerned about any of that right now. I just want to ask you an important question."

He let a moment of silence punctuate what he was about to say.

"Who is the expert on Victoria's heart?"

At this, Charles flashed a quick, white smile. "Victoria."

"So whose student will you be?"

"Victoria's." At this epiphany, he laughed a contagious laugh, and his whole face lit up. Everyone joined in. Delightful.

"Let me give you a starting place," Greg went on. "I would say that at this point, you probably don't have an adequate knowledge base for understanding the issues of her heart. And your tools may not prove to be too effective in that area either. I want to encourage you to be patient in applying the skills you already have to the task, because you may be using a hammer when a hammer is not the right tool. . . . There may be a way she can be a valuable resource for you to get the knowledge you need. You may even learn some new skills that you don't have yet. Are you game?"

"Yes sir, I am."

The whole room seemed to sigh.

Victoria knew she was beaming.

"Charles, look at your wife," Greg said.

He did. And he looked at her as if he were seeing her for the first time.

14

WEDNESDAY, NOON

Ryan hung back as everyone else bounded up the stairs toward the dining room. "Greg, do you mind if I talk to you alone for a minute?"

The morning sessions had ended, and the mood was light. Everyone was ready for the lunch break.

"I'll keep it quick," he promised.

They stepped out into the springtime air. With his hands shoved deep into the front pocket of his sweatshirt, Ryan shivered. "Greg, I know this is my chance. The other couples are proof that I can still have hope of getting it together. I also know that if I don't deal with some of my own stuff—quick—I'm going to lose big time. It's like I see myself stuck headlong in a sandbar. Believe me, nothing in me wants to wade out and start digging, but I need to be free."

"What's up, Ryan?" Greg asked.

The truth needed to be spoken before he chickened out and said something moronic as a cover-up. "I . . . um . . . the affair isn't quite off." There was no turning back now. "I've been involved with this other woman, and—and I want to break it off, but it hasn't been easy." Instead of sounding laid back and casual as he was trying to, his words were tripping over each other. "Honestly, it's hard for me to believe God would create me with this incredible sex drive and then give me this . . . this 'family package.' It's no wonder men have had sex on the side since the beginning of time. Becca's and my sex drives just don't line up anymore. I can't expect her to fulfill this need I have. It's not fair; she can't do it.

"But I don't want to hurt her anymore either. No matter what I do, I hurt her. I care about her, but honestly . . ." Ryan swallowed hard. "I haven't really admitted this to anyone, but I'm not sure I'm in love with Becca anymore." He bounced nervously in place.

"Ryan," Greg replied, "I hear you're really struggling with whether or not you love your wife."

"Yes."

"Would you like some relief?"

"Yes!"

"I often hear people say, 'I don't feel in love with my mate anymore.' Now, as a marriage counselor, I kind of just let that go. It's not real important."

"What?" Ryan asked. "How can you let that go? Not feeling in love with your wife is a huge problem!"

"It's not that I ignore the fact that someone doesn't feel 'love' for the other person; instead, I challenge their beliefs about love and its origins. Let's talk more about this in the next session. I think this is some pretty important stuff that the others will want to hear."

Oh, great, Ryan thought. Now what had he done?

❂ ❂ ❂

Victoria and Charles went for a brief stroll on the deck after lunch. "Hard morning, love?" Charles asked.

"Not as bad as I thought. Oh, Charles, I was so afraid you'd feel betrayed when I spoke about Isaac."

"I appreciated your courage in there."

"Oh?" She stopped. She had thought he'd be angry at her for revealing so much.

The pattern of arguing was so ingrained in Charles. She noticed he almost started to debate again. With visible determination, he softened his tone and looked into her eyes. "Our story needed to be told, V. Somehow, it doesn't hold such power over me after it's been spoken out loud. This morning was definitely the time and the place. Thank you."

Victoria breathed a deep sigh. "Those kids felt your pain, Charles."

"And yours," he said definitively but as gently as he could.

"Yes, ours."

"I'm so sorry I've locked you out, my dear," Charles said. "It kills me to think about all you endured." She loved how he held her hand loosely while they ducked under a low tree branch. "How could I have not seen it?"

"I looked fine, made certain you never saw my grief. Never did I intend to be dishonest, but I guess . . . I was," Victoria reflected. "I didn't think you could handle my emotions. I had such rage at times, I frightened myself."

She picked up a fallen branch and looked at its knobby bark. "I'm still trying to make sense of it all." The necessary steps away from their disjointed marriage dance were becoming more and more visible, especially after watching other couples dance through their dialogues. "It was time for us to roll up our sleeves and really give it a try."

From day one of the Intensive, the Templetons had watched their counselors demonstrate the remarkable process of Heart Talk with each of their clients. Victoria would never forget Bob's dialogue with Chelsea on that first morning when she was so frightened and didn't want to stay. With fascination, she and

Charles recalled together the unmistakable care with which Bob and Greg had listened to each person and reflected back what they thought they heard without getting caught on the words themselves.

Their sole purpose in communicating was to create a safe place wherein the others could open up and speak their hearts. This explained how Bob could remain unruffled by some of Todd's angry outbursts and Becca's accusations, why he wasn't put on the defensive. The best part was that his approach was so effective that even Charles was put at ease. Victoria hoped that someday she would be so graceful with the man she loved.

"No one is born knowing how to communicate effectively; this is something we must learn and improve as we go through life," Greg had said. *"Even after being married thirty-two years, you can be successful at learning how to tenderly care for your mate through listening!"* He said it so confidently that Victoria believed him. And that was exactly what Bob and Greg had walked them through. They had taken Charles and Victoria through each of the steps of Heart Talk so they could learn it themselves and practice until they got it right.

"You did a fine job, Charles, of listening to my heart in there," she said.

"I think I could listen better if I could lay my ear right next to your heart," he said with a coy smile.

Victoria wasn't the touchy-feely type and would have to reckon with how their physical affection fit into the picture of their future. She would have to speak honestly about it, without just stuffing her feelings inside to please Charles and then later resenting it. She would deal with all that another time.

Standing behind his wife, Charles slid his arms around her waist as she stood looking out over the trees still cloaked with mist. "I really do love you, Victoria Templeton, and I care about you, your feelings, your dreams. . . ." They hadn't kissed since before Christmas—not a proper kiss—and Victoria didn't want to mess this one up. In their tight embrace she felt his body communicate his unspoken request. Her heart did double time. She was glad he couldn't see her face.

Charles must have felt her stiffen, because he took his arms away and pretended to be preoccupied with the button on his sleeve. Victoria spun around playfully, holding her stick like a sword, hoping to compensate for her self-consciousness. "Do you have a wheelbarrow, darling?" She looked up at him, her smile tinged with a plea for space.

Her jovial question caught him off guard. With eyebrows raised, a smile crept across his face. He knew she was playing for time. But he understood why and no longer resented it.

"I've got a few bricks I need to remove from that wall around my heart. It may take a little time, but I think it's a project we can do together," she said, propping the small limb against the trunk of a dogwood tree.

Playing at their recent lesson in Heart Talk, he reflected back, "If I'm hearing you right, you're saying my wheelbarrow and I are invited for a visit, but I should leave my bulldozer at home. . . . How does that make you feel?"

She laughed at his silliness and pulled him close. For the first time in months, she wanted him. "A bit feverish and weak in the knees, actually."

"Isn't that something? I feel it too!" He went limp and laughed while nuzzling her neck. "Just watch where you're throwing those bricks."

She liked this new gentle flirting. Her man had initiated, but with an open invitation rather than expectation.

"Oh, my sweet darling." Their kiss was long and sweet.

"Would you like to see my room, Mr. Templeton?" she whispered as if it were off-limits.

"Why, Victoria . . ." He searched her soft brown eyes. "I'd love to."

✧ ✧ ✧

WEDNESDAY, 2:10 P.M.

The afternoon session was already underway, and everyone acted as if they didn't notice Victoria and Charles slipping into their seats twenty minutes late. Becca thought they were adorable—like two naughty children sneaking into Sunday school. Victoria no longer wore her cashmere shell, and she looked suspiciously rumpled.

Becca tried to turn her attention back to the task at hand. It appeared that during the lunch break, her husband had pulled Greg aside and, after chatting for a bit, had requested to work next. She was flabbergasted but promised herself and God she would remain quiet. She had no idea where this session would go.

Greg's voice broke into her thoughts. "Ryan, I said we'd come back and talk about love's origin. Let me ask you a question: Where does love come from—where does love actually originate?"

"I'm not sure. I've never really thought about that." Her husband shrugged.

"I had never thought about that question either, until I realized that there were times in my marriage—when Erin and I were completely into our Fear Dance—that I did not in that moment feel 'in love' with my wife. And it scared me! That is, until I understood where love comes from. Then I felt relief. After thinking about it for a minute or two, do you know where love comes from?"

"I imagine the right answer is *God*."

"That's right. But we easily lose sight of this truth. Instead we start to assume all sorts of other stuff. People tend to think love is magical or that they have the ability to crank up the old love generator and create love. Love is not about chemistry. That's just a fantasy."

Greg continued, "When we don't feel love for our spouse, we

tend to put enormous pressure on ourselves to somehow create love for our mate. And when we fail to feel love, we easily become convinced that there is something wrong with us, because we are incapable of generating love, or there is something wrong with our mate—that he or she is unlovable, or there is something wrong with the marriage itself.

"In reality, there is no love that comes from us. We are not the originators. God is. It says in 1 John 4:7-8 that love comes from God and that God is love! In verse 19 it goes on to say that we love because God first loved us.

"Ultimately, you've got to ask yourself what is true of you. Are you a man of love? Let me ask you, Ryan, are you a follower of Christ?"

"I want to be, even though I screw it up all the time. I've made a commitment to believe in him, if that's what you mean."

"If you have given your life to him, his Spirit is within you. Is this true for you?"

"Yes, I . . . I think so. If he'll still have me."

"Do you want to love other people the way God loves us?"

Ryan looked hesitant about committing to something he might not be able to pull off. "Yeah. I mean, I want to."

A TALK WITH THE DOCTORS

God Is Love

We do not generate a single drop of love. It all comes from God. By receiving God, we receive his love. We can then open our heart and share it with others. Love feels good to us, but we are just passing it through from God to others. And by making a conscious decision, we can pass love through to our spouse.

When people say they no longer feel love for their spouse, we assume they have the door to their heart closed for some reason or another to prevent the flow of love. This is the common link in almost every Intensive couple we see—that individuals have lost "heart."

They are completely disconnected from their heart—especially their emotions. We find people who exist in a black-and-white world—their hearts are closed or shut down. They don't "feel" life; they rationalize or numb themselves to life and to their hearts. Here are other words people use to describe a dead heart:

- Detached
- Indifferent
- Numb
- Lifeless
- Heartless
- Alone
- Emotionally unavailable
- Hard-hearted

Here is the key. We do not make the issue about how to love our spouse. Since we do not have any ability to create love, we instead focus on the state of the heart. The real question becomes, "Is my heart open or closed to my spouse?" If our heart is closed, then God's love does not come from him, through us, to our spouse. And we don't feel "in love."

If our heart is closed, then we have shut out God's love. This is what is actually happening when we do not feel love for our spouse. We have simply closed our heart to our mate (often for good reasons). We must discover why the door to our heart is closed before we can open it up again.

The final step is to ask God to allow us to see our spouse through his eyes and to feel what he feels for him or her. When we can see the things God values and cherishes in our spouse and feel the love he feels, our heart becomes open and full. Loving our spouse is easy and relatively effortless from there.

"Ryan, has anyone ever accused you of being emotionally unavailable, indifferent, numb, or heartless?" Greg asked.

Becca couldn't help nodding. This was wonderful stuff.

"Absolutely," Ryan said. "My wife has said that about me. And quite frankly, it's true. That's how I am."

"Do you see, then, that your feelings toward your wife—or lack thereof—are not about love?"

"I'm not sure, but I think so." His eyes were unreadable.

"Since you can't create love," Greg went on, "I suggest that instead you focus on your heart. The real question I'd encourage you to ask yourself is this: Is my heart open or closed to Becca? If your heart is closed to her, there's no way you can feel 'in love.'"

"I know I look like an insensitive jerk, so I guess it's still closed."

"I'm guessing you feel like a jerk, and that is what bothers you," said Bob bluntly. Becca felt like cheering him on. Maybe Ryan would actually listen to the experts. Bob went on, "You don't like looking like a jerk, so you've become this other person, a person who is trying to please everyone around you. But you do so at a great expense."

Greg stepped in again. "Can you tell us what led up to that moment when you started shutting down? You weren't born this way, so there may be a situation or a series of events that marks the closing of your heart."

Becca wondered too. Had her husband ever been in touch with his emotions enough to know such a thing? She watched as he shook his head, as if trying to physically jar something loose in his brain. But his next words surprised her.

"Nothing makes the memory go away—not lifting weights at the gym, not sailing, not sex. . . . Nothing will erase what happened. . . . Nothing can change the fact that my silence killed a mother and her unborn twin girls!

"At first, nothing about the young mother stood out. Her name was—" Ryan choked up a little—"Lisa. Although she was a typical ob-gyn patient at first, something about her caught my attention. Her eyes seemed distant, like she was removed from her situation. But it wasn't as if she was a teenage mother or low income. She was beautiful and lived in an affluent area of Newport."

Ryan tried to explain how something about Lisa had caused him to care more than he usually would. He told how he rationalized that it must be because she was carrying twin girls. Becca had her own theory.

"At first, she tried to explain away the bruises. 'I'm just clumsy, Dr. Stuart. Don't worry.' But I did worry."

Ryan locked his gaze on Greg's paper-clip figurines and narrated the story without emotion. "Toward the beginning of Lisa's third trimester, I definitely noticed a change. The bruises got bigger, and Lisa seemed to be in a deep, dark fog. I even prescribed Prozac for depression and encouraged her to talk to someone about her feelings."

Imagine that, Dr. Stuart encouraging someone to visit a shrink! Becca thought. *Will wonders never cease?* How much was there about this man that she didn't know?

Ryan shared that he would never forget Lisa's last visit to the clinic. She had several terrible bruises, this time on her face. Again she justified them by saying she'd banged into the side of the crib as she was setting it up. Ryan confronted her directly that day about not being able to get those kinds of injuries from a crib and asked again if she'd gone to see Dr. Oliver at the women's clinic. "I thought I'd done all the right things, but I should have reported my suspicions. . . . Those precious baby girls . . ." His voice trailed off, as though he'd gotten lost in his thoughts.

"It was only a few hours later, that same day, that my nurse buzzed to say there was an emergency and that I was needed in the ER immediately. In my gut, I knew it was Lisa, but I never could have anticipated all three of them."

"What do you mean 'all three'? What happened?" Becca

blurted before she knew what she was saying. She could see that Ryan could barely breathe. He looked as if he might throw up.

"Her rich boyfriend had beat her up pretty bad. She was ultimately pushed down a flight of stairs. The cause of death may have been from injuries sustained during the assault, but more likely it was the fall. She had head injuries and multiple internal injuries. She had dissection of major thoracic and abdominal vessels, liver and splenic lacerations, multiple extremity and pelvic fractures. He did a number on her. I can't believe no one suspected this was going on. They found some old bruises and tissue damage too."

"The babies . . ." Becca prompted.

"The twin girls," Ryan went on, "most likely died from maternal death. But we also found placental abruption . . . and several skull fractures."

Becca held her wad of tissues to her mouth as tears flowed down her cheeks. She never knew. Why hadn't he told her? But she knew the answer. There were so many sad stories at the hospital, and Ryan never liked to speak of them at home.

"Ryan . . ." Bob's voice brought this latest chapter of the nightmare to an end. "You said that when you realized that there was nothing you could do to help save Lisa and her baby girls, that's when you started shutting down. And I'm guessing that's about the same time you started getting reckless and having sexual exploits. Have you ever pieced these events together?"

"I'm not sure," he said in a deadpan voice.

"I want to talk about that for a moment. I wonder if you can go back to that experience. Take yourself forward frame by frame, if you can," Bob coached. "I know it's painful. Be gentle, and let us know if it's too much. Ask yourself what you were feeling during that time. Notice the subtle things that were going on."

Ryan leaned with his elbows on his knees and looked down at the floor. Becca didn't want her husband to have to experience this all over again. Having been an RN, she knew how quickly the replays came in one's mind: the cold sweat, the sirens, the split-second decisions—and this time it had all gone wrong, all wrong. . . . She could imagine the panic that had played over and over in Ryan's mind . . . all alone . . . the horrific details . . . and all the while she had no idea of what he was experiencing.

His face hardened. "I was absolutely overwhelmed. All my education, my training, my prayers . . . everything had failed. I not only lost a patient but her children, too. A mother and her two tiny girls were pronounced dead at 3:02 p.m. on a Thursday afternoon." He continued to stare, noticeably disconnected from all of it. "The only control I had was deciding what time to record on their death certificates. I knew I would go home that night and hold my own wife and daughters. Before I could tell the family— Lisa's mother and father—I lost it. Don't you see? They were left with *nothing*."

He held his jaw, unyielding. "I had no choice but to carry on. But I couldn't care. I didn't care about anything. I could not turn my concern on and shut it off. Life lost its meaning for me that day. Three eternal beings had slipped through my fingers. We physicians are taught to deal with death, and I've seen other deaths since then. But that day it hit too close to home."

"What was it about what happened that was close to home?" Bob asked.

"The babies . . . the girls . . . their beautiful mother. . . . I shut down. I don't know, since then I just don't care."

"Ryan, I'd like you to repeat what you just said, only more slowly," said Bob.

He looked puzzled. "I . . . don't . . . care."

"Is it that you don't care, or is it that you have closed yourself off and have become detached from your heart?"

"I don't know, probably the latter. But I didn't dare start drinking or abusing drugs or doing anything that could alter my precision as a physician. I had a family to support." He gave a sick laugh.

Ryan was finished. He stood and took a swig from his water

bottle. The bottle crackled as it imploded from his sucking the water through the opening. Throwing it down, he stalked out of the room.

Becca sat with her feet tucked underneath her, not uttering a sound except for her quiet sniffling. The room was silent.

In response to several concerned expressions, Greg said, "Ryan's going to be okay. Earlier today he and I talked about what's going on in his heart. He's got to figure some of this stuff out. Some hearts open gently, and some seem more like they shatter from the force of pain built up inside. But the good news is that here in this safe place, we can show compassion while God extends his mercy and healing. When two hearts break open, they can at last be restored. Of course there is no guarantee of the path Ryan and Becca will choose, but at least they have a chance now to mend together." He went on to tell them a story.

"About fourteen months ago, Erin and I had a discussion. Bob and I had been doing Intensives for a long time. We were in the middle of one of our 'discussions-turned-arguments,' and she once again accused me of not being available to her, especially emotionally. I had heard her say things like this before, and it just drove me crazy.

"Every time she would say that, I would get so mad at her. I had no idea what she was talking about. I thought I was very available to her.

"I don't know why it happened that particular night, but finally I had a breakthrough moment. Later on that night, the Lord took me to a place where all of a sudden, for the first time in my life, I understood how totally disconnected and detached I had been from my heart. When Erin and I would talk, my response was like, 'Well, what do we need to solve? How do I fix it?' I could reason, I could guide people through their heart issues. . . . I could write all about it, I could talk to people about it, but literally experiencing marriage, from here in my heart, was different. I could think about how important it was, but I never truly experienced how absolutely central the heart is to life, especially to our marriages.

"I felt like the Tin Man in *The Wizard of Oz*. When Dorothy and the Scarecrow find the Tin Man in the middle of the woods, here is what he says: 'It was a terrible thing to undergo, but during the year I stood there I had time to think that the greatest loss I had known was the loss of my heart. While I was in love I was the happiest man on earth; but no one can love who has not a heart, and so I am resolved to ask Oz to give me one.'

"I began to realize that I, too, was pretty cold and dark at the core of my being. And my desire to understand what I was missing began to grow. So instead of asking Oz for a new heart, I asked the Lord. I prayed, 'If this is so important, God, if my heart really matters this much in my marriage and my life, help me to understand it.'

"I'm here to tell you, it has been the most amazing journey. I finally began to feel my heart wake up. So now one of the most important things I tell people who come to an Intensive is that often our hearts are closed. For many different reasons, we've slowly become detached from or indifferent to our hearts. For some of us, hurt and deep disappointment have caused us to close off and shut down."

A TALK WITH THE DOCTORS

The Heart

First Peter 1:22 says, "Love one another deeply, from the heart." This verse has become the banner for my life and marriage. I realized that I want to love people deeply, with all my heart. So I went on a journey and started studying and reading everything I could find on the heart. I figured if heart matters are so important, the Bible would have something to tell me about it. And do you know what I found? There are over 955 verses about the heart!

I also found research that indicates there are neurons in the heart that are five thousand times more powerful than the ones in the lower part of our brains. This finding and others astounded me and gave me new insight into the Scripture that says, "As he thinketh in his heart, so is he" (Proverbs 23:7, KJV). The more I studied, the more I searched for truth. Where does God dwell? He dwells in our heart, the center of our being. There are many things we don't understand in our heads, but Scripture says we can start to understand them with the heart.

One great book that has changed my life is *Waking the Dead*, by John Eldredge. The premise of the book is about how important our heart is and how damaging it is when we are not connected to it. Eldredge points out Isaiah 61:1, which relates Isaiah's prophesy about the coming Messiah. The prophet says two things: Jesus would come to save us, and—I especially love the second part—Christ came to heal the brokenhearted. This has truly become my prayer for anyone we do Intensives with: that we can participate in healing the brokenhearted.

I am passionate about seeing hearts transformed as they start awakening and coming to life. Much like the movie *Pleasantville*, in which a brother and sister get sucked into a black-and-white television show kind of like *Leave It to Beaver*. The people live in black and white until they start experiencing their hearts and true emotions. All of a sudden they start to live in color.

This is the closest I can come to describing what has happened to me. In many ways I feel as if life is finally in color, and if I can live in color, you can too. You know, we are trained to work hard, invest, and be polite, but no one ever taught me how to deal with my heart. No one ever taught me how to guard it. I think one of the most powerful verses in the entire Bible is Proverbs 4:23, which says,

"Above all else, guard your heart, for it is the wellspring of life." Any verse that starts with "above all else" is something we should pay close attention to.

Until recently, I had no clue about guarding the well-spring of life. Not only did I not guard it, I didn't really pay attention to it. I let it deaden over the years, and every time Erin would say, "I just don't feel you are available to me" or "You seem so emotionless," I didn't understand how totally right she was. We weren't connected in our hearts because I wasn't connected to mine.

This revelation has so dramatically changed my life that I am excited for you to experience it too. If you really want to try to understand and rediscover your wellspring of life, it will have such an amazing relational impact that you'll never be the same.

I truly believe the heart should be the most central thing to deal with in marriage. Yet isn't it strange that the heart is something we hardly ever hear about? That has the mark of the enemy all over it. If he can't get our heart closed or get us detached, he takes us out of the game. And we're a pretty vital part of God's plan.

Here is the risk. The only way you can ever experience true intimacy, true connection with a person, is when your heart and the other person's heart are open together. Anything other than that is not true intimacy. The openness of both hearts is central to the definition of intimacy: Two people with their hearts and spirits open, connecting and sharing something of who they are. It is an extremely vulnerable place. It is very risky. But anything short of this isn't intimacy. Together, work to create a safe place, a safe haven, a sanctuary in your relationship that enables you to take the risk of opening up to connect and experience true intimacy.

The picture we *don't* want to paint is that we should throw open our heart and then leave it hanging wide open, hoping that no one hurts us. We must be able to differentiate between slamming our hearts shut and *guarding* our hearts—much the way we would protect a source of pure springwater from contamination. In times when I don't feel safe around Erin or someone else, I guard my heart and take great care of myself. Then, when I start to feel safe again, I open it back up. My goal is to have my heart open to God, myself, and others as much as possible, which allows me to experience life and relationships to the fullest. But that means that there are times when the most loving thing I can do is to guard and protect my heart and keep it safe. Remember 1 Peter 1:22: "Love one another deeply, from the heart." That's the goal.

The impact of Greg's impassioned story brought the puzzle pieces together for the couples in the room—especially for the men. Becca was surprised to find Todd's expression one of intrigue rather than anger. Though his demeanor was still far from warm, the look of contempt and grave deliberation was gone. The pastor and his wife had requested to be the next couple to work, so together the group discussed what this concept about the heart meant for him and Pam.

Following Ryan's example, Todd also shared about his childhood, which could be described as nothing short of trauma. Among other things, he'd lost his father as a young man. Becca was shocked to discover that after talking long into the night with Ryan, Todd had been able to sort through several issues that had kept him stuck. He had also found the courage to share these deep concerns and inhibitions with his wife.

Shamefaced, Todd admitted that he had been surprised to discover Pam's strength and compassion for what he was going through. Not only that, he was also learning she was capable of handling tough circumstances. He did not need to protect her from everything.

Then Todd shared how he'd consistently been taught that he was called to be a prophet—to proclaim God's displeasure with humanity's lack of holiness. He had always understood this to mean that he would be shunned. He'd learned that prophets should expect to be despised for the righteous stance they took. Though there was an element of truth in that, it had become twisted to the point that Todd didn't feel loved by anyone—not even God.

Becca couldn't keep her distance any longer. Leaving the sofa, she went over to the pastor. She didn't touch him but just stood close. "Todd, that's not true. You *are* loved! Todd, remember when I said I believed I was worthless, that no one wanted me? In just the last of couple days I've been reading in the Bible about how God's loving-kindness is everlasting . . . how he chose me before I was even born. And he has chosen you, too! Not only as a mean old prophet, but as his child. He loves you *so much*."

"I couldn't have said it better," Bob said.

❂ ❂ ❂

WEDNESDAY, 7:30 P.M.

By the end of the third day, the terror had subsided, and Victoria knew each couple, like Charles and herself, could see new direction and a renewed sense of hope. After the last counseling session had adjourned, they were feeling more comfortable with each other and basking in the pronounced feeling of safety they'd never before experienced. With all their issues out in the open, it made for a whole new set of rules while they were chatting in the dining room or out on the balcony. Victoria thought it was interesting how natural it felt to laugh and engage in trivial conversations about their kids, hobbies, towns and neighborhoods, or work. Because no one knew the more normal details of each other's lives, there was plenty of room left to become acquainted. An intimate sense of community was starting to take shape among this odd, mismatched group of people.

Though they all had miles to go, they had made remarkable progress, and most were ready for a break in the intensity. Victoria thought music and lights would be nice. She was accustomed to organizing social events, so she rounded up the troops to do dinner on the town. She'd made reservations at the Candlestick Inn— Charles's and her treat.

The food was scrumptious, and the atmosphere was cozy. Victoria had a hard time not getting emotional. She wanted to laugh and cry all at the same time. To the festive background of clinking silverware, quiet chatter, and a gorgeous view of downtown Branson, Rodney kept the group laughing. And Victoria found Becca, seated across from Charles, to be delightful company.

"Do you have any pictures of your grandchildren?" Becca asked at one point during the evening. "I'd love to see them." The child didn't know she couldn't have asked a more perfect question. Victoria beamed.

Charles said why, yes, he did, and pulled out his wallet to display their beautiful, dark-haired grandchildren. They were not formal portraits, as many people carry, but rather gorgeous candid shots in sepia of the children playing and dancing, taken from different artistic angles.

Becca let out a gasp. "Who took these?"

A shy smile played on Charles's lips. "I did."

"They're all so beautiful," she said. "I'd like to hear their names."

He proudly named each one.

Victoria could see in the lovely girl's face that a difficult question was forming. "Becca, do you want to ask if Charles has a photo of Isaac, too?"

"Oh, yes, please. Charles, is there a picture?" Becca asked. "I'd love for you to tell me more about him . . . that is, if it's not too painful."

Charles pulled out another beautiful photo, and with a voice low and deep, he began to share about their dear Isaac, while laughing and wiping away tears.

Todd surprised them all a little while later when he asked to play the piano and serenaded them with a moving rendition of Mozart's difficult Piano Concerto no. 20. With all defenses gone, he seemed to lose himself in the music while his fingers flew over the keys. The group sat speechless until they broke out into loud applause. Only after Todd had showcased his hidden talent did Victoria nudge Charles to do the same. For twenty minutes more, the two men played spontaneous duets, leaving the entire restaurant spellbound.

The evening was growing late, and the group of new friends strolled along the boardwalk in the cool evening. Down by the river, strains of music floated across the dark, glittering water while a jazz band played. Victoria loved being with these new friends who knew her heart so well, and her husband seemed to be in his glory. He was close but not clingy. Just then the band struck up a familiar tune. Charles held out his hand, beckoning her to dance. This time she was ready. The others watched in wonder as Charles and his bride waltzed in perfect time: intimacy swept into one fluid motion.

❂ ❂ ❂

The men said they wanted to hang out and listen to the music, but Becca and Chelsea were getting chilled down by the water's edge. After putting their heads together, the women decided it would be fun to turn in early for a little pajama party. The group had driven two cars, so the ladies were able to return to the Bradford House without the men.

Bedecked in pajamas and slippers, they rendezvoused in Victoria's room. There Victoria braided Becca's and Pam's hair in cornrows, Becca did pedicures, Chelsea gave back and shoulder rubs, and Pam served snacks. The only rule was that any talk of marriage or anything related to their being at the Intensive was strictly forbidden.

Soon the women were giggling like schoolgirls, sharing fun trivia about their lives, and bonding further as sisters and new friends.

❀ ❀ ❀

"So what did you women talk about?" Rodney asked his wife as they settled in for the night.

"You can relax," Chelsea said, laughing over her shoulder at his curiosity. "We girls promised not to mention anything relating to marriage or anything serious. We did share a little about our kids and our interests—girlie stuff like that. Mainly we laughed a lot. It was wonderful." She examined her toenails, which looked pretty and pink. "Did you know Pam loves horses? Or how about this: Becca won spitting contests when she was a kid! How about you guys? What did you do?"

Rodney looked away until he could push down his smile. He didn't want to reveal what they had actually been doing, and he did feel a bit relieved that the girls hadn't run away to have an intimate crying session. "Todd was so relaxed. I wonder if his headaches will ease up after some of his stuff is dealt with. The tension he's been under is phenomenal! Can you believe his incredible musical talent?" Rodney made exaggerated motions with his fingers up and down an imaginary keyboard. "It was like he expressed everything in his heart through his fingers. I was actually getting choked up." He walked into the bathroom and reached for the toothpaste. "And Charles, is he cool or what?" Rodney called over his shoulder.

"And Ryan? How'd he do?" asked Chelsea, walking to the bathroom doorway.

Rodney finished his story as he brushed. "He hung out with us. Man, at first I thought he was such a jerk, but it's amazing what you discover about a person when they start to open up. I think I could really like him, but he was still quiet. The day's been pretty hard on him, I think. You know that whole I-don't-care thing? Wow." Now he swished a mouthful of water and gargled. "Do you think he and Becca are going to make it?"

Chelsea agreed that she hadn't liked Ryan at first either. "But he really is sensitive. I think he is a tortured soul trying to outrun his love." Then she pointed out that she also couldn't stand Becca at the outset, but now she had come to admire her strength. "She isn't at all frail; she has survived so much."

As was her habit, Chelsea began getting the room in order and setting out things to wear for the next day. "Still," she said as she worked, "I don't get how men can have these flings off to the side and carry on like everything is normal."

Rodney felt his eyebrows rise. Chelsea had room to comment about men who had flings?

She turned his way before he could rearrange his face. "Don't give me that look, Rod! I mean it. I don't go around having flings. One night and I was going crazy. I had to tell the truth after one night."

He shrank back a little, still looking hurt.

"Rod, you don't think I left you because of . . . that accountant, do you? Because I didn't. I said this earlier. It was nothing more than a stupid knee-jerk reaction to my anger toward you and life in general. . . . I don't know what's going on with Ryan, but my story is different."

Rodney saw her look at him earnestly before crossing over to the mirror to apply moisturizer to her face.

Carefully, he responded by saying that he had suspected something was up, and he thought maybe she was merely trying to make a point.

Frowning, she stood motionless. "That wasn't my intention at all. What possessed you to think that?"

"I dunno."

She blinked with indignation. "What can I do to make you believe me?"

Reaching over, he gently swatted her with the brush and said something humorously suggestive.

She narrowed her eyes and crossed her arms. "Come on, I'm being serious."

Whether it was the misty green of her eyes or the gentle curve of her lips, he wasn't sure, but she was irresistible. Rodney got up from the bed and walked around behind her, wrapping his arms around her middle and kissing her silky, copper-colored hair.

"Rodney, it's not true at all, and you must believe me when I say it. I was just so disconnected from you, from me, from God. . . . Like Charles, I felt like my heart was bolted shut. You know that verse that says Jesus came to heal the brokenhearted and set the captives free? I never knew it meant me."

He inhaled deeply, smiled against her neck, and said, "I believe you, Chels. I can see it in your eyes."

"You can't see my eyes."

"Yes, I can, just not right now." He held the woman of his dreams tight. His body enfolded her little frame, and he rested his chin on her head. Seeing their reflection in the mirror, Rodney's eyes began to tear up. It had been far too long since she'd allowed him to hold her.

Only after her body relaxed and turned toward his did he kiss her. Stroking her hair, he made it clear that they didn't need to go any further if she wasn't ready.

"Rodney, it's just that I need space from time to time . . . and I needed to be sure of how I felt before we came together again. Can you understand that?" She pulled away slightly. "I didn't want to be pressured into making this marriage work. But when you found me last night out there in the rain, I was already turning back—to you. I'm glad you came to find me. I really needed you . . . like I do now."

15

THURSDAY, 7:00 A.M.

Day four at the Bradford House dawned with bright rays of sun setting the mood for the final day of the Intensive: a new day for clarity, redemption, and miracles. "Hello, you," Victoria said, nibbling on the edge of Charles's ear as she surveyed the breakfast table set for two. Charles had laid an intimate setting in the front dining area.

Victoria watched her life partner. He squeezed her tea bag with care to make it as strong as she liked it. He then stirred in a spot of milk with a half teaspoon of sugar and reached for a dessert napkin to place under the cup. Charles's precision marked his love for his wife, and she was at last ready to receive it. He served her breakfast exactly the way she would have made it herself: a dollop of yogurt on her fresh fruit, granola on the side.

She smiled as he completed his careful preparations, thinking back to the night before. He'd spoken with awe, saying she was beautiful, and not just as a step toward his own end. Totally attuned to one another, their lovemaking had been familiar, yet extravagant and indulgent. Charles had made her feel like a precious jewel.

"V, are you all right?"

"Darling, I have missed you so terribly . . . and I can't describe how badly I want this for the others," she said. "Do you think they'll find it?"

○ ○ ○

The bathroom was filled with steam as Becca wrapped her hair in a towel. She opened the door, prepared to go into the bedroom to select her clothes. Then she looked up.

There stood Ryan in the doorway.

Startled, she let out a shriek. She hadn't heard him come in. He might as well have been a stalker by her reaction. How dare he walk in on her?

Ryan had been keeping his distance, sleeping on the couch downstairs every night. They hadn't necessarily planned it; they had taken each day as it came, and it had just happened that way. Of course, after her first night of terror, she refused to feel bad for having the comfortable bed. It was merely poetic justice for all the times her husband had chosen to sleep somewhere other than with her.

"Ryan!" In her shock, she had failed to notice his swollen eyes and ashen face. Under closer scrutiny, he looked as if he'd wrestled the devil all night long . . . and she couldn't tell who had won.

His gaze seemed to penetrate right through her.

"Becca, I need to talk to you. I . . . I know you don't want me here . . . not like this." All of a sudden he seemed to realize the precariousness of the situation. "I'm not here to convince you of anything or . . . or to coerce you into making love . . . or even to forgive me."

"No—"

"Just listen, will you? I need to talk to you."

His urgent tone got her attention. She had no idea what direction this was going to take. She wondered what she would say if he asked to come back or begged to return home. She wouldn't go for it. She wasn't ready. He still hadn't even seen the doctor—her one simple request. This was the first time she realized that she could live without Ryan Stuart. She was being healed . . . although the dull ache in her stomach was a good indication of her unrelenting love for him.

She fixed her eyes on his mouth and watched his lips as he spoke.

"I just want you to know that this heart stuff is really beginning to take its toll on me." His voice cracked. "Last night I thought about leaving; I was going crazy." He swore and slammed his fist on the doorjamb. "All night I wrestled with how closed off and unsafe I've been. I don't deserve your trust—I've been such an idiot." He began pacing back and forth, avoiding her eyes. He perched on the side of the bed for only a moment before standing up again and pacing some more.

"Ryan. Stop."

He let out a moan and slammed his fist into the wall. Facing a crumble of white plaster, his body became racked with broken sobs.

Becca stood motionless across the room. For all her acting out and emotional frenzies, she had never seen her husband lose control—ever. She didn't know what to do.

"Something is happening to my heart, Bec," he said, his face against the wall. "It feels like it's literally breaking in half. And it hurts. . . ." He swore again. "But . . . I'm feeling it!" He turned, holding his chest, still looking anywhere but at her. "I've been so closed up. Like Greg said, I've been living out of my head—in a black-and-white world. I've had so many walls up; I haven't felt a thing. I didn't feel any remorse, I couldn't feel my pain, I couldn't feel yours, and . . . and that means I haven't been feeling any real pleasure either. I'm not just saying that, I mean it. I feel like that movie Greg talked about. I'm coming back into color. I just kept thinking about Charles and how Victoria didn't think he could ever love again, and . . ."

Becca started to cry.

"I just gave my shriveled-up heart to God last night. But I did it differently. Instead of just throwing the teddy bear to him, I asked him to join me—and the two of us—in healing my heart. I know he can heal all that pain and disappointment from my past, just like he is healing yours. . . ." He dared to steal a glance at her. "I want to give you what's left of me. But I'm not sure how to do that. Or if you even want it."

Becca remained silent.

"I'm scared. I'm especially afraid to open myself up to you. I don't expect mercy after all I've done—you have every right to hate me. I just didn't care for so long, but even if it's too late, now I do."

"On one hand, that's great," Becca said, "but on the other hand—"

"What other hand?" Ryan said. "There isn't another hand."

"Yes, there is. At least I think there is." Becca twisted her hair.

"Last night God just showed me, over and over, how incredible you are and . . . and the girls, too . . . even how valuable I am to him. He showed me how I've thrown around and mistreated the most precious gifts ever given to me. I've been so angry and disillusioned." His face contorted in agony. "I—I couldn't see you. I've hurt you and the girls, and I've become a man I don't want to be."

He fell to his knees and wept openly, with his face on the floor. "I'm sorry—I'm so . . . sorry."

Becca stood motionless. Repulsed. She wanted to hit him and say something cruel. In discovering her own worth, she was recognizing just how horrible Ryan had been to her. He was no better than her father and all those creeps who . . . It was all wrong, so terribly sick and wrong. All of a sudden she experienced a hatred like nothing she had ever felt before.

But it wasn't Ryan she hated. No. It was the lies.

As if a heavy veil had been lifted, she began to see the lies she had been told, the lies she had believed, the lies she had lived. Hers had been a false, distorted life.

And her hero . . . ? Here on his knees before her, he was just a broken, ordinary man.

Ryan lifted his wet face and met her eyes for the first time since he'd come into their room. Wordlessly, she handed him the towel that had been wound around her hair so he could wipe the tears that were dripping from his chin.

"Why are you angry?" he asked.

"I'm not angry, I'm sad." She didn't know why she was so upset. "You know that story Bob told about holding back his heart from Jenni until he knew she was safe? I think I'm there. My first reaction is to comfort you—but I can't. I have to care for myself now. I don't want to make you prove yourself to me anymore—I don't want you to be my source of safety and security. I want you to journey with God on your own for a while.

"I want to forgive you, Ryan. I do. But I don't know when I'll be ready to be intimate again." She reached out and touched him lightly on the head. "We really need to start over. I've been so struck by what Bob and Greg have been saying about guarding our hearts. Ryan, right now I can't open my heart to you because I don't feel completely safe . . . but I want that to be different, I really do. Remember what Bob shared with us about boundaries yesterday at lunch?" He had said that the goal needed to be creating an environment that felt safe enough for each of their hearts and spirits to be open, rather than Becca's trying to change or control Ryan. "I want that for me, and I want that for us.

"Bob said that the first step was to make a request, which means we can say no. That feels totally bizarre to me, but I do want to ask that you be patient with me, helping me to feel safe again with you and not pushing me until I feel ready."

"I can do that."

She rushed on lest she lose her momentum. "I know now that

part of my insecurity in our relationship is *me* not trusting *me*, so I'm going to work on that, too. And that plan he talked about? I have one now. . . . I know I need to continue to keep you at arm's length until I feel ready. I've never done that. But I have to do this—for me and for the girls. I know God wants me to do this. And, Ryan?"

His face was unreadable, but she had his full attention.

"I really want this to work. I do . . . for both of us." Tears spilled down her cheeks. "I want us to be a family."

Then, spotting the clock, she started tossing clothes out of the armoire onto the bed. "Shoot, Ryan. We need to hurry up or we're gonna be late again."

A TALK WITH THE DOCTORS

Establishing Christ-Centered Boundaries

When a situation appears to warrant setting some sort of boundary, such as Becca was experiencing, it is often difficult to know how to establish that boundary in an effective way. To be effective, a boundary must be one that will take care of you and your interests in a way that best accomplishes your overall personal and relational goals. Thus, the critical initial question is: What am I wanting or trying to accomplish?

The two most common answers are:

- To protect myself from people or circumstances
- To take good care of myself within ongoing relationships in a way that strengthens and builds those relationships

If your answer is the first one, the typical reaction will be to build walls or barriers between you and the people or circumstances that are difficult or threatening (withdrawal) or to attempt to stop or change the current behavior to a preferred behavior (control, manipulation). Either response, withdrawal or control, hurts both relationships and individual self-esteem.

The second answer speaks to a deeper question: Ultimately, what does it look like to take good care of myself?

Truly taking care of yourself requires aligning yourself with what Jesus said are the greatest, foundational commandments: to love the Lord with all your heart, soul, mind, and strength; and to love others as you love yourself. The implication is that we must also love ourselves. The necessary posture to follow these commands, and thus to truly take care of yourself, is to allow love to flow to you and through you by maintaining an open heart.

Often, the difficulty with maintaining an open heart is that openness exposes our vulnerability and therefore is risky. Openness is actually the most natural state of being for humans, but painful experiences in life tend to encourage us to become defensive and protected (various states of being closed). When we feel safe, however, we are naturally inclined to open up because it is more comfortable and takes less energy. When two people who care about each other are open, intimacy occurs and God's love flows easily and naturally in them, through them, and between them.

Therefore, the ultimate goal is to attempt to create a safe space where we are well taken care of that enables our heart to remain open to God, ourselves, and others.

Maintaining an open heart is the essence of a Christ-centered boundary. Christlike boundaries are characterized by love, honor, and respect. They also facilitate movement toward—rather than away from—relationships. Therefore, these boundaries cannot involve withdrawal, manipulation, or control.

Here are the steps to establishing Christ-centered boundaries:

- Make sure you have the right goal: attempting to create a space that enables you to keep your heart open to God, yourself, and others (including those you are setting boundaries with).
- Make a request regarding the behavior or circumstances that are making it difficult for you to keep your heart open. Remember, a request must allow for no to be an acceptable response. If no is not acceptable, you are making a demand, not a request.
- Establish a contingency plan—what you will do if your request is denied. This is an action you can take that is not contingent on other people or circumstances, that moves you to a physical, emotional, or spiritual space that best facilitates the openness of your heart.

THURSDAY, 8:00 A.M.

Becca was still reeling from Ryan's brokenness as she made her way down to the counseling room. The other couples were already there, and Greg was just about to open in prayer. He began by asking a blessing on the now-intimate group who had bonded in so many unexpected and remarkable ways. The mood was an odd mixture of celebration and nostalgia, but there was still work to be done.

While the others began the morning check-in, Becca tried to get her thoughts in order. She knew there was still a ton of work to do in her marriage, and she was afraid there just wouldn't be time. How could she leave for home later today when things were still so unsettled between her and Ryan?

She perked up when Charles gave his update. What a dear man he was! He was saying, "Doc Smalley, Doc Paul, I can't even tell you how happy I am right now. But I must say, I've been caught off guard by how much love hurts." Yeah, Becca could relate to that.

"Can you tell us a little more about that, Charles?" Greg asked.

"You know that heaviness in my chest yesterday? I've been considering that, and I think it's a load of guilt. I've never said this out loud, but I don't know that I can ever forgive myself for what happened to my grandson."

Greg's face was intent as he nodded and allowed a respectful pause before responding.

"I would venture to say—and I am not trying to make this overly simple, because only you know for sure—that what you are experiencing as guilt is actually a form a grief. But not healthy grief. I think maybe you are hating the grief rather than accepting this overwhelming angst as a testimony of the depth of your love. You want to get rid of it instead of saying, 'I loved my Isaac more than life itself, and that is why I hurt like this.'

"You've had many losses to grieve, my friend. But you don't need to feel overwhelmed by them. In our society, we've come to believe grief is cold and empty—that it's a hopeless, helpless experience. But the cold, empty, hopeless feeling is actually fear, not grief. Grief is simply a part of love. We grieve because we love. However, when we are confronted with our grief, we hurt. And like anything else, our fear of the pain triggers our natural fight-or-flight response. As a result, we close our heart to protect ourselves, and that feels very heavy.

"Charles, this heart of yours is astounding; it is so alive. Your grief is evidence of your love. Your heart has so much love still in there, you don't know what to do with it all. I guarantee that if it wasn't, you wouldn't be feeling this indescribable heaviness. You will honor your grandson with your grief and all it encompasses. What do you think of that?"

"I think I haven't grieved properly."

"Why not?"

"I've been afraid that it would overtake me and I wouldn't be able to continue on."

"Do you know that without the fear, grief is not empty, as we might anticipate? It's just the opposite, actually. When we grieve without fear, our hearts are full. Remember, perfect love casts out fear. We may at times feel helpless in our grief, but we never need to feel hopeless. The depth of your grief gives testimony to your love—how deeply you care. In fact, true grief is not a separate emotion; it is merely a facet of love. Notice that you never grieve something you didn't really care about."

Becca could see that Charles was touched by Greg's gentle insight.

"Sometimes there is a private portion of grief," Greg went on, "but there is also a way we can connect deeply with another around shared grief." He looked around the room. "You have all lost . . . and grieving something you care about is an expression of the heart of Christ. Sharing that area of pain together without blame can be a precious sharing of love. Not fun, but deeply intimate and meaningful. That leads to a powerful experience of togetherness and unity. I look forward to that being a central theme for today. So who wants to start working?"

Becca was glad that Ryan was the first to speak up. "I'm beginning to see some of the messed-up things I've done. I know I've brought a lot of this on myself and on my family. I fully admit it now; I own it. I know I can't create love—that it has to flow from Christ through me—but I can't get away from the feeling that I still have to pay penance to earn back Becca's trust and restore all that has been lost. Whether that's reasonable or unreasonable. I really want to figure out how to make this thing work, but I'm afraid that as soon as we leave here, she's going to start making her demands again, and I don't want to start resenting her all over again."

Bob asked, "Is this a question of not understanding fully how to become trustworthy, or are you saying there's no way to win? If you don't feel good about doing something and then you do it anyway, you are not being true to yourself."

"No, I think it's more superficial than that. For instance, when Becca asked me to change my cell phone number, I kind of fought it at first, but then I conceded. But when she wanted me to change my pager number, too, I have to say, it was a royal pain. I tried for two hours, and then I said, 'What is she thinking, and why am I doing this?' Then I got angry and resentful. I started fighting with her, and after a lot of bickering and throwing things around and getting mad, I just gave up. What if something like that happens again?"

"It sounds like even if you don't resent the individual requests, you feel as if to make Becca happy, you have to keep losing you," Greg said.

"Yeah, and I'm afraid it will never end. What am I supposed to do? She has put restrictions on my independence, and honestly, I think maybe I need them. And maybe I owe her this to make her feel comfortable. But I guess I want to decide if all this needs to be in place for my protection or for her comfort. Am I making any sense? Like joining an accountability group—is that for me or for her?"

"Well, the thing that seems to be a problem here is you believe that as a result of what you did, you now have to basically say, 'Okay, Becca, from this point forward, you call the shots on everything. I am not entitled to have a say about anything.' Whether that is actually true or not is irrelevant, because what we are dealing with here is the way you feel. That is itself a fact, and you are going to react to it. Let me ask this: How are you dealing with it now?"

"I'm kind of upset."

Bob stepped in. "Becca said on our first day together that she wanted a faithful husband, which seems like a completely reasonable request. However, she also wanted the marriage to be just like it was. But there is no way you can go back to the way it was before for two important reasons. First, part of her comfort was based on an illusion of perfect trust that has now been shattered. And second, there were clearly things about the marriage that weren't working for either of you—not in light of what happened. If the goal is to have a marriage that both of you are thrilled with, then you've got to come up with something brand new, yet an approach that still works for both of you."

"That sounds good to me," Ryan said with surprising enthusiasm.

"Can the two of you see how you are locked in an intense power struggle? Can you feel that?"

Becca and Ryan looked at each other, and then Becca blurted out, "Yeah, and I hate it!"

"Would you say that the power struggles had begun before the affair?"

Ryan nodded. "We're both strong minded . . . maybe even a little stubborn. . . . I know I am."

Becca nodded, grateful for the understanding smiles she received from several of the others.

Ryan went on, "Actually, though, up until the affair, I probably steamrollered right over Becca most of the time."

"I have come to the conclusion," Bob said, "that power struggles are the single greatest ploy the enemy has ever devised to destroy marriages, and here is why: Who is the enemy of your marriage?"

Becca answered, "Satan."

"And when you and Ryan square off in conflict, who do you perceive as the enemy?"

"Each other," Ryan said.

"Exactly. And at that moment Satan has you right where he wants you. In fact, he doesn't even need to stick around anymore. He can walk out of your house dusting off his hands and go next door and mess with the neighbors, because he's got you both totally covered. Sometimes power struggles are very subtle, but the bottom line is that the moment you perceive each other as the enemy, you're sunk.

"You know, a number of years ago I had a realization that transformed my marriage, and I have a feeling it could easily do that for you two. The interesting thing is that it occurred during an interaction with my eldest son, not with Jenni.

"Chris and I were having a 'discussion' over something that to me felt like a safety issue that he wasn't understanding. He was a younger adolescent at the time, and he was not seeing things my way, so this 'discussion' got a little heated.

"I said, 'Chris, you don't get it, this could really be bad for you.' I was passionate about what I was saying. We went around and around, and I used everything I could think of to make my point. Finally, after an hour and a half, he got it. I was so relieved that I just fell back on the bed and said, 'Thank you, Jesus!'

"A little while later, I noticed Christopher sitting in the dining room by himself with his head in his hands. All of a sudden I felt utterly gripped with conviction. I sat down next to him and asked him, 'Son, who would you say won back there in the bedroom?' He said, 'For the most part, Dad, you did.'

"I looked at him and said, 'Chris, if that's the case, I lost.' He looked at me as if I was an alien.

"My son was playing Little League baseball at that time, and he played with a kid named Chuckie. I asked him, 'When you and Chuckie are playing ball, is there ever a time when you win and Chuckie loses?'

"He said, 'No.'

"'How come?'

"'Dad, we're on the same team,' he said, still looking at me like I was weird.

"'Exactly! Son, I'm not your enemy, I'm your teammate. Therefore, if you lose, I lose. The idea that teammates can have a win-lose outcome is nothing more than an illusion from the pit of hell. And Satan just had his way with us.' I could see it registering in his eyes, and he smiled. We went on to have a great talk and a special father-son time together.

"The amazing part of the story is that over the next several days, it started to dawn on me that for years, I had unknowingly set up almost every single interaction with my wife, Jenni, the way I had with Chris. Jenni is not my enemy either; she's my team-mate, my partner, and I was continually playing right into the real enemy's hands. Satan is the only one who celebrates when Jenni and I get into a power struggle. He not only celebrates, he laughs at how easy we are to defeat!

"This whole concept really got my attention. I decided right then and there that those days were over. That day I adopted what we now call a 'no-losers policy.' Very simply it means this: We have made it 100 percent unacceptable for either of us to ever walk away from an interaction feeling like we've lost a battle. I'm not going to tell you that it hasn't happened since then, because it has, but it is no longer okay with us.

"We've had to sort all this out and come up with a different definition for winning. We've come to recognize that if either of us loses, the whole team loses."

A TALK WITH THE DOCTORS

A No-Losers Policy

Are you at odds with your mate? Do you often feel as if you win—or lose—in your marriage? If you answered yes, you've probably fallen prey to one of the evil one's most common ploys.

In every power struggle, spouses become adversaries; they take on opposing positions and try to crush their opponents. And as soon as a husband and wife set themselves up as antagonists, Satan can just fold his arms and walk away, because he knows spouses-turned-adversaries will hurt and sometimes even destroy each other. He doesn't have to do anything more. Jesus knew this reality when he said, "Any kingdom divided against itself will be ruined, and a house divided against itself will fall" (Luke 11:17).

Never forget that your true enemy is not the other person. It's Satan, the enemy of our souls and marriages. If a struggle for power gives the devil a ridiculously easy way to bring strife and disharmony to a marriage, what kind of strategy can we use to effectively counter such a ploy? "How about a win-win solution?" someone suggests. Sounds good! When everybody wins, power struggles evaporate. Ideally, we all want win-win solutions.

But what happens when a win-win solution looks impossible to achieve? What then? Too many of us settle for what we see as a win-lose option. Not the best, maybe, and we'd really rather avoid it, but at least it's not the worst, either. In other words, we compromise.

When we opt for the win-lose approach, however, we don't really get one winner and one loser. There is no such thing as a win-lose in a marriage. It's either a win-win or a lose-lose. Everybody wins, or everybody loses. Period. There is no other option, because we are on the same team.

Members of a team win together, or they lose together. Marriage partners experience exactly the same thing—except that in marriage, we choose every day whether we will win or lose.

What will you choose?

We encourage you to make a commitment to a new way of doing things and determine to abandon the old failed model. This begins by establishing a no-losers policy. In a no-losers policy, couples agree that it will never be acceptable, from this point on, for either of them to walk away from any interaction feeling as if they lost. Each spouse has to feel good about the solution.

Remember what Paul wrote in Philippians 2:2-4: "Make my joy complete by being like-minded, having the same love, being one in spirit and purpose. Do nothing out of selfish ambition or vain conceit, but in humility consider others better than yourselves. Each of you should look not only to your own interests, but also to the interests of others."

(See appendix C for seven practical steps to a win-win outcome.)

Becca was puzzled as she tried to relate what Bob was saying to the power struggles in her marriage. "Wait a minute, Bob. I'm confused. So you're saying that unless Ryan and I are in complete agreement on an issue . . ." Her voice trailed off.

"Yes."

"But we can't agree on anything at this point!"

"Would you like to see if we can help you get through an issue you are stuck on?"

Becca thought for a second and then said, "How about my need for Ryan to get checked by a doctor? We've been at a total impasse on this."

"Is that okay with you, Ryan?"

"Sure."

"Keep in mind, the goal here is to arrive at a solution that both of you feel great about. So we need to start with each of you working to really understand how the other one feels and why they want what they want, why it's important to them.

"Becca, why did you insist that Ryan get checked by a doctor?"

"So I know he doesn't have AIDS."

"Yes, you are wanting him to get checked so you can find out that he doesn't have AIDS . . . so that . . . you don't get AIDS, right?"

"Yes."

"It's a necessity in taking care of yourself—so it is actually about you."

"Hmm. Okay. I see now that I can't force him to do it, but I still think that from the very beginning he should have done it without question. The really scary part, Bob, is that I've slept with him since then. Stupid, I know, but what's done is done."

"I hear you. But at that point, having sex with him was for you. You chose to put yourself in harm's way."

"But I get really angry with him for putting me in this position. First, I can't have sex because he's unfaithful; second, because he's being a stubborn . . . you-know-what. It's not right. So either I get the whole guilt trip about 'punishing' him by withholding sex—therefore, he has every right to keep fooling around—or I risk my own life."

Becca thought this was a pretty big issue to begin with for Team Building 101, but Bob seemed confident they could bring resolution. He said, "Ryan, I want you to seriously try to understand what Becca is wanting and feeling. Remember that understanding and caring for how she feels doesn't mean you have to agree or do what she wants. This has to work for both of you, or it works for neither.

"To get started, let's replay where the conversation has gone so far. Becca, go ahead and tell Ryan what you want. I'll play the part of Ryan."

"Do I have to try to be nice when I say it?" she asked.

"No, be honest."

"Ryan, I want you to go to the doctor to get checked."

Bob, now playing the part of Ryan, responded, "I've tried to tell you I used condoms. I promise, I have nothing."

"I don't care what 'precautions' you've taken. This is what I need you to do, because I'm scared."

"I feel like you are trying to control me."

She threw her hands up in the air. "See? This is what I have to deal with!"

"Wait. Let me help you with a response," Bob said. "Try this: 'Ryan, this is the only thing I know to do to take care of myself. It is not because I don't love you, because I do. I am afraid that I will be hurt, and I need to know you're clean so I can let go of that. It is not about you, Ryan; it is about me. I'm afraid. I'm hoping that you do love me and care about me. I need to make sure that I am okay, even if you are not willing to make sure that you are.' How did that sound?"

"That is exactly how I feel," said Becca.

Turning to Ryan, Bob said, "Ryan, let me ask you, what do you hear Becca saying? Try to summarize, focusing on her feelings."

Ryan looked straight at Becca and said, "I hear that you are really scared and need me to do this in order to feel safe." He sat quietly for a moment and ran his palms along his thighs. "I think I have been assuming that this was more about you wanting to control me, but I'm hearing it differently now."

Becca was baffled by his lack of resistance. "Ryan, I don't want to control you." She added quietly, "Just don't put me in danger."

"I know. I'm so sorry that I haven't been able to really hear you. I don't know if you ever can, but I want you to feel safe with me."

"Ryan, why has it been so hard for you to do this?" Becca asked. "Right now, I'm not judging, I just want to understand."

The exercise felt awkward, but Ryan was hanging in there. "I've been too afraid to let myself care. Honestly, this whole thing was at the point where I wouldn't even let myself know this. It's been a total surprise to me over the last twenty-four hours. My defense has been to not care, and I've used sex to try to feel alive in the midst of the deadness I was creating. But I want to be alive again. I want to feel my heart again. I want to be a man I can be proud of again."

They both looked at Bob. "What now?" Becca asked.

Bob suggested that Becca ask what Ryan wanted.

"So what do you want from me?"

Ryan paused a moment before answering. "I want you to be patient with me too. I know this isn't going to be easy for me, because I've gotten used to being this way. I want you to learn to take good care of yourself, but I don't want you constantly trying to control me. I'm willing to hear and care about your feelings, but mine have to matter too."

Bob nodded and then looked at Becca. "Becca, how does that sound to you?"

"I'm willing to give it a try. It doesn't sound unreasonable."

"Ryan, how about you?"

He gave a wry smile. "Not only am I willing to go see the doctor, I've already made the appointment."

Becca was stunned. When did that happen?

Ryan added, "I wanted it to be a gift to you, Bec, a message that I care. But I feel even better about it now than I did this morning when I made the appointment, because it's not only for you—it's for us. Maybe—" he drew in a breath—"we can win too."

Ryan reached out his hand for Becca's, and she cautiously offered him hers. He gently squeezed it. A small gesture for some; monumental for Dr. Stuart.

Everyone in the room broke into applause.

Chelsea didn't want to be late for the second part of the morning session. The girls had taken a ten-minute jaunt during the break to stretch their legs and enjoy the fresh spring air. She had run up to her room to freshen up a bit and was now hurrying back to the counseling room.

She came cruising around the corner and then halted abruptly. She had almost interrupted an intimate moment between Victoria and Charles. Careful not to call attention to herself, she began moving quietly in reverse out of earshot so the older couple had another moment before she made her presence known. After returning from her jog early that morning, she'd seen Charles, debonair in his satin robe, give a little skip as he came out of Victoria's room. Now they were laughing and being tender with each other. What an incredible sight! *Love can last,* she thought to herself. *How cool is that?* Yes, she did want to grow old with Rodney.

Just then she felt two strong arms wrap around her tiny waist and lift her off the floor. "Oof, Rodney!" she yelled in a stage whisper. "Put me down!" He turned and locked her in a passionate kiss. He didn't hear Bob and Greg arrive on the scene.

"Hey, you two. Get a room, will you?" Greg winked at Chelsea.

"You heard them, honey. Gotta do what the doc says," Rodney said, playfully tugging her toward the stairs. Chelsea knew her husband would have an impossible time concentrating from this point forward. Truly, it was all so surreal. . . . Just four days prior, they had both been lost and filled with dread. Now they were feeling a little drunk on life, with the keenest urge to go and play. She knew Rodney missed their children, Jack and Hannah, and wanted nothing more than to have them all under the same roof again. All those beautiful days they had spent in the park— days she'd taken for granted. Never again. She knew full well her treasure. When it came to love, she was married to a rich man.

With a broad grin, Rodney pulled her close to his side, and they walked the rest of the way to the counseling room arm in arm.

When Todd and Pam entered, Chelsea noticed that Pam had a sweet, fresh glow about her. That morning in the ladies' room, Victoria had taught her how to tie the pretty new scarf Todd had purchased for her the evening prior.

Now Victoria clucked like a mother hen, "My goodness, you look lovely, dear. Is that a new scarf?" Chelsea caught her secret womanly smile. She knew Victoria had every intention of drawing Todd's attention to his wife.

"That color does look beautiful on you," Becca chimed in.

Pam looked embarrassed but pleased. Her hand went to the new silk scarf, now perfectly knotted by a woman who knew fashion.

❂ ❂ ❂

The no-losers policy story had touched Todd like nothing else had during the Intensive. Well, on second thought, that wasn't entirely true, but it certainly was the capstone challenge for his personal journey. The mental image of Bob's son, Chris, hanging his head in defeat after Bob had lectured him for too long haunted the pastor. What damage had he himself wrought with his words? What victory had Satan gained over the Davis family during all the times Todd insisted they submit to his forceful authority? He had ruled without first being compassionate. The memory of bitter, drawn-out wars between him and his son filled him with remorse.

During the midmorning break, Todd had worked frantically to reach Zach by phone in order to apologize. Zach had refused to speak to his father. It was then that Todd broke, fearing he was too late.

Todd had a lot of work to do. In order to make the no-losers policy effective, he would need to become well enough acquainted with his wife and kids to hear their hearts so they could all determine together what would be a win for them.

It was time to update the group on where he was. "I spent the night searching my heart about whether or not I should stay in the ministry," he began, "and what that decision would mean for my family." He shared the need he felt for them to have a private retreat as a family—a time away from ministry to rediscover who they were and to let them know how genuinely sorry he was for being angry and locking them out of his heart. "I'm planning to speak with the elder board when we get back and request a six-week sabbatical. I thought maybe we could spend two or three weeks camping in the mountains together, kind of getting reacquainted."

Everyone listened attentively. Todd couldn't believe how supportive they were, especially after how judgmental he'd been the first day.

"Pam, how are you doing with this?" Bob wanted to know.

Todd and Pam had talked through the night, discussing his plans and how their family would be affected.

Now she told the group, "I fully desire to be on the same team as Preacher, but I realize I must first remove some obstacles that

The DNA of Relationships for Couples

are standing in the way. Like Becca, I feel a little defensive now that my husband has all of a sudden made a radical turnaround."

❁ ❁ ❁

Pam was trying to be truthful in what she shared, but she supposed that deep down, she wasn't sure exactly how or if she wanted to be on Todd's team. Even with a heart change, his personality brought with it the promise of being on a team with a forceful captain.

She could reason through all the whys of what Todd had done; still, she felt like she'd lost twenty years of herself to this man. She wasn't casting blame but rather, just by acknowledging who she had become, was in a process of grieving. The path to learning to love and care for herself seemed filled with roadblocks of righteous indignation. Not only did she need to acknowledge the conflict and draw Christ-centered boundaries, she also needed to forgive the past wrongs in her marriage as much as Becca did. Granted, her husband hadn't been unfaithful. But emotionally, she felt just as betrayed. She wasn't sure she was ready to forgive Todd. If she was as valuable and precious as Bob said, she could not stand by and let her husband's rude tone or poor treatment go unaddressed.

Bob could sense her discomfort. "Have you been able to forgive Todd?" he asked suddenly, catching her off guard.

A TALK WITH THE DOCTORS

Forgiveness

Forgiveness follows closely on the heels of personal responsibility, because taking great care of ourselves includes forgiving a spouse who has wronged us. We do not wait to determine whether the person "deserves" it, whether the person has suffered enough, or whether we are feeling especially gracious today. We forgive because we see forgiveness as a matter of personal responsibility. When we forgive, we ourselves are the primary beneficiaries. This is why it's a part of good self-care.

How many marriages have floundered because one or both partners refused to forgive? The Bible makes it clear that every believer has a personal responsibility to forgive those who hurt us—and it does not exempt husbands and wives.

When we refuse to forgive, we think that we hurt the one who wounded us—but that is rarely the case. In fact, the one we hurt most is ourselves. An unwillingness to forgive leads to a bitter spirit, and a bitter spirit languishes in a fetid prison of its own making. When we decide to forgive, we extend unmerited grace and mercy to another as Jesus has done for us. The willingness to forgive frees both parties involved and creates the possibility for a restored relationship.

Do you want to escape the torture of your personal prison? Jesus has one word for you: Forgive. He offers you no other key.

Forgiveness gives us the power to break the bonds of anger, rage, hatred, and vengeance, which all lead down the path of destruction. They are like toxins to the soul, toxins for which forgiveness is the only antidote.

Remember, true forgiveness is a part of caring for yourself.

(See appendix D for some practical suggestions on overcoming the roadblocks to forgiveness.)

"Pam," Bob gently continued, "it looks like you have not been able to forgive Todd. I want you to hear my heart. I'm not judging you. There are many, many good reasons why you haven't been willing to forgive him—not the least of which is that you haven't felt safe."

Pam nodded in agreement.

"And I imagine that you've also felt vulnerable, that your heart has been at risk of getting hurt."

Again, she nodded.

This time, Bob stared right into Pam's eyes and asked, "Are you ready for some relief?"

He had everyone's attention.

"First and foremost, if I am going to forgive someone, it is for me. I want to release myself from dragging around the burden of unforgiveness. It's heavy, and I get tired of carrying it after a while. Often the one I need to forgive is myself."

Greg added, "You know, forgiveness is a complicated topic . . . but I think that when we get first things first, it's really not so hard. I have difficulty forgiving when I feel as if I don't know what to do with the situation, when I still feel threatened, when I don't know how to take care of myself should the situation occur again. I still feel vulnerable, and letting go at that point is really tough."

"That's exactly how I feel," Pam admitted. "How can I say, 'Everything is okay, I forgive you,' when I'm not sure if it's going to happen again?"

Greg nodded and went on, "When I figure out what it was that I could have done differently or how I could take care of myself in the event that something like this happens again, I am free to forgive and move on. The offender has lost their power over me, because I have taken personal responsibility to care for myself. Again, we are talking about the issue of safety.

"When you acquire the skills of really caring for your heart, you can find rest under the wings of God's perfect love, letting him fill all those broken places while you let go of the fear. I guarantee that at this point you will start becoming free, and the process of forgiveness can begin. Forgiveness is in God's nature, so if you are filled with his Spirit, you won't have to force it to happen."

Bob spoke up, "My sense is that if you could honestly say, 'I am awesome at taking great care of myself emotionally, mentally, spiritually, and physically. I am doing that well, and I feel full and alive, and I know how to truly take care of my heart,' then forgiveness just kind of happens. It does. Like I said, the topic of forgiveness is huge and deserves its own careful study. I hope you will pursue the understanding of forgiveness for yourself and others, but for now focus on staying in touch with your heart."

Pam smiled at Bob and Greg for making this difficult issue a little easier to understand. After hearing about forgiveness for the majority of her life, for the first time it made sense to her in terms of becoming free rather than forcing herself to be righteous.

With a nod from Bob, Todd resumed sharing his plans and decisions with the group. Pam watched, wanting to know exactly what he meant. He still wasn't gentle with his words. He knew his tone was sharp, and catching himself, he backed up in hopes of softening what he was saying. But it had a way of gaining momentum until it could fill an auditorium. What decisions would he make about the ministry? Where would they live if he left his church?

"I want you to see why I have to do this," he was saying with marked force. His wife typically checked out when he said something like that, but she saw something else this time. She heard passion behind a voice that still had Wizard of Oz–like tendencies. Todd truly did care about her—her feelings, her needs, her desires. Despite all they had been through, despite his undying devotion to the bride of Christ—the church—Pam was still his bride.

She smiled. She was beginning to understand.

"Todd, do you find your wife fascinating?" Bob shifted the focus to Todd.

"When we first arrived here, Pam felt like a terrible burden," the preacher replied, with his customary lack of tact. "I didn't know what to do with Pam—especially because she was filled with so much contempt for herself. But since we've been here, I've seen the freedom and boldness in her that I was drawn to in the beginning of our relationship." He looked at her, and she felt her heart warm. "I'd like to see it return for good. So yes, after last night when Pam revealed to me things she's kept hidden in fear of me trampling over them or criticizing them, I was more baffled than fascinated. But I think once I can make sense of it all, I will be fascinated."

"I want to take an art class," Pam announced out of the blue. This was the time to ask, when she had people to back her up. She waited for Todd's response.

She had wanted him to smile and be as excited as she was about her newfound courage to pursue her dreams. He was her husband, and she had invited him into her heart. But he only looked confused, while steepling his fingers and assuming his judicial expression. She knew exactly what had happened. Disciplined man that he was, he was trying to figure out how and when she had decided this and what it would cost—monetarily, as well as emotionally.

She stopped short, and her smile faded. Inching forward self-consciously, she said, "I know we will need to discuss these types of things, but I feel more alive now than I have in a long time. It's like—like when you play the piano, honey." She turned to the others with reddened cheeks. "I've come to realize that if my husband wants me vibrant and well, I need to pursue the passions God has placed within me. I must love myself before I know how to love others."

Now Todd smiled at her, and though she could tell it took some effort, at least it was a start. She began to relax.

❂ ❂ ❂

Rodney listened as everyone gave their final updates and the counselors offered their last words of wisdom. He could hardly believe that after lunch, in just an hour or two, all four couples would go their separate ways. How could so much growth, bonding, and healing have taken place in four days? And for that matter, how had he even gotten Chelsea to agree to come? He thought back to how hopeless he had felt that day he phoned the Marriage Institute for help. Looking back, he could see that God had been working on their miracle even then.

He looked around as people began saying their good-byes and expressing their thanks to Bob and Greg. It was obvious that Rodney was not alone in crediting these insightful, compassionate, and godly men with facilitating the huge miracle God had begun to work in their marriages.

Charles shared that he and Victoria had plans to honeymoon on their way back to Dallas, and they had mapped out a few little romantic stops along the way. The beautiful Texan couple laughed and hugged each person in the room. When Victoria said she would stay in touch, they weren't empty words. Rodney knew they would be together again if she had her way. Rodney was so happy to see Charles's heart opening up not only to Victoria but to the love surrounding him on all sides.

Pam, whose plight had nearly broken Rodney's heart on the first day, looked pretty and self-assured now. And she was holding her husband's hand! Pam said she hated leaving the three dear couples who in four short days had become like family. She laughed and said she wished she could sneak Bob and Greg home to help referee for a few more days in the Davis's real-life parsonage environment. Rodney could relate!

And the California supermodel couple, Ryan and Becca . . . Rodney recalled how flamboyant and unusual they had appeared to him at first. The closest he'd ever come to seeing people like them was on TV. But over the past few days, they had become real people, real friends. He knew their hearts as well as they knew his. Rodney hoped they'd be able to keep making progress on their issues and avoid some of the pitfalls they'd talked about in their sessions. Ryan had publicly made a renewed commitment to his wife, promising to see a doctor, as she had asked, as well as continuing with personal counseling.

Finally Rodney's eyes fell on the love of his life, the only woman he had ever wanted to grow old with. Chelsea was capturing candid moments with her digital camera and talking about how anxious she was to get home to their sweet kids. Rodney felt his eyes tearing up as he recalled how helpless he had felt when they had first arrived. How good God was to them. Rodney knew there was plenty of work ahead to build the Promised Land marriage Bob and Greg had talked about, but he knew now that it was possible. Yes, he could be *thrilled* with his marriage. And he couldn't wait to take the next step of that journey.

"So Where Do We Go from Here?"

WE WANT TO TALK about where you, the reader, go from here.

First, we are convinced, after all these years of doing Intensives, that one of the keys to success is the sense of community the couples experience. Real community is a place where you are accepted and cared for, where you feel safe to be just who you are. Community is a place where you can share your deepest feelings, fears, wounds, longings, and so forth. We think the Lord wants us to experience that feeling of community—really connecting—and our society doesn't make this very easy.

We want to encourage you to find ways to bring community into your life, whether by being involved in a small group, finding a great church, or getting plugged into a neighborhood or community organization.

We also want to give you a couple of tips on how to put into practice the issues addressed in the Intensive. The key is to have a clear understanding of this model and the specific steps to use it.

The best way to summarize all that was taught during the Intensive is to revisit the analogy of the Israelites' journey to the Promised Land.

Marriage represents the hope of entering the Promised Land—

the land flowing with milk and honey. Unfortunately, many find themselves disappointed and discouraged along the way. Basically, they feel "stuck," as if they're trapped in slavery. The marriage may be characterized by turmoil and misery or it may simply be disappointing and boring, but either way it is a far cry from what they had hoped for. What keeps us stuck is the Fear Dance.

Each individual has his or her own fear buttons and reactions. And in a marriage, these feelings and reactions tend to play off one another. In other words, the things you do in response to your buttons being pushed seem as if they will be helpful in the moment and perhaps create more safety. Instead, when you see the complete process, it becomes obvious that your natural reactions actually set in motion a cycle that spins around and around, and ends up feeling far from safe.

FEAR DANCE

HUSBAND'S FEARS
(e.g., being controlled)

WIFE'S REACTION
(e.g., pursuing)

HUSBAND'S REACTION
(e.g., withdrawal)

WIFE'S FEARS
(e.g., abandonment)

For example, let's say we have a husband whose fear button is being controlled and a wife whose fear button is being abandoned. When the husband's fear of being controlled gets pushed, his natural reaction is to close his heart and withdraw. When the wife's fear of being abandoned gets pushed, she pursues. The couple's Fear Dance begins when either of them has their fear button pushed. If the husband's fear of being controlled gets pushed, he withdraws. His withdrawal in turn pushes his wife's fear of abandonment, which triggers her natural coping reaction of pursuing. Her pursuing retriggers his fear of being controlled, and the cycle continues. After many times through the cycle, the pain increases, and eventually the couple closes their hearts toward one another.

The key, then, is to clearly identify your Fear Dance. We encourage you to turn to appendix A and take the test. Once you've both completed the test, you can diagram your dance by following the directions.

One of the most powerful things about seeing your Fear Dance mapped out is that you can begin to recognize how the very things you do in reaction to your buttons getting pushed, in turn, push your partner's buttons. When a couple accurately identifies their Fear Dance, it becomes clear that the same fears and reactions appear in almost every conflict, no matter what the topic is.

The Promised Land

The Promised Land represents all that God intended marriage to be. Although many things need to go into your relationship to make it a marriage you're both thrilled with, the biggest factor is safety. There are two paths your relationship can take. In fact, in every interaction between you and your spouse, you have a choice to make. You can move toward creating and maintaining a safe environment for your relationship, or you can fall into the trap of reacting to one another in ways that make the relational environment feel insecure and unsafe.

Why is safety so important? The heart is the epicenter of life and relationships. When the heart feels safe, it opens. When the heart feels afraid or threatened, it closes. Safety and fear each set into motion chain reactions that lead to different destinations when it comes to marriage. The sense of safety will determine the heart of a couple's marriage. When people feel safe, they are naturally inclined to open their hearts and spirits. Intimacy occurs effortlessly and naturally when hearts and spirits open to one another. Below is a simple representation of what we are talking about:

Safety ⇒ Openness ⇒ Connection/Intimacy

One of the main goals in a Couples Intensive is to create a safe environment in which people are inclined to open up. In a typical

Intensive situation, couples share intimate details of their lives and relationships because they feel safe. As a result, the people in the group begin to feel close and connected with one another.

We encourage you to make these same efforts to create safety in your marriage. In the optimal setting, your home will feel like the safest place on earth, where your hearts thrive and beat with life. Take some time to answer the following questions about safety:

- How have I made our relationship unsafe for my spouse?
- How do I damage the safety of my marital environment?
- What do I do in response to feeling unsafe?
- What could I do for myself to make myself feel safe?

Discussions about fear and safety in a marriage relationship can be very helpful. Many people, however, get to the point where they see how they have helped create an unsafe environment in their marriage, but they don't know how to turn it around and get "unstuck."

Steps to the Promised Land

After working with thousands of couples and individuals, our clinical team has found that there are four main steps that help us move from feeling stuck and unsafe to the safe, open, and connected marriage we want. Below is a model of how we understand these steps to work.

Step 1: Personal Responsibility—The Power of One

The first step out of the Fear Dance is personal responsibility, also called the power of one, which empowers each individual in the marriage to become the person God has created him or her to be. This happens when we accept the job of being responsible for our own behavior and well-being. We truly become an adult when we assume that mantle of responsibility.

Personal responsibility is the key to personal empowerment. Allowing your ultimate well-being, emotions, and behavior to be dependent on others is to be disempowered. When we give our responsibility away, we essentially give away the "wellspring" of our lives too. Proverbs 4:23 states, "Above all else, guard your heart, for it is the wellspring of life." It is your job to care for your heart. Giving away that responsibility or taking on the responsibility for someone else is not guarding your heart and will leave you feeling disempowered.

JOURNEY TO THE PROMISED LAND

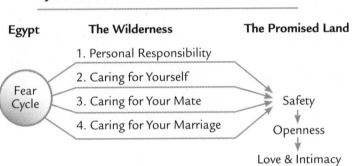

Answer the following four questions about personal responsibility:

- As you reflect on your marriage, what areas of your life/ behavior/reactions would you like to work on to become more personally responsible?
- Refer back to the diagram you made of your Fear Dance. Is it easier to point the finger at your partner and see how he or she should change than to look closely at yourself?
- To what degree have you felt disempowered because you are waiting for your spouse to do things differently?

How much energy have you spent trying to change
your spouse?
- Consider your relationships with friends, family, and
significant others. In what ways have you struggled
with your behavior, words, or actions? How do you
want these areas to be different in your marriage?

In terms of breaking out of the Fear Dance, personal responsibility occurs when we are clear what we should focus on—our own selves. When we focus on getting our spouse to change, we are disempowered. On the other hand, separating my stuff from his or her stuff allows me to concentrate on things I can actually control. And that is personal responsibility. Turn back to your Fear Dance diagram and, as shown in the diagram below, draw a diagonal line separating your fears and reactions from your spouse's. Everything on your side of the dance is what you are responsible for. Notice that your spouse's "stuff" isn't on your side!

FEAR DANCE
Good *personal* focus

HUSBAND'S FEARS
(e.g., being controlled)

WIFE'S REACTION
(e.g., pursuing)

HUSBAND'S REACTION
(e.g., withdrawal)

WIFE'S FEARS
(e.g., abandonment)

Step 2: Caring for Yourself

The first step out of the Fear Dance is personal responsibility, which means accepting the job of caring for ourselves. The second step, then, is to actually care for ourselves.

Caring for yourself, sometimes referred to as self-care, is the process of fully receiving God's love and provision and sharing them with others. It involves being filled in all aspects of your being: mental, physical, spiritual, and emotional.

When self-care is exercised, there is more safety in a marriage, because we stop looking at our spouse as the source of our fulfillment. That is God's job. When we mistakenly look to another person to fill us up, we place a burden on that person and on the relationship that neither can bear.

Self-care begins when we focus on our own side of the Fear Dance— our own spiritual, emotional, mental, and physical well-being. Notice in the diagram below where the focus is. Turn to your

FEAR DANCE
Good *personal* care

HUSBAND'S FEARS
(e.g., being controlled)

HUSBAND'S REACTION
(e.g., withdrawal)

WIFE'S REACTION
(e.g., pursuing)

WIFE'S FEARS
(e.g., abandonment)

Fear Dance diagram and circle your side of the dance. That is what you are responsible to care for.

The ultimate goal of personal care is the fulfillment of the greatest commandments: Love the Lord your God with all your heart, soul, mind, and strength (an act of giving and receiving, and the ultimate act of self-love), and love your neighbor in the same way you now love yourself. This process enables us to become and remain full vessels and then to give from our abundance. Self-care is about wholeness.

We are called to love the Lord with our whole being, but since love comes only from God, we must first be filled with his love. As we allow ourselves to be filled with God's love—the essence of life—we are truly loving ourselves. Once we are filled with his love, loving him and others becomes a natural outflow. At that point, we are fulfilling the call.

However, if we hoard the love of God, it becomes stale and useless to everyone. If we give and don't receive, we become empty. Therefore, if we give and then receive again from God, then give some more, our water stays fresh and we stay full. Thus, taking good care of ourselves is good for us, and giving to others is good for us. This is why we say that taking good care of ourselves is *always* in the best interest of all parties involved.

This pattern of receiving and giving, receiving and giving is the way God created the world to operate, and thus all human life is based on this model. A healthy, sustainable relationship is one in which two people look to God as their source of fulfillment, actually get full, and then share the blessings with each other and the world.

Excellent self-care, then, requires finding a healthy balance between giving and receiving. The natural cycle—and necessary components—of self-care are:

- Attending: responsibly attending to the state of your heart and determining what it needs and desires
- Receiving: opening your heart to receive from God and others

- Giving: responsibly responding to the needs and
  desires of others

People often avoid fully caring for themselves because they think it is selfish. In fact, the opposite is true. The fuller you are, the more you have to give. The more you have to give, the more you are able to serve God and others. There is nothing selfish about that. Jesus says, "I have come that they may have life, and have it to the full" (John 10:10). His desire is for our hearts to be full so that when we give, we are giving out of the abundance of our hearts instead of from a diminishing reservoir. Answer the following questions about self-care:

- How empty, tired, or exhausted do you feel? How
  whole do you feel?
- Consider the categories mentioned: physical, mental,
  emotional, and spiritual. How well are you taking
  care of yourself in each of these areas? Comment
  on each.
- Think of at least three ways you could be (or are) taking good care of yourself in each of the four categories: physical, mental, emotional, and spiritual.
- In what ways would good self-care improve your marriage and make it safer?

Step 3: Caring for Your Mate

The third step out of the Fear Dance is caring for our spouse. As personally empowered and fulfilled people, we can effectively care for our spouse as a precious child of God. We can seek to understand, encourage, and assist our spouse in managing their needs by caring deeply about their feelings on the journey toward becoming a full expression of the person God created them to be.

One of the first opportunities to show care for our spouse's feelings is through the skill of emotional communication, or what we call Heart Talk. Oftentimes, our communication focuses on details that are distracting and making progress more difficult. Focusing on who is right, whose fault it is, or what really happened—particularly when strong emotions are involved—encourages defensiveness and makes people feel like adversaries. Communication proceeds more easily and effectively when participants are able to trust that they are truly being understood and that their feelings matter. When we care about another person's feelings, it is a form of caring for their heart. When our spouse expresses an emotion, we may want to ask, "What is their heart trying to say?"

In Heart Talk, the goal is to fully understand one another on an emotional level. Notice in the diagram below that the focus isn't on reactions but instead on the deep emotions (e.g., fears).

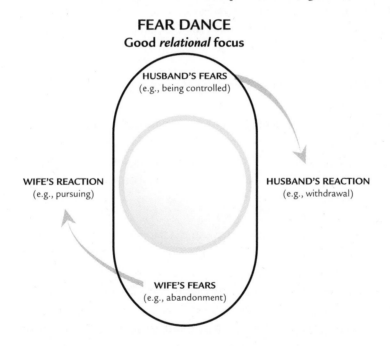

FEAR DANCE
Good *relational* focus

HUSBAND'S FEARS
(e.g., being controlled)

WIFE'S REACTION
(e.g., pursuing)

HUSBAND'S REACTION
(e.g., withdrawal)

WIFE'S FEARS
(e.g., abandonment)

Once people believe that their feelings are understood and that they actually matter, they tend to relax and become more cooperative. They are more likely to care about the feelings and needs of the other person. Healthy relationships work at building a foundation of trust so each person has room to be who they are and feel how they feel. They know that fundamentally they will be respected, understood, and cared for. They are confident that they will not be steamrollered, judged, or rejected. (See appendix B for more details on using Heart Talk.) Answer the following questions about caring for your spouse:

- How effective has the communication in your marriage felt?
- Do you usually walk away feeling deeply understood and cared for?
- How often do you truly seek to understand and care for your spouse's feelings?
- How could the Heart Talk method bring safety to your communication?

Step 4: Caring for Your Marriage

The fourth and final step out of the Fear Dance is caring for our marriage. As personally empowered and fulfilled people who effectively care for our spouse, we accept our role as a member of the marital team. We also accept our responsibilities to constantly strive to be the best we can be, to assist our spouse in being the best they can be, and to do everything in our power to make the team successful.

Power struggles seem to be one of Satan's greatest ploys to cause trouble in a marriage. The problem is that power struggles encourage us to assume an adversarial position against one another. Because marriage is designed to be a team effort, assuming an adversarial posture with our partner sets up a hopeless situation; the outcome is already set. There is no such thing as a win-lose outcome in a marriage. As teammates, married partners either both win or both lose in any given situation.

Therefore, we encourage you to adopt a no-losers policy: Either both partners win or no one wins. With this policy, it is unacceptable for either partner to walk away feeling as though they have lost. Both recognize that if either loses, the whole team loses.

In order to establish a no-losers policy, couples need to come up with a new definition of winning. Winning cannot be about getting our own way, because if the goal is to get our way, we lock ourselves into an adversarial position. Therefore, winning has to be redefined as finding a solution that both parties feel good about. In the end, it can be our way, our spouse's way, some combination of the two, or some creative alternative. As long as both spouses feel good about the solution and neither feels as if they are losing, the outcome is a win for the team. Notice that in the diagram on the next page, the focus is on finding solutions that both people feel great about—win-win. (See appendix C for more practical steps on implementing a no-losers policy.)

Remember what Paul wrote in Philippians 2:2-4: "Make my joy complete by being like-minded, having the same love, being one in spirit and purpose. Do nothing out of selfish ambition or vain conceit, but in humility consider others better than yourselves. Each of you should look not only to your own interests, but also to the interests of others."

The ideal for a good marriage, as for a good team, is unity. Differences are often viewed as the enemy of marriage because they are capable of upsetting the unity of the team. However, differences are vital for a team to be efficient and effective. The problems we experience on our teams are caused not by the differences but by a lack of knowledge and skill for how to use them.

Answer the following questions about caring for your marriage by working as a team:

- Are there times in your relationship when you've felt more like competitors or adversaries than teammates?
- How does your relationship lose when you forget that you're teammates?
- How is teamwork related to safety?

FEAR DANCE
Good *relational* goal: No-losers policy

HUSBAND'S FEARS
(e.g., being controlled)

WIFE'S REACTION
(e.g., pursuing)

WIN-WIN
SOLUTIONS

HUSBAND'S REACTION
(e.g., withdrawal)

WIFE'S FEARS
(e.g., abandonment)

Casting a Vision for Your Marriage

When we embrace the purpose of marriage as a means by which God can reflect his image, there is so much hope beyond the daily grind.

There is something about seeing the bigger picture that can be freeing and inspiring. It gives us motivation to keep growing. This is not unlike a teenager working in a grocery store, earning money for college. It is similar to a waiter or waitress working in a restaurant at night while auditioning in the day for acting parts, with the dream of becoming a Hollywood star. It is the purpose behind cooking another meal or washing another load of laundry that helps a parent stay motivated. If the purpose is to create an environment of security where the children can thrive, the most meaningless jobs can feel rewarding and significant.

So again: Embracing a purpose for your marriage can be powerful!

We can stop and ask poignant questions: How is this conflict, this challenge, this transition in our lives being used to transform us into the people God created us to be? How is our marriage inspiring people to draw closer to God—we ourselves, our children, and people outside our home?

Asking the questions takes courage. Answering the questions takes even more courage. But God is available to help—and celebrate—as you confront the essence and purpose of your marriage.

Identifying Your
Fear Dance

1. Describe a recent conflict or negative situation with your spouse—something that really "pushed your buttons." For the purpose of this exercise, be sure that you and your spouse write down the same conflict.

_____

_____

_____

_____

_____

2. What were the buttons that got pushed during the conflict? Another way to look at it is, How did what happened during the conflict make you feel about *yourself*? What did the conflict say about *you*? What was the message it sent to *you*? Look through the following options and use them to fill in the blanks in this statement: "As a result of this conflict, I felt _____ or feared feeling _____, or I thought _____ would happen." Check all that apply—but put an asterisk beside the most important feelings.

✓ or *	"As a result of the conflict, I felt . . ."	What That Feeling Sounds Like
	Rejected	I am discarded; I am useless; my spouse doesn't need me; I am not necessary in this relationship; my spouse doesn't desire intimacy with me.
	Unwanted	My spouse doesn't want me; my spouse does not choose me; my spouse is staying in the marriage out of duty, obligation, or because it's the "right" thing to do.
	Abandoned	I am alone; my spouse will ultimately leave me; my spouse won't be committed to me for life.
	Disconnected	We are emotionally detached or separated; there are walls or barriers between us in the marriage.
	Like a failure	I am not successful as a husband/wife; I do not perform right or correctly; I fall short in my relationship; I don't make the grade.
	Helpless or powerless	I cannot do anything to change my spouse or my situation; I do not possess the power, resources, capacity, or ability to get what I want.
	Controlled	I am controlled by my spouse; my spouse exercises authority over me; I am made to "submit"; my spouse restrains me; I am treated like a child or my spouse acts like my parent.
	Defective	Something is wrong with me; I'm the problem; I am unlovable.
	Inadequate	I am not capable; I am incompetent.

✓ or *	"As a result of the conflict, I felt . . ."	What That Feeling Sounds Like
	Inferior	Everyone else is better than I am; I am less valuable or important than others.
	Invalidated	Who I am, what I think, what I do, or how I feel is not valued by my spouse.
	Unloved	My spouse doesn't love me anymore; my spouse has no affection or desire for me; my relationship lacks warm attachment, admiration, enthusiasm, or devotion.
	Dissatisfied	I do not experience satisfaction within the relationship; I will exist in misery for the rest of my life; I am not pleased within my marriage; I feel no joy in my relationship.
	Taken advantage of	I am cheated by my spouse; my spouse takes advantage of me; my spouse withholds things I need; I feel like a doormat; I don't get what I want.
	Worthless or devalued	I am useless; my spouse fails to recognize my value and worth; I feel cheapened or undervalued in the marriage; I have little or no value to my spouse; my mate does not see me as priceless.
	Not good enough	Nothing I do is ever satisfactory or sufficient for my spouse; there are always more "hoops" to jump through; I am never able to meet my spouse's expectations of me; my efforts are never enough.
	Unaccepted	My spouse does not accept me; my partner is not pleased with me; my spouse does not approve of me.

✓ or *	"As a result of the conflict, I felt . . ."	What That Feeling Sounds Like
	Judged	I am always being unfairly judged or misjudged; my spouse forms faulty or negative opinions about me; I am always being evaluated; my spouse does not approve of me.
	Humiliated	This marriage is extremely destructive to my self-respect or dignity.
	Ignored	My spouse will not pay attention to me; I feel neglected.
	Unimportant	I am not important to my spouse; I am irrelevant, insignificant, or of little priority to my spouse.
	Useless	I am of no use in my marriage; I am ineffective; I am not needed.
	Afraid of intimacy	I am afraid of opening up emotionally to my spouse; I will be hurt emotionally if I allow my spouse past my walls.
	Misunderstood	My spouse fails to understand me correctly; he/she has the wrong idea or impression about me; I am misinterpreted or misread.
	Disrespected	I feel insulted; my spouse does not admire me; my spouse has a low opinion of me; I am disregarded; my spouse does not respect me; my spouse does not look up to me.
	Out of control	My marriage is wild, unruly, or hectic; my spouse is unmanageable or uncontrollable; things feel disorganized or in disorder.
	Alone	I am by myself or on my own; I am without help or assistance; I am lonely and isolated.

✓ or *	"As a result of the conflict, I felt . . ."	What That Feeling Sounds Like
	Insignificant	I am irrelevant to my spouse; I am of no consequence to my spouse; I am immaterial, not worth mentioning, trivial in the eyes of my spouse; I am of minor importance to my spouse.
	Unknown	My spouse does not know me; it's like I'm a stranger to my spouse; I am nameless or anonymous to my spouse; I am unfamiliar to my spouse.
	Boring	There is no passion in our marriage; my spouse perceives me as dull and dreary; our marriage is uninteresting; my spouse believes that he/she knows everything there is to know about me; I feel as if we are just roommates; there are no romantic feelings between us.
	Disappointing	I am a letdown in the marriage; my spouse is disppointed in me.
	Phony	My spouse sees me as fake or not genuine; my spouse believes that I'm a fraud, a pretender, or an imposter; my spouse perceives that I'm not who I say I am; I'm viewed as a hypocrite.
	Unfairly treated	My spouse treats me unfairly; my spouse wants me to do things he/she is unwilling to do; there is a double standard; I am asked to do things that are unreasonable or excessive; my spouse treats me differently from others; I am not treated equally.

✓ or *	"As a result of the conflict, I felt . . ."	What That Feeling Sounds Like
	Deceived	Our relationship lacks truth, honesty, or trustworthiness; my spouse willfully perverts truth in order to decieve, cheat, or defraud me; my spouse misleads me or gives a false appearance.
	Betrayed	My spouse is disloyal or unfaithful; my spouse has given up on the relationship; I feel let down; my spouse shares or reveals private information with others.
	Unaware	I do not know what is going on in the relationship; I do not have the necessary information; I'm in the dark; I'm clueless; things feel secretive, hidden, or undisclosed; I'm ignorant or uninformed.
	Other	

3. What do you *do* when your buttons get pushed? (Your buttons are the items you marked in question #2.) How do you *react* when you feel that way? Identify your common *coping strategies* to deal with that feeling. Check all that apply. Put an asterisk next to the most important reactions or coping behaviors.

✓ or *	"When I am in conflict I . . ."	Explanation
	Withdraw	I avoid others or alienate myself without resolution; I am distant; I sulk or use the silent treatment.
	Stonewall	I turn into a stone wall by not responding to my spouse.
	Escalate	My emotions spiral out of control; I argue, raise my voice, or fly into a rage.
	Emotionally shut down	I detach emotionally and close my heart toward my spouse; I numb out; I become devoid of emotion; I have no regard for others' needs or troubles.
	Pacify	I try to soothe, calm down, or placate my spouse; I try to get him or her to not feel negative emotions.
	Go into earn-it mode	I try to do more to earn others' love and care.
	Belittle	I devalue or dishonor someone with words or actions; I call my spouse names, use insults, ridicule, take potshots at, or mock him or her.
	Form negative beliefs	I believe my spouse is far worse than is really the case; I see my spouse in a negative light or attribute negative motives to him or her; I see my spouse through a negative lens.
	Become arrogant	I posture myself as superior to or wiser than my spouse.
	Blame	I place responsibility on others, not accepting fault; I'm convinced the problem is my spouse's fault.

✓ or *	"When I am in conflict I . . ."	Explanation
	Feel like an innocent victim	I see my spouse as an attacking monster and myself as put upon, unfairly accused, mistreated, or unappreciated.
	Control	I hold back, restrain, oppress, or dominate my spouse; I "rule over" my spouse; I talk over or prevent my spouse from having a chance to explain his/her position, opinions, or feelings.
	Become dishonest	I lie about, fail to reveal, give false impressions of, or falsify my thoughts, feelings, habits, likes, dislikes, personal history, daily activities, or plans for the future.
	Withhold	I withhold my affections, feelings, sexual intimacy, or love from my spouse.
	Demand	I try to force my spouse to do something, usually with implied threat of punishment if he/she refuses.
	Use annoying behavior	I use irritating habits or activities to infuriate, annoy, upset, or get on my spouse's nerves.
	Provoke	I intentionally aggravate, hassle, goad, or irritate my spouse.
	Isolate myself	I shut down and go into seclusion or into my "cave."
	Exaggerate	I make overstatements or enlarge my words beyond bounds of the truth; I make statements like "You always . . ." or "You never . . ."

✓ or *	"When I am in conflict I . . ."	Explanation
	Throw tantrums	I have a fit of bad temper; I become irritable, crabby, or grumpy.
	Go into denial	I refuse to admit the truth or reality.
	Invalidate	I devalue my spouse; I do not appreciate who my partner is or what he/she feels, thinks, or does.
	Maintain distress	I replay the argument over and over; I can't stop thinking about the conflict or what my spouse does that frustrates or hurts me.
	Exercise independence	I become independent (separate from my spouse) in my attitude, behavior, and decision making.
	Rewrite history	I recast our earlier times together in a negative light; my recall of previous disappointments and slights becomes dramatically enhanced.
	Become defensive	Instead of listening, I defend myself by providing an explanation; I make excuses for my actions.
	Become clingy	I develop a strong emotional attachment or dependence on my spouse; I hold tight to my spouse.
	Become passive-aggressive	I display negative emotions, resentment, and aggression in passive ways, such as procrastination, forgetfulness, and stubbornness.
	Use avoidance	I get involved in activities to avoid my spouse.

✓ or *	"When I am in conflict I . . ."	Explanation
	Caretake	I become responsible for others by giving physical or emotional care and support to the point where I am doing everything for my spouse, and my partner does little to care for himself or herself.
	Become pessimistic	I become negative, distrustful, cynical, and skeptical in my view of my spouse and marriage.
	Act out	I engage in negative behaviors like drug or alcohol abuse, extramarital affairs, excessive shopping, or overeating.
	Go into fix-it mode	I focus almost exclusively on what is needed to solve the problem.
	Complain	I express unhappiness or make accusations.
	Criticize	I pass judgment, condemn, or point out my spouse's faults; I attack his/her personality or character.
	Strike out	I lash out in anger; I become verbally or physically aggressive, possibly abusive.
	Manipulate	I control, influence, or maneuver my spouse for my own advantage.
	Get angry	I display strong feelings of displeasure or violent and uncontrolled emotions.
	Catastrophize	I use dramatic, exaggerated expressions to depict that the relationship is in danger or that it has failed.

✓ or *	"When I am in conflict I . . ."	Explanation
	Pursue the truth	I try to determine what really happened or who is telling the truth, instead of trying to understand my spouse's feelings.
	Judge	I negatively critique, evaluate, or conclude something about my spouse.
	Become selfish	I become overly concerned with myself and my own interests, feelings, wants, or desires.
	Lecture	I sermonize, talk down to, scold, or reprimand my spouse.
	Cross-complain	I meet my spouse's complaint (or criticism) with an immediate complaint of my own, totally ignoring what my spouse has said.
	Whine	I express myself by using a childish, high-pitched nasal tone and stress one syllable toward the end of the sentence.
	Use negative body language	I give a false smile, shift from side to side, or fold my arms across my chest.
	Use humor	I use humor as a way of not dealing with the issue at hand.
	Use sarcasm	I use negative or hostile humor, hurtful words, belittling comments, cutting remarks, or demeaning statements.
	Minimize	I assert that my spouse is overreacting to an issue; I intentionally underestimate, downplay, or soft-pedal the issue or how my spouse feels.

✓ or *	"When I am in conflict I . . ."	Explanation
	Rationalize	I attempt to make my actions seem reasonable; I try to attribute my behavior to credible motives; I try to provide believable but untrue reasons for my conduct.
	Say, "Yes, but . . . "	I start out agreeing (*yes*) but end up disagreeing (*but*).
	Become indifferent	I become cold and smug; I show no concern for my spouse or my marriage.
	Dump	I emotionally "vomit," unload, or dump on my spouse.
	Abdicate	I give away responsibilities; I deny my commitments.
	Self-deprecate	I run myself down or become very critical of myself.
	Mind-read	I make assumptions about my spouse's private feelings, behaviors, or motives.
	Repeat myself	I repeat back my own position over and over instead of understanding my spouse's position.
	Debate right vs. wrong	I argue about who is right and who is wrong; I debate whose position is the correct one.
	Neglect myself	I desert myself; I neglect myself; I take care of everyone except myself.
	Show righteous indignation	I believe that I deserve to be angry, resentful, or annoyed with my spouse because of what he/she did.

✓ or *	"When I am in conflict I . . ."	Explanation
	Become stubborn	I will not budge from my position; I become inflexible or persistent.
	Emphasize righteousness	I make everything a moral issue or argue about issues of morality or righteousness.
	Play dumb	I pretend not to understand or know what my spouse is talking about.
	Nag	I badger, pester, or harass my spouse to do something I want.
	Other	

4. Instead of experiencing the feelings you marked in question #2, how do you *want* to feel in your marriage? These feelings are usually the opposite of the buttons or fears you checked in question #2 (e.g., the opposite of feeling like a failure is success; the opposite of feeling helpless is power; the opposite of feeling rejected is acceptance, etc.). Check all that apply. Put an asterisk next to the most important wants/desires.

✓ or *	"I want . . ."	What That Feeling Sounds Like
	Acceptance	I want to be warmly received without condition.
	Grace	I want something good (i.e., forgiveness) that I don't deserve.
	Connection	I want to be united to others.

✓ or *	"I want . . ."	What That Feeling Sounds Like
	Companion-ship	I want deep, intimate relationships.
	Success	I want to achieve or accomplish something; I want to be successful as a spouse.
	Self-determination	I want to have independence and free will.
	To be cared for	I want my spouse to watch out for me; I want to be well cared for.
	Understanding	I want to be known and understood at a deep level.
	To be a hero	I want to be the knight in shining armor; I want to be my spouse's champion.
	Love	I want to feel attractive to my spouse; I want to be admired; I want to feel lovable.
	Validation	I want be valued for who I am, what I think, and how I feel.
	Competence	I want to have skills and abilities that bring success.
	Respect	I want to be admired and esteemed.
	To be important	I want to feel relevant, significant, and of high priority to my spouse.
	To be valued	I want to be honored and to feel like a priceless treasure.

✓ or *	"I want . . ."	What That Feeling Sounds Like
	Commitment	I want to have unconditional security in relationships.
	Passion	I want excitement, fascination, intrigue, romance, and adventure.
	Significance	I want to have meaning and purpose.
	Attention	I want to be noticed and attended to.
	Comfort	I want to feel a sense of well-being.
	Support	I want my spouse to back me up and care about what matters to me.
	Approval	I want to be liked and accepted.
	To be wanted	I want to be sought after.
	Safety	I want to feel protected and secure.
	Affection	I want to feel fondness and warmth.
	Trust	I want to have faith in my spouse.
	Hope	I want confidence that I will get what I love and desire.
	Joy	I want to feel satisfied and happy; I want to be thrilled with my marriage.
	Power	I want to feel that I have the ability to control the outcome or influence the direction of my marriage.
	Partnership	I want to feel like my spouse is my teammate or partner; I want us both to have equal responsibility for our marriage.

✓ or *	"I want . . ."	What That Feeling Sounds Like
	To feel adequate	I want to feel like I measure up or am good enough.
	Appreciation	I want my spouse to notice what I do in the marriage and to feel gratitude.
	To feel useful	I want to feel needed in the marriage.
	Accurate portrayal	I want to be seen correctly; I want my spouse to represent me in a true and accurate manner; I want to be seen in a positive light.
	Assistance	I want to have a helpmate; I want support, backing, and assistance from my spouse.
	Peace	I want serenity and tranquility; I want my marriage to be relaxed.
	Intimacy	I want to open my heart and not have walls in my marriage; I want a deep closeness.
	Other	

5. Now it's your turn to diagram your personal Fear Dance. Turn to the blank chart called "Your Fear Dance" on the next page. Fill in the feelings you marked in question #2 (e.g., *rejected, unwanted, abandoned,* etc.) on the blank lines under "Husband's [or Wife's] Fears." Have your spouse fill in the other section based on his or her responses. Then fill in the coping strategies you marked in question #3 (e.g., *withdraw, stonewall, escalate,* etc.) on the blank

lines under "Husband's [or Wife's] Reaction." Again, have your spouse fill in the other section based on his or her responses.

YOUR FEAR DANCE

HUSBAND'S FEARS

_____
_____
_____
_____
_____

WIFE'S REACTION

_____
_____
_____
_____
_____

HUSBAND'S REACTION

_____
_____
_____
_____

WIFE'S FEARS

_____
_____
_____
_____
_____

Putting Heart Talk into Action

Heart Talk, or emotional communication, is focused on connecting and caring for one's relationships. It stands in sharp contrast to Work Talk, in which we are communicating simply for productivity or in order to reach a predetermined outcome. Heart Talk involves listening and speaking with open hearts. You must ask, what is this person feeling? We recommend using five simple steps.

1. Make safety the first priority.

You can have the best tools, the latest insights, the greatest determination, and the most powerful strategies and still fail if the environment is wrong. In a safe environment, no one has to worry about being shamed, rejected, punished, or attacked for stating personal beliefs and feelings. A safe environment makes Heart Talk easier, which in turn creates more safety.

2. Listen to the words the speaker is saying.

You don't have to agree with what your spouse is saying or fear that you will have to change your behavior because of it. You are simply listening to gain a greater understanding of who this person is and what feelings are being expressed.

3. Listen with your heart.

Listen with your heart to the point that the other person feels deeply understood and cared for. This is exactly what the Bible says to do: "Love one another deeply, from the heart" (1 Peter 1:22).

4. Reflect back to the speaker what you hear him or her saying.

Don't react to any particular word; rather, start trying to identify the emotions underneath the words. Repeat back to the speaker what you heard, using different words, and then say, "Is that what you said?" After the speaker confirms that you heard the words right, ask about feelings. Ask questions such as, "What were you feeling when that happened to you?" or "How does that make you feel?" or "When that happens to me, I sometimes feel like this or that; is that how you feel?"

5. Allow the other's emotions to touch you.

It is one thing to hear these emotions and say, "Boy, I can tell you are really upset." But it is another to allow these emotions to penetrate your heart, to allow yourself to feel the pain or the sadness. The key is not merely to understand these feelings but also to allow the feelings to touch you.

What Stops Us?

There are several factors that make us hesitant to use Heart Talk. Some people are afraid that . . .

- they'll have to do what the other person wants them to do.
- this means that they are agreeing with the other person.
- they might be made to feel guilty if too many feelings come out during the conversation.

- they will be too vulnerable in the presence of deep emotion.

Heart Talk Saves Time

Does this sound like a lot of work or like it will take far too much time? Be careful about trying to "save time"! Just making a quick decision will not solve your problem. When people don't feel understood and cared for, they may "agree" to some decision, but they won't get on board with it. Relationally, it doesn't feel to them like a satisfying or effective solution. And in the end, you'll have to talk about these things all over again.

If you shut down the dialogue, you might not have to deal immediately with more words—but you *will* have to deal with a cold shoulder, distance, or other consequences of not taking the time to attend to a person's feelings. This is why Heart Talk actually *saves* tremendous amounts of time.

Practice Makes Perfect

Is this method easy? Not in one sense: It's probably very different from what you've done to this point in your life. Therefore, it will take some effort to begin to put these ideas into practice. At first it may feel awkward, and you may be clumsy at it. But as you get more practice, it gets easier.

Communicating from the heart is a complex business. If you go into it expecting things to flow easily and without a lot of effort, you're kidding yourself. We recommend that you adjust your expectations.

Expect problems and misunderstandings.

Even the best communicators sometimes fail to understand others and fall short of making themselves understood.

Expect that you'll need a lot of patience.

Heart Talk takes time. You and your spouse may not connect or get on the same wavelength on the first or second (or third or even fourth) attempt. Impatience can doom the goal of genuine understanding. Instead, recognize that emotional communication deserves patience and a deliberate attempt to understand not only the words being said but also the emotions behind the words.

Expect a lot of trial and error.

People have different ways of communicating. While all of us can master and use a powerful set of tools for emotional communication, the way we use those tools varies from person to person. (For some effective communication tools, you might want to check out the book *Men's Relational Toolbox* by Gary Smalley, Greg Smalley, and Michael Smalley.) We get the best use out of communication tools by adapting them for our own style and personal bent—and that requires trial and error.

Would you like to enjoy your relationships for the rest of your life? Would you like to ride them out for the long haul? You can! When you choose to master the art of Heart Talk rather than Work Talk, you can help all your loved ones *feel* truly loved and cared for. And a loving relationship is a growing relationship!

Guys, Take Note

Men often feel frustrated when their wives seem to go on and on. So we have a special word here for the guys reading this book: *Heart Talk is ultimately more efficient and takes less time than any other method.* Think about it: If you don't have to repeatedly go over the same old ground, you can spend your time on other things. Often, the reason women keep revisiting subjects is because they don't feel *emotionally* understood. If husbands take the time to actually uncover their wives' heartfelt concerns, the conversation can move on and men won't have to hear the same thing a dozen times, from six different angles. When guys finally "get" this, the lightbulb goes on for us. We get excited about our ability to condense the conversation.

If your wife repeats the same thing over and over, we can almost guarantee that she does not believe you understand her heart. You could say at that point, "I noticed that you are repeating yourself, and that causes me to question whether you feel I understand you. Am I missing something?" It is amazing what happens when a woman feels deeply understood emotionally.

So learn to put your problem-solving urges on hold for a while, and listen with your heart. Problem-solving skills remain extremely valuable, of course, but they are much more effective *after* you understand the emotions involved. So save time! Get efficient! And look for the emotional nugget.

Steps to a No-Losers Policy

A win-win solution makes both parties feel good, gives positive movement to the marriage, and leaves it in a different (and better) place than it was before. How do you create a win-win solution? We have found seven steps that help both partners in the marriage feel great about the solution.

Step 1: Establish a no-losers policy.

First, remember you're on the same team. This is huge! Just keeping this in mind can change the way you treat one another as you communicate and negotiate. A no-losers policy says that it is not acceptable for one of you to walk away feeling as if you've lost. You could say, "I need you to know that I will not feel okay with any solution that you do not also feel good about." If either one of you says, "I don't feel good about this decision" or "I feel as if I'm losing here," that's it. You back up and start over. It is simply unacceptable for either of you to feel as if you're losing.

This first step instantly creates a positive tone that tends to radically improve how you treat one another. As a matter of fact, if you did nothing more than this, you would see an enormous improvement in your relationship. The worry simply dissipates and is replaced by a feeling of safety.

Step 2: Listen to how the other person feels.

Talk to each other. Listen for the heart. Take time to understand how your spouse feels and why he or she prefers a particular solution. Why does it seem like the right way to go? Why is it important? Usually there are reasons why your spouse's position is so critical—but you usually have to dig for them. The key is to keep asking questions and being curious. "Why is your solution so important?" "What will it help you to accomplish?" "What is it that you really want?"

Work at it until both of you feel completely understood. It's likely that your conflict will melt away as you go deeper and understand one another's core feelings and concerns. Often, couples find that they are really not as far apart as they thought.

Once you get to the underlying feelings, take your separate ideas and set them aside. Put them on the shelf. You don't throw them away or pursue them; you simply set them aside. Keep them handy in case you want to go back to them at a later time.

Step 3: Ask God for his opinion.

Pray together. Share your perspectives about what you think the Bible says about the issue, remembering that the Bible does not speak specifically to every issue. If God has an opinion, wouldn't his answer be the best?

Some conflicts resolve at this point, when you discern God's leading on the issue. Furthermore, it is almost impossible to want to pray with someone when you're really angry or when your heart is closed. This step is a good internal check-in time. If you don't want to pray together, you probably shouldn't be trying to resolve the conflict at this time—you're probably not very safe and are likely to say or do something that will get you back into the Fear Dance.

But do you want to know something really amazing? In the end, God's opinion on the matter at hand may well prove to be less important than the act of seeking his opinion together. For in the very act of coming together to discover God's perspective, you've instantly restored unity—you are now seeking God together. We love the verse that reads, "Let the peace of Christ rule in your hearts, since as members of one body you were called to peace. And be thankful" (Colossians 3:15).

Step 4: Brainstorm about a win-win solution.

Brainstorm solutions. Get creative. Now that you each understand where the other person is coming from, you can begin to generate ideas that have the potential of being win-win solutions. Don't judge or criticize the ideas at this stage; the idea is to be creative and generate a list of options. Give each person an opportunity to express any suggestion he or she thinks might work. Make sure this is a green-light session—a time when both of you feel safe to share ideas. Then revisit them all, highlighting the ones that might help you solve your dilemma. If you feel you need more input, do some research at the library or on the Internet. You might consult with an expert. The goal is to explore lots of options.

Step 5: Select a win-win solution.

Now it's time to evaluate the options and pick a win-win solution—something you both can feel good about. It doesn't matter who suggests the proposed solution; the important thing is that both of you feel it's a win.

There will be plenty of times when you end up doing exactly what your spouse wanted to do from the beginning, but by the time you get there, you feel great about it—win-win. At other times, the opposite will happen: You do exactly what you wanted in the first place, but by the time you get there, your spouse feels great about it—win-win. Sometimes you'll come up with creative solutions that neither one of you thought about beforehand. At other times you'll negotiate and piece something together—a little of his, a little of hers. But the goal—both of you feeling good about your final decision—remains the same, no matter how you get there.

Step 6: Implement your solution.

Just do it! After you hammer out something that looks as if it might work for both of you, try it out. But go into it with the same spirit that helped you to identify this option: making sure that both of you still consider it a win-win.

Step 7: Evaluate and rework your solution, if necessary.

A real win-win has to stay a win-win. Many times we think we have dreamed up a really great idea, only to find out that it doesn't work as well as we'd hoped. "I didn't think about that," we say, or "That's not nearly as good as I thought it would be." If you make such a discovery, don't sweat it. Just rework your solution. Remember, you want to start and end with a win-win. You want to make sure that your team stays on the successful side of things.

Two Objections Answered

Some people who have never seen a no-losers policy at work hesitate to implement it in their marriage. The following are two of the most common objections we see.

It will take too much time.

"I don't have the time to go through all these steps," some say. "With all the disagreements we have, it would take *forever!*"

But do you know what we've discovered? A no-losers policy actually saves huge chunks of time, especially once it becomes a habit. Here's why.

When you feel as if you have to defend your territory, you tend to dig in your heels for a protracted and tiring tug-of-war. The battle continues until one party just wears out—and that can take a long, long time. When you implement a no-losers policy, however, you stop having to worry about protecting your agenda. You no longer feel anxious that your feelings won't be considered. And when those issues go away, the substance of your disagreement usually turns out to be pretty small. Since you now have very little to fuss about, you move through the process quickly. It's very efficient and doesn't take much time at all.

What if we cannot come to an agreement and somebody has to make a decision?

You know what? That hardly ever happens. Remember, the problem is rarely the problem. If you follow through on the seven steps, you'll hardly ever end up in a stalemate.

But what if you do? Let us tell you something else we've discovered. Most "urgent" decisions—things that drive us to hurry up, that tell us we're almost out of time, that insist we're about to miss the opportunity of a lifetime—end up being less than urgent. Either the opportunity was not as good as it looked or another, even better opportunity had not yet presented itself. We often realize that if we had moved on the first decision, we would have missed out on the second.

In general, it is wise to hold off on such decisions until we can arrive at a place of unity. But if the decision really does need to be made, we try to determine who appears to be the most qualified to make it—based on experience or training or something else—and let that person decide. Too often guys say things such as, "Listen, I'm the man, so you need to submit!" (The dreaded *s* word.)

A quick word for the husband who is trying to follow biblical truths: Ephesians 5:21 says, "Submit to one another out of reverence for Christ." We are both to submit to each other. But the man does more than submit to his wife; he actually follows Christ's example and lays down his life. Ephesians 5:25 goes on to say, "Husbands, love your wives, just as Christ loved the church and gave himself up for her."

It's like the chicken and the pig. Who gives the biggest sacrifice for breakfast? The pig does. The chicken only submits an egg daily. But the pig gives his life. So men, we need to be like the pig. (The next time your wife calls you a pig, say thank you!) The man who is willing to die for his wife finds a wife who is willing to discover a win-win solution and submit to the final decision—one that they both feel great about. Remember, the only other possibility is for your team to lose. Don't make the issue about submitting; make it about finding a win-win. That is honor. That makes the marriage feel safe.

In our own marriages, if we feel compelled to make a decision that our wives oppose, we do it with great caution. We say, "I feel led to make this decision, but I have to tell you that because you and I are not together on this, I'm open to the possibility that I might be wrong. Therefore, I will make the decision, but I want you to know that I will also take the heat if I'm wrong. And I will be the one to answer to God. You are off the hook." This is very different from saying, "I'm the man, so back off and submit, because I make the decisions around here!"

Again, in a marriage, there is no such thing as a win-lose solution. It is either win-win or lose-lose. No other options exist. The apostle Paul labored to get his young churches to understand this basic principle. In passage after passage, he pled with them to cooperate, work together, and find solutions that benefited everyone. "Do nothing out of selfish ambition or vain conceit," he told one church, "but in humility consider others better than yourselves. Each of you should look not only to your own interests, but also to the interests of others" (Philippians 2:3-4).

Overcoming Roadblocks to Forgiveness

"Why can't I forgive?" people often ask. "I know that God wants me to, but I just can't find the strength to go through with it." We each have a choice to make when our spouse offends us in some way. We can refuse to forgive because of past mistakes. We can let the offense tear apart our most prized relationship. Or we can decide to forgive and allow the work of Christ to heal both our spouse and ourselves.

Let's be honest. No one finds forgiveness an easy task. Yet we find five main roadblocks that cause most of our hesitancy to forgive.

The Five Main Roadblocks to Forgiveness
1. We fear that forgiveness somehow lets the guilty partner off the hook.

Some people confuse forgiveness with acceptance of the wrong. We believe that to forgive is to excuse. We feel as if we're being asked to condone what should never be condoned. We think, *If I forgive my spouse, then I'm excusing what he [or she] did!* The fear is that if we pardon the offender's behavior and let them off the hook, then they won't learn their lesson and will most likely hurt us again.

But true forgiveness has nothing to do with condoning someone's sinful actions. It has everything to do with freeing us to move beyond the offense and gain the strength and stability available only through God's grace.

2. We believe that forgiving means forgetting.

How many times have we heard someone say, "Forgive and forget!" Such a thing is next to impossible—barring serious brain injury. We don't want to forget what happened, because we are afraid the offense will happen again if we let it go and forgive. But if we hold on to the hurt and pain, we reason, it will remind us to protect ourselves, or it will remind the other person not to hurt us again.

But forgiving does not mean forgetting. God did not wire our brains to completely forget painful events. Our Lord uses trials and painful experiences to help his people mature. When we believe that we can forget painful events and stuff away our hurts, we only prolong the inevitable. By stuffing hurts deep down in our inner self, we simply set ourselves up for an explosion. Like a volcano, the intense heat and pressure from past hurts build up until they finally erupt. And the hot ashes and molten lava cover everything in their path.

Another version of this roadblock is believing that to forgive means to reconcile. We falsely believe that in order to forgive, we must also reconcile with the person who hurt us. This ultimately creates more fear and makes us feel more unsafe. The reality is that it would be extremely dangerous and personally reckless if the victim reconciled or reunited with the offender before that person took personal responsibility for his or her actions.

We are commanded by God to forgive, but we are not commanded to reconcile. Scripture says only, "If it is possible, as far as it depends on you, live at peace with everyone" (Romans 12:18). Reconciliation happens only in cases where the victim feels safe—when they trust themselves to always take good care of themselves—and when the offender takes personal responsibility for the hurtful behavior and validates the victim's pain.

3. We fail to own up to our own fallenness.

If we cannot see our own faults and mistakes, how can we possibly move toward forgiveness in our marriage? We must first genuinely admit that we are not perfect and that we are quite capable of hurting our spouse. Remember what Jesus said: "Why do you look at the speck of sawdust in your brother's eye and pay no attention to the plank in your own eye? How can you say to your brother, 'Let me take the speck out of your eye,' when all the time there is a plank in your own eye?" (Matthew 7:3-4).

4. We have unresolved anger.

People who have unresolved anger have various ways of showing it. One way is to cruelly or unreasonably insist on their rights. Such people are said to be demanding their "pound of flesh" (based on a reference to Shakespeare's play *The Merchant of Venice*). Others want to get revenge, to want to make the person pay for what happened. If it costs the offender something, then perhaps he'll remember not to do that again. Some people struggling with unresolved anger want to teach the other person a lesson. They think, *If the person really learns their lesson, then they won't do it again.*

Another facet of unresolved anger is wanting the offender to validate our hurt and pain. If we don't feel validated by the offender or if we don't feel the person really understands and cares about our pain, then we're afraid the offender may hurt us again.

If we refuse to let go of bitterness, rage, or hatred, we hold on to enormously destructive forces. These forces stand in direct opposition to the power of forgiveness. The two forces cannot coexist; there can be no harmony and no truce between them.

5. We are afraid of becoming helpless and vulnerable.

This is one of the most powerful reasons why some people refuse to forgive. It stems from the fact that we do not think we can take care of ourselves in the face of further pain, hurt, or rejection. If we cannot adequately care for ourselves in the presence of pain, we feel helpless and vulnerable, and we do not extend forgiveness.

The solution is to find the real source of power. It will never be in another person. It is only found in the Lord and in his work in our lives.

We build walls and fortresses for protection. When we feel threatened, our instinctive protective/survival mechanism triggers, and we are inclined to shield or close our hearts. If you want to deal with your helplessness and vulnerability, focus on creating a safe place for yourself. This is done by honoring your own feelings and making it okay to be in a place where you're not willing to forgive at this time. While God does command us to forgive, it's not an instantaneous or easy process. The key is not to view your walls as obstacles you need to eliminate but rather as temporary strategies employed to protect a valuable person—you. In other words, care about the person behind the wall and honor your right to use whatever coping method (i.e., not forgiving) you choose to take care of yourself.

Take the focus off of forgiveness and make the issue about your fear (feeling helpless and vulnerable). Put down the self-judgment about not forgiving and replace it with curiosity about why you are having a hard time forgiving ("I feel helpless and vulnerable"). When we judge ourselves ("I should be able to forgive"), this naturally leads to defensiveness, which makes progress harder. Curiosity without judgment feels safer and tends to encourage openness, which makes progress easier.

You always have the option to validate your own pain. This is exactly what Joseph in the Old Testament did as he dealt with having been rejected by his brothers.

> So they sent word to Joseph, saying, "Your father left these instructions before he died: 'This is what you are to say to Joseph: I ask you to forgive your brothers the sins and the

wrongs they committed in treating you so badly.' Now please forgive the sins of the servants of the God of your father." When their message came to him, Joseph wept. His brothers then came and threw themselves down before him. "We are your slaves," they said. But Joseph said to them, "Don't be afraid. Am I in the place of God? You intended to harm me, but God intended it for good to accomplish what is now being done, the saving of many lives. So then, don't be afraid. I will provide for you and your children." And he reassured them and spoke kindly to them. (Genesis 50:16-21)

Joseph is a great example of someone who took good care of himself and did not need to control or manipulate his brothers so they would take responsibility or admit they were wrong for selling him into slavery. Again, you can validate your own pain. Although it's wonderful when the offender validates our pain, real power and confidence come from our ability to do that for ourselves. Admit that someone has hurt you. Notice that's exactly what Joseph did when he said, "You intended to harm me. . . ."

Furthermore, listen to the psalmist David: "My friends and companions avoid me because of my wounds; my neighbors stay far away. Those who seek my life set their traps, those who would harm me talk of my ruin; all day long they plot deception" (Psalm 38:11-12). He is validating his pain.

Listen to the apostle Paul: "You know that everyone in the province of Asia has deserted me, including Phygelus and Hermogenes. . . . Demas, because he loved this world, has deserted me and has gone to Thessalonica. . . . Alexander the metalworker did me a great deal of harm. . . . He strongly opposed our message" (2 Timothy 1:15; 4:10, 14-15).

Even Jesus Christ himself cried out from the cross, "My God, my God, why have you forsaken me?" (Matthew 27:46).

These are not the cries of people who tried to hide or deny the fact that they were victims. They deeply felt the pain caused by others and expressed it openly and without shame. So should you.

Ultimately, the goal is to open your heart to God, yourself, and others. This is exactly what happened to Joseph. His heart was truly open to God, himself, and his brothers. He got there by plugging into God's endless resources and getting filled by him, and by doing great self-care, long before he reconciled with his brothers.

In terms of forgiveness, we find that when people . . .

- honor their own walls and make it okay not to forgive the offender for a season
- make the issue less about forgiveness and more about understanding and caring for their fears (i.e., feeling helpless and vulnerable)
- take responsibility for their fears, pain, and feelings
- learn how to trust themselves to do a great job of caring for their own well-being
- plug into God for their source of true fulfillment
- see the hurt and painful experience from God's perspective ("but God intended it for good")
- release the offender from ever making it "right"

. . . forgiveness seems to occur naturally.

When you take great care of yourself and feel safe with yourself, forgiveness is not something you have to force. Ultimately, you no longer feel helpless and vulnerable. When we have confidence and know that we can take care of ourselves, when we believe in our own capacity and ability to care for ourselves in the face of further pain, hurt, or rejection, when we adequately care for ourselves in the presence of pain, we feel fundamentally empowered (the opposite of helpless), and we will feel safe and at peace (the opposite of vulnerable).

Do you recognize any of these roadblocks to forgiveness in your marriage? Are they keeping you from forgiving your husband or wife? How easy is it for you to say, "I was wrong" or "I am wrong"? When was the last time you told your spouse, "What you did made me angry" or "I feel bitter about what you said"?

Don't let these roadblocks stop your journey to forgiveness. Your marriage can't afford the delay.

Seeking Forgiveness

Every marriage, no matter how mature or healthy, has to make forgiveness an ongoing priority. Times of hardship and emotional strain will come, but as long as the two of you remain committed to seeking forgiveness from one another, the hard times will become assets, not deficits. We recommend that you keep three things in mind when seeking forgiveness.

1. Remember that your approach sets the tone of the conversation.

Proverbs 15:1 says, "A gentle answer turns away wrath, but a harsh word stirs up anger." When you make your voice soft and receptive to your partner's feelings and attitudes, you're bound to get a better hearing. Be gentle, tender, soothing, calm, and temperate. We like to ask ourselves, *How humble am I right now? How willing am I to hear what my wife [or husband] is saying?* If we have rehearsed a rebuttal, we're probably not ready.

Remember what King Solomon says: "Through patience a ruler can be persuaded, and a gentle tongue can break a bone" (Proverbs 25:15).

2. Ask for specifics on how you hurt your spouse.

We often misdiagnose how we hurt our spouse. It helps to validate our partner's feelings and needs when we ask how our words or actions caused the pain. If your spouse doesn't immediately want to describe the hurt, don't force the issue. Give them some time to build their thoughts. Sometimes you can ask questions that might help them understand more clearly how you hurt him or her.

Proverbs 20:5 reminds us, "The purposes of a man's heart are deep waters, but a man of understanding draws them out." How can these "deep waters" be drawn out? Through patience, genuine concern, and good questions.

3. Don't focus on what your spouse did to you.

Remember, forgiveness grows out of personal responsibility. You do not control your spouse; thus you can't make them seek or accept forgiveness. You control only yourself and how you behave toward your spouse. By humbly seeking forgiveness and acknowledging every aspect of your wrongdoing, you clean up your end of the mess. God does not hold you responsible for your spouse's sin, but he does hold you responsible for your own choices and behavior.

Forgiveness Is a Process

Forgiveness is not a onetime event; it is a process. Too often we hear some version of "If he really forgave me, then he would be over this by now!"

But that simply is not realistic. We shouldn't expect immediate healing or instant forgiveness, especially if we've done something extremely hurtful. Your spouse will not get over the hurt right away; it takes time.

The pain of some hurts never fully goes away. When an event sparks an old memory, the pain may return with it. This may be one way God keeps us humble. It's hard to get overconfident about our emotional or spiritual maturity when we remember how things used to be.

We need to dispense with the belief that once we say those magic words, "I forgive you," all pain and hurt instantly disappear. Forgiveness is a process, and only by going through it can we begin to heal.

National Institute of Marriage

www.nationalmarriage.com
417-335-5882

The National Institute of Marriage was originally founded as the Smalley Marriage Institute under the leadership of Dr. Greg Smalley. Because of the growth of this ministry and its growing national presence, we renamed the organization National Institute of Marriage (NIM), which more accurately represents the goals of the ministry. Led by copresidents Dr. Robert S. Paul and Mark Pyatt, NIM team members have a wide variety of training and expertise but one single passion: making an eternal difference in the lives of couples.

Through our nationally recognized Intensive programs, the team members accomplish two very important goals: to remain dependent on God's transforming power in the restoration of marriages and to continually learn, apply, and teach the life-changing concepts that result in successful marriages.

Exponentially expanding the impact of the ministry, NIM is focusing on presenting the principles, concepts, and tools from the Intensive program to professional counselors, chaplains, pastoral leaders, marriage mentors, and small group leaders. We believe that as we enrich and equip these leaders who are influencing a multitude of couples, a marriage revival will take place that could change the world.

For more information on these programs, to inquire about speaking engagements, or to become a ministry partner, visit www.nationalmarriage.com or call 417-335-5882.

The Center for Relationship Enrichment John Brown University

ENRICHING RELATIONSHIPS FOR A LIFETIME

The Center for Relationship Enrichment (CRE), under the leadership of Dr. Gary Oliver, equips people for healthy relationships through biblically based consulting, education, enrichment, resources, research, and assessment. The CRE uses several of the following initiates or programs to accomplish its mission and vision.

1. Church Relationship Initiative

An important part of the mission of the CRE is to partner with church leaders to increase their effectiveness in ministering to the wide range of personal and interpersonal needs represented in their congregations. As a part of this mission, the CRE has designed the Church Relationships Survey.

2. Consulting and Training Services

The CRE offers consulting and training services to Christian leaders and organizations in order to contribute to the effectiveness and health of personal and interpersonal ministries. As part of our Church Initiative, we administer the CRE Church Relationship Assessment. This survey gives us detailed information on the health and effectiveness of the relational ministries that are being offered to the church congregation. This information is then given to the staff, pastors, elders, deacons, and lay leaders.

For more information about the Church Survey, the Church Relationships Survey, or consulting and training services, please contact us at 479-524-7105 or CRE@jbu.edu.

3. Special Speaking Team

The CRE speaking team, which includes Dr. Gary and Carrie Oliver and Dr. Greg and Erin Smalley, is well equipped to provide you with the necessary tools for enriching marriage and family relationships in your church. We would love the opportunity to discuss your specific needs and customize a speaking event that will have maximum impact for you. To schedule our speakers, please contact us at 479-524-7105 or CRE@jbu.edu.

THE DNA OF RELATIONSHIPS
BY DR. GARY SMALLEY

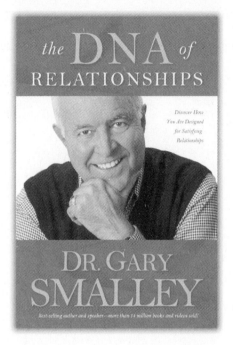

HAVE YOU EVER FELT AS IF YOU'RE . . .

Repeating the Same Mistakes in Your Relationships?

DR. GARY SMALLEY TELLS YOU
THE WHYS AND HOWS OF RELATIONSHIPS:

· Discover the fear dance that occurs in all relationships.

· Explore how to create safety in relationships.

· Cultivate healthy habits that care for your emotional needs.

· Find out how to listen to other people's emotions.

ABOUT THE AUTHORS

 DR. GREG SMALLEY serves as the vice president of marriage and family formation at Focus on the Family. In this role, he develops and oversees initiatives that prepare individuals for marriage, strengthen and nurture existing marriages, and help couples in marital crises. He is the author or coauthor of seventeen books, including *Fight Your Way to a Better Marriage, The DNA of Parent-Teen Relationships,* and *The Wholehearted Marriage.* He and his wife, Erin, co-created *Ready to Wed,* a complete premarital curriculum for engaged couples, and the online Focus on Marriage Assessment. They also released *Crazy Little Thing Called Marriage: 12 Secrets for a Lifelong Romance* in 2015. He received his doctorate at the Rosemead School of Psychology at Biola University in Southern California and a counseling degree from Denver Seminary. Married since 1992, Greg and Erin live in Colorado with their three daughters, Taylor, Murphy, and Annie, and their son, Garrison.

DR. ROBERT S. PAUL is vice president of the Focus on the Family Marriage Institute. Bob received his bachelor's degree from Evangel University, his master's degree from Georgia State University, and a diploma in Christian counseling and an honorary doctorate from Psychological Studies Institute. He holds a license in the state of Missouri and the state of Georgia as a professional counselor. Bob is an accomplished speaker who presents regularly at professional conferences and enrichment events both nationally and internationally. He has appeared on numerous radio and television programs and has coauthored three books: *The DNA of Relationships*, with Drs. Gary, Greg, and Michael Smalley, *The DNA of Relationships for Couples*, with Dr. Greg Smalley, and *Finding Ever After*. He is a former professor at Evangel University, where he taught in both the biblical studies and psychology departments, specializing in marriage and family counseling, human sexuality, and the integration of faith into all areas of life. Bob and his wife, Jenni, live in Springfield, Missouri, having been married for more than thirty-seven years. They have four children and five grandchildren.